CHOCTAW BY BLOOD

ENROLLMENT CARDS

1898-1914

VOLUME VIII

TRANSCRIBED BY

JEFF BOWEN

NATIVE STUDY
Gallipolis, Ohio
USA

Originally published:
Baltimore, Maryland
2016

Reprinted by:

Native Study LLC
Gallipolis, OH
www.nativestudy.com

Library of Congress Control Number: 2020911767

ISBN: 978-1-64968-011-2

Made in the United States of America.

Other Books and Series by Jeff Bowen

1901-1907 Native American Census Seneca, Eastern Shawnee, Miami, Modoc, Ottawa, Peoria, Quapaw, and Wyandotte Indians (Under Seneca School, Indian Territory)

1932 Census of The Standing Rock Sioux Reservation with Births And Deaths 1924-1932

Census of The Blackfeet, Montana, 1897- 1901 Expanded Edition

Eastern Cherokee by Blood, 1906-1910, Volumes I thru XIII

Choctaw of Mississippi Indian Census 1929-1932 with Births and Deaths 1924-1931 Volume I

Choctaw of Mississippi Indian Census 1933, 1934 & 1937, Supplemental Rolls to 1934 & 1935 with Births and Deaths 1932-1938, and Marriages 1936-1938 Volume II

Eastern Cherokee Census Cherokee, North Carolina 1930-1939 Census 1930-1931 with Births And Deaths 1924-1931 Taken By Agent L. W. Page Volume I

Eastern Cherokee Census Cherokee, North Carolina 1930-1939 Census 1932-1933 with Births And Deaths 1930-1932 Taken By Agent R. L. Spalsbury Volume II

Eastern Cherokee Census Cherokee, North Carolina 1930-1939 Census 1934-1937 with Births and Deaths 1925-1938 and Marriages 1936 & 1938 Taken by Agents R. L. Spalsbury And Harold W. Foght Volume III

Seminole of Florida Indian Census, 1930-1940 with Birth and Death Records, 1930-1938

Texas Cherokees 1820-1839 A Document For Litigation 1921

Visit our website at **www.nativestudy.com** to learn more about these and other books and series by Jeff Bowen

This series is dedicated to
Mike Marchi,
who keeps my spirits up.

CREEK CENSUS.

SECOND NOTICE.

Members of the Dawes Commission will be present at the following times and places for the purpose of enrolling Creek citizens, as required by Act of Congress of June 10, 1896:

At Muskogee, Nov. 8 to 30, 1897, inclusive.
At Wagoner, Nov. 8 to 13, " inclusive.
At Eufaula, Nov. 8 to 13, " inclusive.
At Sapulpa, Nov. 15 to 20, " inclusive.
At Wetumpka, Nov. 15 to 20, " inclusive.
At Okmulgee, Nov. 22 to 30, " inclusive.

All persons who have not heretofore enrolled before the Dawes Commission should appear and enroll. Parents and guardians can enroll their families and wards.

TAMS BIXBY,
FRANK C. ARMSTRONG,
A. S. McKENNON,
THOS. B. NEEDLES,
Commissioners.

The above illustration is similar in nature to what was found throughout Indian Territory for different tribes as far as postings on bulletin boards, public centers, or wherever they could be read so people would be notified of where and when they needed to be for enrollment with the Dawes Commission.

This is a picture of the Dawes Commission at Camp Jones in Stonewall, Indian Territory on September 8, 1898.

The images below are of two of the original cards given on the microfilm. The cards given in this book have been formatted to fit on one page and still give all the information found on the original cards.

Introduction

This series of Choctaw Enrollment Cards for the Five Civilized Tribes 1898-1914 has been transcribed from National Archive Film M-1186 Rolls 39-46.

The series contains more than 6100 Choctaw enrollment cards. All of the cards list age, sex and degree of blood, the parties' Dawes Roll Numbers, and date of enrollment by the Secretary of Interior for each person. The contents also give the enrollee's parents' names as well as miscellaneous notes pertaining to the enrollee's circumstances, when needed. Most entries indicate whether or not a spouse is an Intermarried White, with the initials I.W.

Enrollment wasn't as simple a process as most would think just by going through these pages. The relationships between the Five Tribes and the Dawes Commission were weak at best. There were political battles going on between the tribes and the U.S. Government as it was, but the struggles didn't stop there. Each tribe had its own political factions pulling it from every direction. On top of everything else, people from every corner of the United States were trying to figure how to get in on the spoils (Money and Land Allotment) by means of political favor. Kent Carter, author of *The Dawes Commission*, describes the continuous effort required to enroll the different tribes and the pressure the Commission incurred from people all over the country who tried to insinuate themselves into the equation:

"In May 1896 the Dawes Commission Returned To Indian Territory for its third visit, establishing its headquarters at Vinita in the Cherokee Nation. It now had to process applications for citizenship in addition to negotiating allotment agreements; these circumstances make the narrative of events more confusing because the commission attempted the two tasks concurrently. The commissioners resumed making their usual speeches to tribal officials and public gatherings to promote negotiations, but now they inevitably had to respond to questions about how the application process for citizenship would work. They also began receiving letters from people all over the United States asking how they could 'get on the rolls' so they could 'get Indian land'."[1]

For the actual process of Choctaw enrollment, "A commission was appointed in each county of the Choctaw Nation under an act of September 18 to make separate rolls of citizens by blood, by intermarriage, and freedmen; it was to deliver them to recently elected Chief Green McCurtain by October 20, but he rejected them even before they were completed because of charges that people were being left off for political reasons. On October 30, the National Council authorized establishment of a five-member

---

[1] *The Dawes Commission* by Kent Carter, page 15, para. 1

ix

commission to revise the rolls within ten days and then directed McCurtain to turn them over to the Dawes Commission on November 11, 1896. The Choctaws hired the law firm of Stuart, Gordon, and Hailey, of South McAlester to represent the tribe at all proceedings held by the Dawes Commission,"[2] another indication that throughout the Commission's efforts there was always controversy between the tribes and the negotiators.

When completed, this multi-volume series will contain thousands of names, all of them accounted for in the indexes carefully prepared by the author. Hopefully this work will help many researchers find their ancestors and satisfy the questions that so many have had about their Native American heritage.

Jeff Bowen
Gallipolis, Ohio
NativeStudy.com

---

[2] *The Dawes Commission* by Kent Carter, page 16, para. 5

Choctaw By Blood Enrollment Cards 1898-1914

RESIDENCE: Wade POST OFFICE: Talihina I.T. COUNTY. **Choctaw Nation** Choctaw Roll (Not Including Freedmen) CARD NO. FIELD NO. **2101**

Dawes' Roll No.		NAME		Relationship to Person	AGE	SEX	BLOOD	TRIBAL ENROLLMENT		
								Year	County	No.
6053	1	Nicholas, Wilson	26	First Named	23	M	Full	1896	Blue	9806
6054	2	" Elissie	19	Wife	16	F	"	1896	Wade	6706
15833	3	Potts, Alfred		Son of No2	1	M	"			
	4									
	5									
	6									
	7									
	8									
	9									
	10									
	11	ENROLLMENT								
	12	OF NOS. ~~~ 3 ~~~ HEREON APPROVED BY THE SECRETARY								
	13	OF INTERIOR Jun 12 1905								
	14									
	15	ENROLLMENT								
	16	OF NOS. 1,2 HEREON APPROVED BY THE SECRETARY								
	17	OF INTERIOR Jan 17 1903								

TRIBAL ENROLLMENT OF PARENTS

	Name of Father	Year	County	Name of Mother	Year	County
1	Willis Nicholas	Ded	Blue	Sadie Nicholas	Ded	Blue
2	Jimpson Jones	"	Wade	Annie Jones	"	Wade
3	Watson Potts			No 2		
4						
5			For child of No.2 see N.B. (Apr 26, 1896) Card No. 225.			
6						
7						
8			No2 on 1896 rolls as Elissie Jones.			
9			Nos 1 and 2 have seperated[sic].			
10			No3 was born Sept 6 1902: application received and No3 placed			
11			on this card April 28, 1902 under Act of Congress approved March 3, 1905			
12			Father of No3 on Choctaw card No 2129, final roll No 6154.			
13						
14						#1&2 inc
15						Date of Application for Enrollment.
16						2/29/99
17						

1

Choctaw By Blood Enrollment Cards 1898-1914

RESIDENCE: Wade COUNTY.
POST OFFICE: Talihina I.T.

Choctaw Nation

Choctaw Roll
(Not Including Freedmen)

CARD NO.
FIELD NO. 2102

Dawes' Roll No.	NAME	Relationship to Person First Named	AGE	SEX	BLOOD	TRIBAL ENROLLMENT		
						Year	County	No.
6055	1 Push Sylvester T.		23	M	Full	1896	Sugar Loaf	10158
	2							
	3							
	4							
	5							
	6							
	7							
	8							
	9							
	10							
	11							
	12							
	13							
	14							
	15	ENROLLMENT OF NOS. 1 HEREON						
	16	APPROVED BY THE SECRETARY OF INTERIOR JAN 17 1903						
	17							

TRIBAL ENROLLMENT OF PARENTS

	Name of Father	Year	County	Name of Mother	Year	County
1	Tennis Push	Ded	Nashoba	Lina Push	Ded	Nashoba
2						
3						
4						
5						
6						
7		On 1896 roll as Silway Push				
8		No1 is the husband of Susan McCurtain on Choc Card #2100 Nov 7, 1901				
9						
10						
11						
12						
13						
14						
15						
16				DATE OF APPLICATION FOR ENROLLMENT 5/29 /99		
17						

2

Choctaw By Blood Enrollment Cards 1898-1914

RESIDENCE: Wade   COUNTY. **Choctaw Nation**   **Choctaw Roll** (Not Including Freedmen)   CARD NO.
POST OFFICE: Lenox, I.T.   FIELD NO. 2103

Dawes' Roll No.	NAME	Relationship to Person First Named	AGE	SEX	BLOOD	TRIBAL ENROLLMENT Year	County	No.
6056	1 Milton, Willis ~~DIED PRIOR TO SEPTEMBER 25, 1902~~		40	M	Full	1896	Wade	8583
6057	2 " Sylon 25	Wife	22	F	"	1896	"	8584
6058	3 " George 15	Son	12	M	"	1896	"	341
6059	4 " Malinda 13	Dau	10	F	"	1896	"	8586
6060	5 " Lacin 11	"	8	"	"	1896	"	8582
6061	6 " Lymon 6	Son	3	M	"	1896	"	8585
	7							
	8							
	9							
	10							
	11							
	12							
	13							
	14							
	15	ENROLLMENT OF NOS. 1,2,3,4,5,6 HEREON						
	16	APPROVED BY THE SECRETARY OF INTERIOR JAN 17 1903						
	17							

TRIBAL ENROLLMENT OF PARENTS

	Name of Father	Year	County	Name of Mother	Year	County
1	A-mah-li	Dead	Skullyville	Sti-ah-mi	Dead	Wade
2	James Beams	"	Wade	Jamesy Beams	"	"
3	No 1			Elsie Milton	"	"
4	No 1			" "	"	"
5	No 1			" "	"	"
6	No 1			No 2		
7						
8						
9						
10			No3 on 1893 Pay Roll Wade Co, No 341			
11			No5 " 1896 Roll as Lyin Milton			
12	No1 died - - 1900: Enrollment cancelled by Department July 8, 1904					
13						
14						
15			For child of No5 see NB (April 26, 1906) #821		Date of Application for Enrollment.	
16			For child of No3 see NB (March 3, 1905) #1491		May 29/99	
17						

3

Choctaw By Blood Enrollment Cards 1898-1914

RESIDENCE: Nashoba POST OFFICE: Octavia I.T. COUNTY. **Choctaw Nation** **Choctaw Roll** *(Not Including Freedmen)* CARD NO. FIELD NO. 2104

Dawes' Roll No.	NAME		Relationship to Person First Named	AGE	SEX	BLOOD	TRIBAL ENROLLMENT Year	TRIBAL ENROLLMENT County	No.
6062	1 Ludlow Henry J	57	First Named	54	M	Full	1896	Nashoba	7997
6063	2 " Mason	59	Wife	56	F	"	1896	"	7998
6064	3 " Linsey	32	Dau	29	"	"	1896	"	7999
6065	4 " Lisarney	27	"	24	"	"	1896	"	8001
6066	5 " Silward	25	Son	22	M	"	1896	"	8002
6067	6 " Marsey	22	Dau	19	F	"	1896	"	8003
6068	7 " Marlie	20	"	17	"	"	1896	"	8004
	8								
	9								
	10								
	11								
	12								
	13								
	14								
	15								
	16								
	17								

ENROLLMENT
OF NOS. 1,2,3,4,5,6,7 HEREON
APPROVED BY THE SECRETARY
OF INTERIOR JAN 17 1903

TRIBAL ENROLLMENT OF PARENTS

	Name of Father	Year	County	Name of Mother	Year	County
1	Mahintubbee	Ded	Nashoba	Chinalihona	Ded	Nashoba
2	Lewis Frazier	"	"		"	"
3	No 1			No 2		
4	No 1			No 2		
5	No 1			No 2		
6	No 1			No 2		
7	No 1			No 2		
8						
9	No5 is Male Sex changed under Departmental authority of March 4, 1907					
10	(ITD 6280-1907) DC 13389-1907					
11				No3 on 1896 roll as Simpsie Ludlow		
12				No4 " " " " Liseanie "		
13				No6 " " " " Mersie "		
14						
15						
16				Date of Application for Enrollment 5-29-99		
17						

Choctaw By Blood Enrollment Cards 1898-1914

RESIDENCE: Nashoba COUNTY. **Choctaw Nation** **Choctaw Roll** CARD NO.
POST OFFICE: Octavia I.T. *(Not Including Freedmen)* FIELD NO. 2105

Dawes' Roll No.	NAME		Relationship to Person	AGE	SEX	BLOOD	TRIBAL ENROLLMENT		
							Year	County	No.
6069	1 Samuel Sicelry	42	First Named	39	F	Full	1896	Nashoba	11412
6070	2 " Esther	17	Dau	14	"	"	1896	"	11413
6071	3 " Lillie	11	"	8	"	"	1896	"	11414
6072	4 " Lymon	18	Son	15	M	"	1896	"	11415
15855	5 " Timothy	6	"	2	"	"			
	6								
	7	ENROLLMENT							
	8	OF NOS. ~~~ 5 ~~~ HEREON APPROVED BY THE SECRETARY							
	9	OF INTERIOR JUN 12 1905							
	10								
	11								
	12								
	13								
	14								
	15	ENROLLMENT OF NOS. 1,2,3,4 HEREON							
	16	APPROVED BY THE SECRETARY OF INTERIOR JAN 17 1903							
	17								

TRIBAL ENROLLMENT OF PARENTS

	Name of Father	Year	County	Name of Mother	Year	County
1	Makintubbee	Ded	Nashoba	Chinalihona	Ded	Nashoba
2	Cephas Samuel	"	"	No 1		
3	"			No 1		
4	"			No 1		
5	"			No 1		
6						
7	No5 Born in January 1897 Proof of birth filed April 3 1905					
8						
9			No1 on 1896 roll as Cisby Samuel			
10			No4 " " " " Lamon "			
11			Affidavit for No5 to be supplied Recd Aug 9/99			
12	For two children of No2 see NB (Apr 26-06) Card #855					
13						
14						
15						
16				Date of Application for Enrollment.	5/29/99	
17						

5

Choctaw By Blood Enrollment Cards 1898-1914

RESIDENCE: Wade   COUNTY. **Choctaw Nation**   **Choctaw Roll** CARD NO.
POST OFFICE: Talihina I.T.   *(Not Including Freedmen)*   FIELD NO. 2106

Dawes' Roll No.	NAME	Relationship to Person First Named	AGE	SEX	BLOOD	TRIBAL ENROLLMENT Year	County	No.
6073	1 Harkins Benjamin ⁴³	First Named	40	M	Full	1896	Wade	5397
~~6074~~	DIED PRIOR TO SEPTEMBER 25, 1902 2 ~~Elsie~~	~~Wife~~	~~38~~	~~F~~	"	~~1896~~	"	~~5398~~
6075	3 " Panson ¹⁰	Son	7	M	"	1896	"	5399
	4							
	5							
	6							
	7							
	8							
	9							
	10							
	11							
	12							
	13							
	14							
	15 ENROLLMENT OF NOS. 1, 2, 3 HEREON							
	16 APPROVED BY THE SECRETARY							
	17 OF INTERIOR JAN 17 1903							

TRIBAL ENROLLMENT OF PARENTS

	Name of Father	Year	County	Name of Mother	Year	County
1	Mahlatubi	Ded	Wade		Ded	Wade
2	Machintubi	"	"		"	"
3	No 1			No 2		
4						
5						
6						
7						
8			No2 died in November 1901: Enrollment cancelled by Department May 2, 1906			
9						
10			No3 on 1896 roll as Penson Harkins			
11						
12						
13						
14						
15					Date of Application for Enrollment.	
16					5/29/99	
17						

Choctaw By Blood Enrollment Cards 1898-1914

RESIDENCE: Wade   COUNTY. **Choctaw Nation**   **Choctaw Roll**   CARD NO.
POST OFFICE: Muse I.T.   (Not Including Freedmen)   FIELD NO. **2107**

Dawes' Roll No.	NAME		Relationship to Person First Named	AGE	SEX	BLOOD	TRIBAL ENROLLMENT		
							Year	County	No.
6076	1 Johnson Hagan	36	First Named	33	M	Full	1896	Wade	6695
6077	2 " Rhoda	32	Wife	29	F	"	1896	"	6696
6078	3 " Laura	11	Dau	8	"	"	1896	"	6697
6079	4 " Lorena	6	"	2	"	"			
	5								
	6								
	7								
	8								
	9								
	10								
	11								
	12								
	13								
	14								
	15	ENROLLMENT OF NOS. 1,2,3,4 HEREON							
	16	APPROVED BY THE SECRETARY OF INTERIOR Jan 17 1903							
	17								

TRIBAL ENROLLMENT OF PARENTS

	Name of Father	Year	County	Name of Mother	Year	County
1	Tushuehambi	Ded	Wade	Atobe	Ded	Wade
2	William Beams	"	"	Hannah Beams	"	"
3	No 1			No 2		
4	No 1			No 2		
5						
6						
7						
8						
9						
10						
11						
12						
13						
14						Date of Application for Enrollment.
15						
16						5/29/99
17						

7

Choctaw By Blood Enrollment Cards 1898-1914

RESIDENCE: Wade

POST OFFICE: Talihina I.T.

COUNTY. **Choctaw Nation**

Choctaw Roll
(Not Including Freedmen)

CARD No.

FIELD No. 2108

Dawes' Roll No.	NAME		Relationship to Person	AGE	SEX	BLOOD	TRIBAL ENROLLMENT		
							Year	County	No.
6080	1 Parton Gabrial	38	First Named	35	M	Full	1896	Wade	10277
	2								
	3								
	4								
	5								
	6								
	7								
	8								
	9								
	10								
	11								
	12								
	13								
	14								
	15	ENROLLMENT							
	16	OF NOS. 1 HEREON APPROVED BY THE SECRETARY							
	17	OF INTERIOR JAN 17 1903							

TRIBAL ENROLLMENT OF PARENTS

	Name of Father	Year	County	Name of Mother	Year	County
1	Achafantubby	Ded	Jacks Fork	Molsy	Ded	Jacks Fork
2						
3						
4						
5						
6			N°1 is now husband of Susan Wells on Choctaw card #2160, Oct 14, 1902			
7						
8			For child of No1 see NB (Mar 3 1905) Card No 53			
9						
10						
11						
12						
13						
14						
15						
16				Date of Application for Enrollment		5/29/99
17						

Choctaw By Blood Enrollment Cards 1898-1914

RESIDENCE: Wade
POST OFFICE: Talihina I.T.

COUNTY. **Choctaw Nation**

Choctaw Roll
(Not Including Freedmen)

CARD NO.
FIELD NO. 2109

Dawes' Roll No.	NAME	Relationship to Person	AGE	SEX	BLOOD	TRIBAL ENROLLMENT Year	County	No.
6081	1 Wilkin Josephine 20	First Named	17	F	Full	1896	Wade	976
14718	2 Ludlow John 2	Son	29mo	M	Full			
14719	3 " Ellis 1	"	8mo	M	"			
	4							
	5		ENROLLMENT					
	6		OF NOS. 2 and 3 HEREON					
	7		APPROVED BY THE SECRETARY OF INTERIOR MAY 20 1903					
	8							
	9							
	10							
	11							
	12							
	13							
	14							
	15	ENROLLMENT OF NOS. 1 HEREON						
	16	APPROVED BY THE SECRETARY OF INTERIOR JAN 17 1903						
	17							

TRIBAL ENROLLMENT OF PARENTS

	Name of Father	Year	County	Name of Mother	Year	County
1	Madison James	Ded	Wade	Martha James	Ded	Wade
2	Austin Ludlow	1896	Nashoba	N° 1		
3	" "	1896	"	N° 1		
4						
5			For child of No.1 see NB (Apr 26-06) Card #572			
6						
7			On 1896 roll as Josephine Bruton			
8			Also " 1893 " " " James Wade Co page 9, No 89			
9			N° 1 wife of Austin Ludlow Choc card 2057			
10			N°2 Born July 17, 1900. Enrolled Dec 24, 1902			
11			N°3 Born April 15, 1902. Enrolled Dec 24, 1902			
12						
13						
14						
15					#1	
16				Date of Application for Enrollment.	5/29/99	
17						

9

Choctaw By Blood Enrollment Cards 1898-1914

RESIDENCE: Wade   COUNTY. **Choctaw Nation**   **Choctaw Roll** CARD No.
POST OFFICE: Talihina, I.T.   (Not Including Freedmen)   FIELD No. 2110

Dawes' Roll No.	NAME	Relationship to Person First Named	AGE	SEX	BLOOD	TRIBAL ENROLLMENT		
						Year	County	No.
6082	1 Alexander, Eastman 23	First Named	20	M	Full	1896	Wade	150
	2							
	3							
	4							
	5							
	6							
	7							
	8							
	9							
	10							
	11							
	12							
	13							
	14							
	15							
	16							
	17							

ENROLLMENT
OF NOS. 1 HEREON
APPROVED BY THE SECRETARY
OF INTERIOR JAN 17 1903

TRIBAL ENROLLMENT OF PARENTS

	Name of Father	Year	County	Name of Mother	Year	County
1	Jos Alexander	Dead	Sugar Loaf	Lotie Alexander	Dead	Sugar Loaf
2						
3						
4						
5						
6						
7						
8						
9						
10						
11						
12						
13						
14						
15						
16						
17						

Date of Application for Enrollment.

5/29/99

RESIDENCE: Wade		COUNTY.					CARD No.	
POST OFFICE: Lenox, I.T.		**Choctaw Nation** (Not Including Freedmen)				Choctaw Roll	FIELD No. 2111	

Dawes' Roll No.	NAME	Relationship to Person First Named	AGE	SEX	BLOOD	TRIBAL ENROLLMENT		
						Year	County	No.
6083	1 Lewis, Sampson ~~DIED PRIOR TO SEPTEMBER 25, 1902~~	First Named	41	M	Full	1896	Wade	7889
6084	2 " Rhoda 21	Wife	24	F	"	1896	"	7890
6085	3 " Catherine 4	Dau	9mo	"	"			
6086	4 Wright, Lena ~~DIED PRIOR TO SEPTEMBER 25, 1902~~	S.Dau	6	"	"	1896	Wade	13110
6087	5 Nicholas, Rosie 1	Dau	6wks	F	"			
	6							
	7							
	8							
	9							
	10							
	11							
	12							
	13							
	14							
	15	ENROLLMENT OF NOS. 1,2,3,4,5 HEREON						
	16	APPROVED BY THE SECRETARY						
	17	OF INTERIOR JAN 17 1903						

TRIBAL ENROLLMENT OF PARENTS

Name of Father	Year	County	Name of Mother	Year	County
1 Lewis Harge	Dead	Wade	Bessie Harge	Dead	Wade
2 Abel Williams	1896	"	Annie Williams	"	"
3 No 1			No 2		
4 Joseph Wright	1896	Wade	No 2		
5 Wilson Nicholas	1896	Blue	No 2		
6					
7	No5 Born March 22, 1901: Enrollment April 9, 1902				
8					
9	No1 died in fall of 1901; proof of death filed Dec 15, 1902				
10	No4 " " Summer of 1901; " " " "				
	No2 is now wife of William James Choc #2018				
11	No1 died - - 1901;No4 died - - 1901: Enrollment cancelled by Department July 8, 1904				
12	For child of No2 see NB 973 (Act Apr 26 06)				
13					
14					
15					
16			Date of Application for Enrollment.	5/29/99	
17	PO of 2,3&5 Talihina I.T. 12/10/02			1 to 4	

Choctaw By Blood Enrollment Cards 1898-1914

RESIDENCE: Wade   COUNTY. **Choctaw Nation**   **Choctaw Roll**   CARD NO.
POST OFFICE: Muse I.T.   *(Not Including Freedmen)*   FIELD NO.   2112

Dawes' Roll No.	NAME	Relationship to Person First Named	AGE	SEX	BLOOD	TRIBAL ENROLLMENT			
						Year	County		pNoR
6088	1 Williams, Sallie Ann 53	First Named	50	F	Full	1893	Wade		477
	2								
	3								
	4								
	5								
	6								
	7								
	8								
	9								
	10								
	11								
	12								
	13								
	14								
	15								
	16								
	17								

ENROLLMENT
OF NOS. 1 HEREON
APPROVED BY THE SECRETARY
OF INTERIOR JAN 17 1903

TRIBAL ENROLLMENT OF PARENTS

Name of Father	Year	County	Name of Mother	Year	County
1 Alixon Vaughn	Ded	Wade	Falamahona	Ded	Wade
2					
3					
4					
5	No1 also on 1896 Choctaw roll, page #344: No 13098 as Selina J Williams				
6					
7					
8		On 1893 Pay Roll for Wade County as			
9		Sallian Williams			
10					
11					
12					
13					
14				Date of Application for Enrollment,	
15					
16				5/29/99	
17					

Choctaw By Blood Enrollment Cards 1898-1914

RESIDENCE: Wade
POST OFFICE: Albion, I.T
COUNTY. **Choctaw Nation**
Choctaw Roll (Not Including Freedmen)
CARD NO.
FIELD NO. 2113

Dawes' Roll No.	NAME	Relationship to Person First Named	AGE	SEX	BLOOD	TRIBAL ENROLLMENT Year	County	No.
6089	1 Thompson, Allen	First Named	27	M	1/2	1896	Wade	12059
6090	2 " Josephine 24	Wife	21	F	1/2	1896	"	12060
6091	3 " Louvina 6	Dau	3	"	1/2	1896	"	12062
	4							
	5							
	6							
	7							
	8							
	9							
	10							
	11							
	12							
	13							
	14							
	15							
	16							
	17							

DIED PRIOR TO SEPTEMBER 25, 1902

ENROLLMENT OF NOS. 1, 2, 3 HEREON APPROVED BY THE SECRETARY OF INTERIOR JAN 17 1903

TRIBAL ENROLLMENT OF PARENTS

	Name of Father	Year	County	Name of Mother	Year	County
1	Jack Thompson	Dead	Sugar Loaf	Mary Thompson	Dead	Sugar Loaf
2	Stephen Woods	"	Wade	Winnie Woods	1896	Non Citz
3	No 1			No 2		
4						
5						
6						
7						
8			No3 on 1896 roll as Lou Thompson			
9						
10			See testimony of G. W. Dukes as to marriage			
11			of parents of No 2			
12						
13		No1 died July 6, 1899: proof of death filed Dec 12, 1902				
14		No1 died July 6 1899: Enrollment cancelled by Department July 8, 1904				
15					Date of Application for Enrollment.	
16					5/29/99	
17						

13

Choctaw By Blood Enrollment Cards 1898-1914

RESIDENCE: Nashoba   COUNTY. **Choctaw Nation**   Choctaw Roll *(Not Including Freedmen)*   CARD NO.
POST OFFICE: Smithville, I.T.   FIELD NO. **2114**

Dawes' Roll No.	NAME		Relationship to Person First Named	AGE	SEX	BLOOD	TRIBAL ENROLLMENT		
							Year	County	No.
DEAD	1 Wilkin, George DEAD			24	M	3/4	1896	Nashoba	13394
15416	2 " Melvina	35	Wife	32	F	1/4	1896	"	15175
6092	3 " John	6	Son	3	M	1/2	1896	"	13395
6093	4 " Raymond	4	"	1	"	1/2			
15417	5 Watson, Martin	17	Step son	17	M	1/2	1893	Nashoba	827
15418	6 Wilkin Alfred	10	Son "	10	"	1/2	1893	"	828
15419	7 " Henry	2	Son of, No 2	2	"	1/4			
	8								
	9	ENROLLMENT OF NOS. 2-5-6-7 HEREON APPROVED BY THE SECRETARY							
	10	OF INTERIOR May 9 1904							
	11								
	12	No.1 hereon dismissed under order of the Commission to the Five Civilized							
	13	Tribes of March 31, 1905.							
	14								
	15	ENROLLMENT OF NOS. 3, 4 HEREON APPROVED BY THE SECRETARY							
	16	OF INTERIOR Jan 17 1903							
	17								

TRIBAL ENROLLMENT OF PARENTS

	Name of Father	Year	County	Name of Mother	Year	County
1	Dennis Wilkin	Dead	Nashoba	Manda Wilkin	1896	Nashoba
2	Joseph Watson	"	"	Rosa A Watson	Dead	Non Citz
3	No 1			No 2		
4	No 1			No 2		
5	Isom Going	dead	Nashoba	No 2		
6	No 1			No 2		
7	Illegitimate			No 2		
8	No6 on 95 Roll as Alfred Watson					
9	As to marriage of No2 with No1 see testimony of Amesiah Wilkin.					
10	No2 is the daughter of Joseph Watson a Choctaw and Rosa Ann Watson, a white woman See card of David Whale, whose wife is a sister of No2, and evidence there taken; see evidence on					
11	7D185					
12	Nos 5 and 6 originally applied for in December 1899 Placed on this card March 16 1904					
13	No4 affidavit of birth to be supplied: Recd Dec 18/99 but irregular and returned for correction Evidence of birth of N°4 received and filed Aug 15 1902					
14						#1 to 4 inc
15						Date of Application for Enrollment.
16	N°1 Died Dec 10 1899: proof of death filed Dec 16, 1902 filed Aug 15, 1902					5/30/99
17	No7 application originally made Aug 15 '02. Proof of birth filed March 15-04					

P.O. Cove Ark 6/8/03

Choctaw By Blood Enrollment Cards 1898-1914

RESIDENCE: Wade   COUNTY, **Choctaw Nation**   **Choctaw Roll**   CARD No.
POST OFFICE: Albion, I.T.   *(Not Including Freedmen)*   FIELD No. **2115**

Dawes' Roll No.	NAME	Relationship to Person First Named	AGE	SEX	BLOOD	TRIBAL ENROLLMENT Year	County	No.
6094	1 Harrison, Lymon ²⁹	First Named	26	M	Full	1896	Wade	5406
I.W. 899	2 " Lorena ㉕	Wife	22	F	I.W	1896	"	14620
6095	3 " Amanda ⁵	Dau	2	"	1/2			
6096	4 " Benjamin ³	Son	1mo	M	1/2			
	5							
	6							
	7	ENROLLMENT OF NOS. 2 HEREON APPROVED BY THE SECRETARY						
	8	OF INTERIOR Aug 3 1904						
	9							
	10							
	11							
	12							
	13							
	14							
	15	ENROLLMENT OF NOS. 1, 3, 4 HEREON						
	16	APPROVED BY THE SECRETARY OF INTERIOR Jan 17 1903						
	17							

TRIBAL ENROLLMENT OF PARENTS

	Name of Father	Year	County	Name of Mother	Year	County
1	Pisa-hi-ya	Dead	Wade	Sukey	Dead	Wade
2	McCoy	1896	Non Citz	Sarah McCoy	"	Non Citz
3	No 1			No 2		
4	No 1			No 2		
5						
6	2 Affidavits as to marriage between Nos 1&2 filed April 22 04					
7	As to marriage, see testimony of No 1					
8						
9	No 3 Affidavit of birth to be supplied. Recd May 30/99					
10	For children of Nos 1&2 see NB (Mar 3, 1905) #648					
11						
12						
13						
14	P.O. Talihina IT 4/7/05					#1 to 3 inc
15					Date of Application for Enrollment.	
16					5/29/99	
17	No2 Status Sept 25/02 requested 3/31/04			No 4 enrolled Nov 1/99		

15

Choctaw By Blood Enrollment Cards 1898-1914

RESIDENCE: Nashoba	COUNTY.								
POST OFFICE: Smithville, I.T.	**Choctaw Nation**				Choctaw Roll *(Not Including Freedmen)*		CARD NO. FIELD NO.		2116

Dawes' Roll No.	NAME	Relationship to Person First Named	AGE	SEX	BLOOD	TRIBAL ENROLLMENT		
						Year	County	No.
6097	₁ Watson, Calvin ¹⁸	Named	16	M	1/4	1896	Nashoba	13392
6098	₂ " Amanda ¹⁴	Sis	11	F	1/4	1896	"	13393
	3							
	4							
	5							
	6							
	7							
	8							
	9							
	10							
	11							
	12							
	13							
	14							
	15							
	16							
	17							

ENROLLMENT OF NOS. 1, 2 HEREON APPROVED BY THE SECRETARY OF INTERIOR JAN 17 1903

TRIBAL ENROLLMENT OF PARENTS

Name of Father	Year	County	Name of Mother	Year	County
₁ Joseph Watson	Dead	Nashoba	Rosa A Watson	Dead	Non Citz
₂ " "	"	"	" " "	"	" "
3					
4					
5					
6					
7		See Card No 2114 as to marriage of			
8		parents of above parties			
9					
10					
11					
12					
13					
14					
15					
16			Date of Application for Enrollment.	5/30/99	
17					

16

RESIDENCE: Wade   COUNTY. **Choctaw Nation**   Choctaw Roll   CARD NO.
POST OFFICE: Talihina, I.T.   *(Not Including Freedmen)*   FIELD NO. 2117

Dawes' Roll No.	NAME	Relationship to Person	AGE	SEX	BLOOD	TRIBAL ENROLLMENT		
						Year	County	No.
6099	1 Pitchlynn Agnes ³²	First Named	29	F	Full	1896	Wade	6704
6100	2 Jones Alfred ¹⁰	Son	7	M	"	1896	"	6707
6101	3 " Nora ⁸	Dau	5	F	"	1896	"	6708
Dead	4 " ~~Minnie DEAD~~	"	2	"	"			
6102	5 Pitchlynn Sissie	Dau	2mo	F	"			
	6							
	7							
	8							
	9							
	10							
	11							
	13							
	14							
	15							
	16							
	17							

No. 4 HEREON DISMISSED UNDER ORDER OF THE COMMISSION TO THE FIVE CIVILIZED TRIBES OF MARCH 31, 1905.

ENROLLMENT
OF NOS. 1, 2, 3, 5 HEREON
APPROVED BY THE SECRETARY
OF INTERIOR JAN 17 1903

TRIBAL ENROLLMENT OF PARENTS

	Name of Father	Year	County	Name of Mother	Year	County
1	James Wright	Dead	Wade	Levina Wright	Dead	Wade
2	Jimson Jones	"	"	No 1		
3	" "	"	"	No 1		
4	" "	"	"	No 1		
5	Allington P Pitchlynn	1896	"	Nº 1		
6						
7						
8	Nº1 is now the wife of Allington Pitchlynn on Choctaw card #2167 Evidence					
9	of marriage filed May 8, 1902.					
10	Nº5 Born March 11, 1902: enrolled May 8, 1902					
11	Nº4 Died Aug 1900, proof of death filed Dec 16, 1902 filed May 8, 1902.					
12						
13						
14					Date of Application for Enrollment.	
15					For No's 1 to 4	
16					5/30/99	
17						

Choctaw By Blood Enrollment Cards 1898-1914

RESIDENCE:	Wade		COUNTY.					CARD NO.	
POST OFFICE:	Talihina, I.T.		Choctaw Nation		Choctaw Roll (Not Including Freedmen)			FIELD NO.	2118

Dawes' Roll No.	NAME		Relationship to Person	AGE	SEX	BLOOD	TRIBAL ENROLLMENT		
							Year	County	No.
I.W. 1296	1 Rose Nancy J	39	First Named	36	F	I.W.	1896	Wade	15135
6103	2 Vaughn George	15	Son	12	M	3/8	1896	"	12599
6104	3 " Larkin	10	"	7	"	3/8	1896	"	12600
6105	4 " Sarah E	8	Dau	5	F	3/8	1896	"	12601
	5								
	6								
	7								
	8								
	9								
	10								
	11	ENROLLMENT							
	12	OF NOS. 1 HEREON							
	13	APPROVED BY THE SECRETARY OF INTERIOR Mar 14 1905							
	14								
	15	ENROLLMENT OF NOS. 2, 3, 4 HEREON							
	16	APPROVED BY THE SECRETARY							
	17	OF INTERIOR Jan 17 1903							

TRIBAL ENROLLMENT OF PARENTS

Name of Father	Year	County	Name of Mother	Year	County
1 George Myers	1896	Non Citz	Sallie Myers	1896	Non Citz
2 Davis Vaughn	Dead	Wade	No 1		
3 " "	"	"	No 1		
4 " "	"	"	No 1		
5					
6	No.1 formerly wife of Davis Vaughn: 1893 Wade, No 473				
7	and who died about 1896				
8	Notify George Myers, Talihina the father of No1 of the action of the Commission				
	No1 on 1896 roll as Nancy Vaughn				
9	No4 " 1896 " " Della "				
10	No1 is now married to a man named Rose 12/24/02				
11					
12					
13					
14					
15					
16			Date of Application for Enrollment.	5/30/99	
17					

18

Choctaw By Blood Enrollment Cards 1898-1914

RESIDENCE: Wade
POST OFFICE: Lenox, I.T.
COUNTY. **Choctaw Nation**
Choctaw Roll *(Not Including Freedmen)*
CARD No.
FIELD No. 2119

Dawes' Roll No.	NAME	Relationship to Person	AGE	SEX	BLOOD	TRIBAL ENROLLMENT Year	County	No.
6106	1 Graham, Thomas 45	First Named	42	M	Full	1896	Wade	4710
6106	2 " Motsey 41	Wife	38	F	1/2	1896	"	4711
6108	3 DIED PRIOR TO SEPTEMBER 25 1902 Handy	Son	18	M	3/4	1896	"	4709
6109	4 " Eliza 7	Dau	4	F	3/4	1896	"	4712
6110	5 " Sina 5	"	1	"	3/4			
6111	6 Sockey, Robert 23	S.Son	20	M	3/4	1896	Wade	11324
6112	7 Hancock, Sikey 15	S.Dau	13	F	3/4	1896	"	5403
6113	8 Sockey, William 21	S.Son	18	M	3/4	1896	"	11325
6114	9 Graham, Martha 2	Dau	2	F	3/4			
	10 No.3 died May 9 1902. Enrollment cancelled							
	11 by Department May 2, 1906							
	12							
	13 ENROLLMENT OF NOS 1,2,3,4,5,6,7,8,9 HEREON							
	14 APPROVED BY THE SECRETARY OF INTERIOR JAN 17 1903							
	15							
	16 Nos 6 and 8 now spell their surnames "Sockey"							
	17							

TRIBAL ENROLLMENT OF PARENTS

Name of Father	Year	County	Name of Mother	Year	County
1 Not Graham	Dead	Wade	Liney Graham	Dead	Wade
2 Alex McCann	"	Sans Bois		"	Sans Bois
3 No 1			Melinda Graham		Wade
4 No 1			No 2		
5 No 1			No 2		
6 George Sakki	Dead	Sans Bois	No 2		
7 Morris Hancock	"	" "	No 2		
8 George Sakki	"	" "	No 2		
9 No 1			No 2		

10	
11 No2 on 1896 roll as Mulcey Graham	
No6 " 1896 " " Bob Sakky	For child of No7 see NB (Apr26-06) Card #740
12 No7 " 1896 " " Silky Hancock " " " Nos1&2" " (Mar 3-05) " #1166	
13 No8 " 1896 " " Billy Sakky " " " No8 " " " " #1219	
14 It is claimed that mother of No2 is a Chickasaw #1 to 8	
No9 Born April 9 1900, Enrolled April 14, 1902 Date of Application for Enrollment.	
15 No6 is now the husband of Rhoda Potts on Choctaw card #2156 June 14 1902	
16 No8 is now the husband of Josephine Holson on Choctaw card #2856 Sept 9 1902 5/30/99	
17 PO Muse IT 4/19/02	

Choctaw By Blood Enrollment Cards 1898-1914

RESIDENCE: Wade COUNTY.
POST OFFICE: Mountain Fork, Arkansas

Choctaw Nation

Choctaw Roll *(Not Including Freedmen)*

CARD NO.
FIELD NO. **2120**

Dawes' Roll No.		NAME		Relationship to Person First Named	AGE	SEX	BLOOD	TRIBAL ENROLLMENT		
								Year	County	No.
6115	1	Parnell, Haywood P	45	First Named	42	M	1/8	1896	Wade	10294
I.W. 19	2	" Roxie	31	Wife	28	F	I.W	1896	"	14935
6116	3	" Jesse H	13	Son	10	M	1/16	1896	"	10295
6117	4	" Thomas O	11	"	8	"	1/16	1896	"	10296
6118	5	" Eliza E	7	Dau	4	F	1/16	1896	"	10297
	6									
	7									
	8									
	9									
	10									
	11									
	12									
	13	ENROLLMENT OF NOS. 1,3,4,5 HEREON APPROVED BY THE SECRETARY OF INTERIOR Jan 17 1903			ENROLLMENT OF NOS. ~~2~~ HEREON APPROVED BY THE SECRETARY OF INTERIOR June 13 1903						
	14									
	15									
	16									
	17	See Choctaw card D269								

TRIBAL ENROLLMENT OF PARENTS

	Name of Father	Year	County	Name of Mother	Year	County
1	Robert Parnell	Dead	Non Citz	Beckie Parnell	Dead	Sugar Loaf
2	Jesse Nichols	1896	" "	Caroline Nichols	1896	Non Citz
3	No 1			No 2		
4	No 1			No 2		
5	No 1			No 2		
6						
7			No1 on 1896 roll as H. P. Parnell			
8			No4 " 1896 " " Thomas "			
9			Evidence of marriage to be supplied. Recd June 1/99			
10			Evidence of divorce of N°1 from his former wife Mary Parnell received and filed Jany. 26, 1903			
11						
12						
13						
14						
15					Date of Application for Enrollment.	
16					5/30/99	
17						

20

Choctaw By Blood Enrollment Cards 1898-1914

RESIDENCE: Wade COUNTY. **Choctaw Nation** **Choctaw Roll** CARD No.
POST OFFICE: Talihina, I.T _(Not Including Freedmen)_ FIELD No. 2121

Dawes' Roll No.	NAME		Relationship to Person	AGE	SEX	BLOOD	TRIBAL ENROLLMENT		
							Year	County	No.
6119	1 Vaughn, Loren	32	First Named	29	M	3/8	1896	Wade	12597
6120	2 " Elsie	33	Wife	30	F	3/8	1896	"	12598
6121	3 Colbert, Simon	14	S.Son	11	M	11/16	1896	"	2402
	4								
	5								
	6								
	7								
	8								
	9								
	10								
	11								
	12								
	13								
	14								
	15	ENROLLMENT OF NOS. 1, 2, 3 HEREON APPROVED BY THE SECRETARY OF INTERIOR JAN 17 1903							
	16								
	17								

TRIBAL ENROLLMENT OF PARENTS

Name of Father	Year	County	Name of Mother	Year	County
1 Davis Vaughn	Dead	Wade	Phoebe Benton	1896	Wade
2 John Davis	"	Gaines		Dead	Gaines
3 Winchester Colbert	"	Wade	No 2		
4					
5					
6		No 1 on 1896 roll as Louis Vaughn			
7					
8					
9					
10					
11					
12					
13					
14					
15					
16			Date of Application for Enrollment.	5/30/99	
17					

Choctaw By Blood Enrollment Cards 1898-1914

RESIDENCE: Gaines COUNTY.	Choctaw Nation	Choctaw Roll	CARD NO.
POST OFFICE: Wilberton[sic], I.T		(Not Including Freedmen)	FIELD NO. 2122

Dawes' Roll No.	NAME	Relationship to Person First Named	AGE	SEX	BLOOD	TRIBAL ENROLLMENT		
						Year	County	No.
6122	1 Hampton, Watson ³⁹	First Named	36	M	Full	1896	Gaines	5301
	2							
	3							
	4							
	5							
	6							
	7							
	8							
	9							
	10							
	11							
	12							
	13							
	14							
	15							
	16							
	17							

ENROLLMENT
OF NOS. 1 HEREON
APPROVED BY THE SECRETARY
OF INTERIOR JAN 17 1903

TRIBAL ENROLLMENT OF PARENTS

	Name of Father	Year	County	Name of Mother	Year	County
1	Willis Hampton	Dead	Sugar Loaf	Charity Hampton	Dead	Sugar Loaf
2						
3						
4						
5						
6						
7						
8						
9						
10						
11						
12						
13						
14						
15						
16			Date of Application for Enrollment.	5/30/99		
17						

22

Choctaw By Blood Enrollment Cards 1898-1914

RESIDENCE: Wade   COUNTY. **Choctaw Nation**   **Choctaw Roll** CARD NO.

POST OFFICE: Talihina, I.T   *(Not Including Freedmen)*   FIELD NO. 2123

Dawes' Roll No.	NAME		Relationship to Person	AGE	SEX	BLOOD	TRIBAL ENROLLMENT		
							Year	County	No.
6123	₁ Bacon, Jefferson	27	First Named	24	M	Full	1896	Wade	953
6124	₂ " Melvina	24	Wife	21	F	"	1896	"	3328
6125	₃ " Melton		Son	1	M	"			
6126	₄ " Charles E	3	Son	7mo	M	"			
6127	₅ " Elmira G	1	Dau	1mo	F	"			
	6								
	7								
	8								
	9								
	10								
	11								
	12								
	13								
	14								
	15								
	16								
	17								

(6125 DIED PRIOR TO SEPTEMBER 25, 1902)

ENROLLMENT OF NOS. 1,2,3,4,5 HEREON APPROVED BY THE SECRETARY OF INTERIOR JAN 17 1903

TRIBAL ENROLLMENT OF PARENTS

	Name of Father	Year	County	Name of Mother	Year	County
1	Reuben Bacon	Dead	Wade	Manda Bacon	1896	Sugar Loaf
2	Dan Daney	1896	"	Nancy Daney	Dead	Wade
3	No 1			No 2		
4	No 1			No 2		
5	No 1			No 2		
6						
7			For child of Nos 1&2 see NB (Mar 3-05) #913			
8			No2 on 1896 roll as Melvina Daney			
9			No.4 Enrolled Aug 6th 1900			
10			No 5 Born June 19th 1902. Enrolled July 19th 1902			
11			No3 died Nov 28, 1900: proof of death filed Dec 12, 1902			
	No3 died Nov 28 1900: Enrollment cancelled by Department July 8, 1904					
12						
13						
14						
15					#1 to 3	
16				DATE OF APPLICATION FOR ENROLLMENT.	5/30/99	
17						

23

Choctaw By Blood Enrollment Cards 1898-1914

RESIDENCE: Wade COUNTY.
POST OFFICE: Talihina, I.T

Choctaw Nation

Choctaw Roll
(Not Including Freedmen)

CARD No.
FIELD No. 2124

Dawes' Roll No.	NAME	Relationship to Person First Named	AGE	SEX	BLOOD	TRIBAL ENROLLMENT		
						Year	County	No.
6128	1 Burney, David DIED PRIOR TO SEPTEMBER 25, 1902		56	M	Full	1896	Wade	956
6129	2 " Abigail 11	Dau	8	F	"	1896	"	958
6130	3 " Frances DIED PRIOR TO SEPTEMBER 25, 1902	"	5	"	"	1896	"	960
6131	4 " Mary R 6	"	3	"	"	1896	"	959
6132	5 McDaniel, Albert 15	S.Son	12	M	"	1896	"	957
	6							
	7							
	8							
	9							
	10							
	11							
	12							
	13							
	14							
	15 ENROLLMENT OF NOS. 1,2,3,4,5 HEREON							
	16 APPROVED BY THE SECRETARY OF INTERIOR JAN 17 1903							
	17							

TRIBAL ENROLLMENT OF PARENTS

Name of Father	Year	County	Name of Mother	Year	County
1 Ho-tubbee	Dead	Wade	Siney	Dead	Wade
2 No 1			Susan Burney	"	"
3 No 1			" "	"	"
4 No 1			" "	"	"
5 Thos McDaniel	1896	Wade	" "	"	"
6					
7	No4 on 1896 roll as Mary Burney				
8	No5 " 1896 " " Albert "				
9	No1 died April 30,1901; proof of death filed Dec 12, 1902				
	No3 " July 4, 1902; " " " " 12, 1902				
10	Nos 2 and 4 are now wards of Crawford J Anderson Choctaw card #1924				
11	Letters of guardianship filed January 13, 1903				
12	No1 died April30,1901: No3 died July 4,1902: Enrollment cancelled by Department July 8, 1904				
13					
14					
15					
16			Date of Application for Enrollment.	5/30/99	
17					

24

RESIDENCE: Wade	COUNTY,	Choctaw Nation	Choctaw Roll	CARD NO.
POST OFFICE: Lenox, I.T.			(Not Including Freedmen)	FIELD NO. **2125**

Dawes' Roll No.	NAME		Relationship to Person	AGE	SEX	BLOOD	TRIBAL ENROLLMENT		
							Year	County	No.
6133	1 Willis James	30	First Named	27	M	1/2	1896	Wade	13104
6134	2 " Cillen	32	Wife	29	F	Full	1896	"	13105
6135	3 " Dixon	8	Son	5	M	3/4	1896	"	13106
6136	4 " Ennet	6	Dau	3	F	3/4			
6137	5 " Allie	4	"	1	"	3/4			
6138	6 Norman, Houston	14	S.Son	11	M	Full	1896	Wade	9623
6139	7 " Malinda	11	S.Dau	8	F	"	1896	"	9624
6140	8 Willis, Mary	2	Dau	13mo	F	3/4			
	9								
	10								
	11								
	12								
	13								
	14								
	15	ENROLLMENT OF NOS. 1,2,3,4,5,6,7,8 HEREON							
	16	APPROVED BY THE SECRETARY							
	17	OF INTERIOR Jan 17 1903							

TRIBAL ENROLLMENT OF PARENTS

	Name of Father	Year	County	Name of Mother	Year	County
1	Tom Willis	Dead	Non Citz	Sallie Willis	Dead	Wade
2	Wilson Tom	"	Skullyville	Phoebe Tom	1896	Sans Bois
3	No 1			No 2		
4	No 1			No 2		
5	No 1			No 2		
6	Willie Norman	Dead	Sugar Loaf	No 2		
7	" "	"	" "	No 2		
8	Nº 1			Nº 2		
9						
10						
11		Nº 8 Born Feby 8, 1901; enrolled March 21, 1902				
12		For child of Nos 1&2 see NB (Mar 3 ;05) #529				
13						
14						#1 to 7
15					Date of Application for Enrollment.	
16					5/30/99	
17	P.O. Muse I.T. 3/21/02					

RESIDENCE: Wade	COUNTY.								
POST OFFICE: Talihina, I.T	**Choctaw Nation**					Choctaw Roll *(Not Including Freedmen)*	CARD No. FIELD No. 2126		

Dawes' Roll No.	NAME		Relationship to Person	AGE	SEX	BLOOD	TRIBAL ENROLLMENT		
							Year	County	No.
6141	1 Benton, George	25	First Named	22	M	Full	1896	Wade	975
6142	2 " Eliza	20	Wife	17	F	"	1896	"	13081
6143	3 " Horace	DIED PRIOR TO SEPTEMBER 25, 1902	Son	5mo	M	"			
6144	4 " Amanda	1	Dau	2mo	F	"			
	5								
	6								
	7								
	8								
	9								
	10								
	11								
	12								
	13								
	14								
	15	ENROLLMENT OF NOS. 1, 2, 3, 4 HEREON							
	16	APPROVED BY THE SECRETARY OF INTERIOR JAN 17 1903							
	17								

TRIBAL ENROLLMENT OF PARENTS

	Name of Father	Year	County	Name of Mother	Year	County
1	Jacob Benton	1896	Wade	Eliza Benton	1896	Wade
2	John Woods	1896		Selina Woods	Dead	"
3	No 1			No 2		
4	No 1			No 2		
5						
6						
7			No2 on 1896 roll as Eliza Woods			
8			No4 Enrolled June 26, 1901			
9			No3 died Aug 8, 1902: proof of death filed Dec 16, 1902			
10	No.3 died Aug 8, 1902. Enrollment cancelled by Department July 8, 1904					
11			For child of Nos 1&2 see NB (Apr 26-06) Card #349			
12		" " "	" " " " (Mar 3 '05) " #767			
13						
14						#1 to 3
15						Date of Application for Enrollment.
16						5/30/99
17						

26

Choctaw By Blood Enrollment Cards 1898-1914

RESIDENCE: Wade   COUNTY. **Choctaw Nation**   Choctaw Roll   CARD NO.
POST OFFICE: Talihina, I.T.   *(Not Including Freedmen)*   FIELD NO. **2127**

Dawes' Roll No.		NAME		Relationship to Person First Named	AGE	SEX	BLOOD	TRIBAL ENROLLMENT Year	County	No.
DEAD	1	Johnico, Isham	DEAD	Named	45	M	Full	1896	Wade	6683
DEAD	2	" Serena	DEAD	Wife	25	F	Full	1896	"	6684
6145	3	" John H	13	Son	10	M	"	1896	"	6685
6146	4	" Annie	8	Dau	5	F	"	1896	"	6686
6147	5	" Grant	5	Son	2	M	"			
6148	6	" Aaron	4	"	7mo	"	"			
6149	7	Pitchlynn, Ebenezer DIED PRIOR TO SEPTEMBER 25, 1902		Ward	12	"	"	1896	Wade	10287
6150	8	" Peter	12	"	9	"	"	1896	"	10288
	9	No.1and2 hereon dismissed under order								
	10	of the Commission to the Five Civilized								
	11	Tribes of March 31, 1905.								
	12	No7 died May - 1902: Enrollment								
	13	cancelled by Department July 8, 1904								
	14									
	15	ENROLLMENT OF NOS. 3,4,5,6,7,8 HEREON								
	16	APPROVED BY THE SECRETARY								
	17	OF INTERIOR Jan 17 1903								

TRIBAL ENROLLMENT OF PARENTS

	Name of Father	Year	County	Name of Mother	Year	County
1	A-pe-sa-tubbee	Dead	Wade	Winey	1896	Nashoba
2	Wilson Tom	"	Skullyville	Phoebe Tom	1896	Sans Bois
3	No 1			No 2		
4	No 1			No 2		
5	No 1			No 2		
6	No 1			No 2		
7	Peter Pitchlynn	Dead	Wade	Sillen Pitchlynn	Dead	Wade
8	" "	"	"	" "	"	"
9						
10	No3 on 1896 roll as John Johnico					
11	No7 " 1896 " " Ebeneezer Pitchlynn					
12	No1 died Jany 29,1902 Proof of death filed April 19, 1902					
	No2 died May 11, 1900: Proof of death filed May 8, 1902					
13	Wife and child of No1 on 7-2132					
14	No7 died May - 1901: Proof of death filed Dec 12, 1902					
15						
16					Date of Application for Enrollment. 5/30/99	
17	No3 P.O. Panama, I.T. 1/26/06					

27

Choctaw By Blood Enrollment Cards 1898-1914

RESIDENCE: Wade   **COUNTY.** **Choctaw Nation**   **Choctaw Roll**   **CARD No.**
POST OFFICE: Talihina, I.T.   *(Not Including Freedmen)*   **FIELD No.** **2128**

Dawes' Roll No.	NAME		Relationship to Person First Named	AGE	SEX	BLOOD	TRIBAL ENROLLMENT		
							Year	County	No.
6151	1 Hitcher, Catherine	28	First Named	25	F	Full	1896	Wade	5401
6152	2 " Thompson	9	Son	6	M	1/2	1896	"	5402
6153	3 " Eddie	4	"	4mo	"	1/2			
	4								
	5								
	6								
	7								
	8								
	9								
	10								
	11								
	12								
	13								
	14								
	15	ENROLLMENT OF NOS. 1, 2, 3 HEREON APPROVED BY THE SECRETARY OF INTERIOR Jan 17-1903							
	16								
	17								

TRIBAL ENROLLMENT OF PARENTS

	Name of Father	Year	County	Name of Mother	Year	County
1	Timpson Jones	Dead	Wade	Rachel Dyer	Dead	Nashoba
2	Harrison Hitcher	1896	Chick Roll	No 1		
3	" "	1896	" "	No 1		
4						
5						
6						
7						
8	Husband, Harrison Hitcher on Chickasaw Card No1441 – Transferred					
9	For child of No1 see NB (March 3, 1905) #769 } to Choctaw Card #5470					
10						
11						
12						
13						
14						
15						
16				Date of Application for Enrollment	5/30/99	
17						

Choctaw By Blood Enrollment Cards 1898-1914

RESIDENCE: Wade   COUNTY. **Choctaw Nation**   Choctaw Roll   CARD No.
POST OFFICE: Lenox, I.T   (Not Including Freedmen)   FIELD NO. 2129

Dawes' Roll No.	NAME		Relationship to Person First Named	AGE	SEX	BLOOD	TRIBAL ENROLLMENT		
							Year	County	No.
6154	1 Potts, Watson	25		22	M	Full	1896	Wade	10302
	2								
	3								
	4								
	5								
	6								
	7								
	8								
	9								
	10								
	11								
	12								
	13								
	14								
	15								
	16								
	17								

ENROLLMENT
OF NOS. 1 HEREON
APPROVED BY THE SECRETARY
OF INTERIOR JAN 17 1903

TRIBAL ENROLLMENT OF PARENTS

	Name of Father	Year	County	Name of Mother	Year	County
1	Charles Potts	Dead	Wade	Melvina Potts	1896	Wade
2						
3						
4						
5						
6		Wife on Chickasaw Card No 1442				
7						
8		For child of No.1 see N.B. (Apr 26 1896) Card No 225				
9						
10						
11						
12						
13						
14						
15					Date of Application for Enrollment.	
16					5/30/99	
17						

29

Choctaw By Blood Enrollment Cards 1898-1914

RESIDENCE: Wade   COUNTY. **Choctaw Nation**   **Choctaw Roll**   CARD NO.
POST OFFICE: Lenox, I.T.   *(Not Including Freedmen)*   FIELD NO.   **2130**

Dawes' Roll No.	NAME		Relationship to Person	AGE	SEX	BLOOD	TRIBAL ENROLLMENT		
							Year	County	No.
6155	1 Woods, Simon	31	First Named	28	M	1/2	1896	Wade	13075
6156	2 " Nancy	21	Wife	18	F	1/2	1896	"	152
6157	3 " Stephen A	4	Son	5mo	M	1/2			
6158	4 DIED PRIOR TO SEPTEMBER 25, 1902 " Gilbert Marvin		Son	3mo	M	1/2			
	5								
	6								
	7								
	8								
	9								
	10								
	11								
	12								
	13								
	14								
	15	ENROLLMENT OF NOS. 1, 2, 3, 4 HEREON APPROVED BY THE SECRETARY OF INTERIOR JAN 17 1903							
	16								
	17								

TRIBAL ENROLLMENT OF PARENTS

	Name of Father	Year	County	Name of Mother	Year	County
1	Benj Woods	1896	Wade	Josephine Woods	1896	Wade
2	Houston Anderson	1896	"	Lucinda Anderson	Dead	"
3	No 1			No 2		
4	No 1			No 2		
5						
6						
7			No2 on 1896 roll as N Ada Anderson			
8						
9			No3 Affidavit of birth to be supplied Recd May 31/99			
10			No.4 born Aug 21 1901: Enrolled Nov 18, 1902			
11			No.4 died May 26 1902: Enrollment cancelled by Department July 8, 1904 For child of Nos 1 and 2 see NB (March 3 1905) #1234			
12						
13						
14						
15				#1 to 3 inc		
16				Date of Application for Enrollment.	5/30/99	
17	P.O. Talihina	4/22/05				

30

RESIDENCE: Skullyville   COUNTY. **Choctaw Nation**   **Choctaw Roll**   CARD No.
POST OFFICE: Cameron, I.T   *(Not Including Freedmen)*   FIELD No.   2131

Dawes' Roll No.	NAME		Relationship to Person	AGE	SEX	BLOOD	TRIBAL ENROLLMENT		
							Year	County	No.
I.W **20**	1 Smith, James A	56	First Named	53	M	I.W.	1896	Skullyville	15025
6159	2 " Mary A	55	Wife	52	F	1/2	1896	"	11131
	3								
	4								
	5								
	6								
	7								
	8								
	9								
	10								
	11								
	12								
	13								
	14								
	15	ENROLLMENT OF NOS. 2 HEREON APPROVED BY THE SECRETARY OF INTERIOR JAN 17 1903	ENROLLMENT OF NOS. 1 HEREON APPROVED BY THE SECRETARY OF INTERIOR JUN 13 1903						
	16								
	17								

TRIBAL ENROLLMENT OF PARENTS

	Name of Father	Year	County	Name of Mother	Year	County
1	Joshua Smith	Dead	Non Citz	Ann S Smith	Dead	Non Citz
2	S.E. Watkins	"	" "	Charlotte Watkins	"	Skullyville
3						
4						
5						
6						
7			No1 on 1896 roll as Jas. A. Smith			
8						
9			As to marriage under Choctaw Law, see testimony of No1			
10						
11						
12						
13						
14						
15						
16			Date of Application for Enrollment.	5/30/99		
17						

Choctaw By Blood Enrollment Cards 1898-1914

RESIDENCE: Wade   COUNTY.   **Choctaw Nation**   Choctaw Roll *(Not Including Freedmen)*   CARD NO.

POST OFFICE: Talihina, I.T.   FIELD NO. 2132

Dawes' Roll No.	NAME		Relationship to Person	AGE	SEX	BLOOD	TRIBAL ENROLLMENT		
							Year	County	No.
6160	1 Bohanan, William	40	First Named	37	M	1/2	1896	Wade	1001
6161	2 " Emiline	37	Wife	34	F	Full	1896	"	1002
6162	3 Johnico, Caroline	16	Dau	13	"	3/4	1896	"	1003
6163	4 Bohanan Eli	12	Son	9	M	3/4	1896	"	1004
6164	5 " Pearl	9	Dau	6	F	3/4	1896	"	1005
6165	6 " Margaret	7	"	4	"	3/4	1896	"	1006
6166	7 " Beulah	5	"	1	"	3/4			
6167	8 " Joshua D	1	Son	2mo	M	3/4			
6168	9 Johnico, Aline	1	GrDau	6mo	F	7/8			
	10								
	11								
	12								
	13								
	14								
	15	ENROLLMENT OF NOS. 1,2,3,4,5,6,7,8,9 HEREON							
	16	APPROVED BY THE SECRETARY OF INTERIOR JAN 17 1903							
	17								

TRIBAL ENROLLMENT OF PARENTS

	Name of Father	Year	County	Name of Mother	Year	County
1	Sam'l Bohanan	1896	Jacks Fork	Margaret Bohanan	1896	Jacks Fork
2	Alfred Sexton	Dead	Wade	Julie A Sexton	Dead	Sugar Loaf
3	No 1			No 2		
4	No 1			No 2		
5	No 1			No 2		
6	No 1			No 2		
7	No 1			No 2		
8	No 1			No 2		
9	Isham Johnico	1896	Wade	Nº3		
10	Nº3 was married to Isham Johnico Oct 9 1900. Evidence of marriage filed May 8 1902					
11	Nº9 Born Oct 21, 1901: Enrolled May 8 1902					
12	No6 on 1896 roll as Henrietta Bohanan					
	No7 Affidavit of birth to be supplied. Recd June 8/99					
13	No8 Enrolled June 18 1901					
14	Full name of No1 is William Johnson Bohanan, and that of No8 Joshua Daniel Bohanan. See					
15	letter of No1 filed this day July 16, 1901					
	For child of No3 see NB (March 3, 1905) #1211					
16					#1 to 7	
17				Date of Application for Enrollment	5/30/99	

32

RESIDENCE: Wade   COUNTY. **Choctaw Nation**   **Choctaw Roll** *(Not Including Freedmen)*   CARD NO.

POST OFFICE: Talihina, I.T   FIELD NO. 2133

Dawes' Roll No.	NAME		Relationship to Person First Named	AGE	SEX	BLOOD	TRIBAL ENROLLMENT		
							Year	County	No.
6169	₁ James, Silas	28		25	M	Full	1896	Wade	6732
6170	₂ " Mary	20	Wife	17	F	"	1896	"	1039
6171	₃ " Delia	4	Dau	6mo	"	"			
	4								
	5								
	6								
	7								
	8								
	9								
	10								
	11								
	12								
	13								
	14								
	15	ENROLLMENT OF NOS. 1, 2, 3 HEREON APPROVED BY THE SECRETARY OF INTERIOR JAN 17 1903							
	16								
	17								

TRIBAL ENROLLMENT OF PARENTS

	Name of Father	Year	County	Name of Mother	Year	County
₁	Jones James	Dead	Nashoba	Ilfie James	1896	Nashoba
₂	Minko-a-che-tubby	"	Wade4	Miley Beans	Dead	Wade
₃	No 1			No 2		
₄						
₅						
₆						
₇	No2 on 1896 roll as Phoebe James: (should be Phoebe Beams)					
₈	For children of Nos 1&2 see NB (March 3 1905) #567					
₉						
₁₀						
₁₁						
₁₂						
₁₃						
₁₄						
₁₅					Date of Application for Enrollment.	
₁₆					5/30/99	
₁₇						

33

RESIDENCE: Wade	COUNTY.								
POST OFFICE: Talihina, I.T.	**Choctaw Nation**					Choctaw Roll *(Not Including Freedmen)*	CARD NO. FIELD NO. 2134		

Dawes' Roll No.	NAME		Relationship to Person First Named	AGE	SEX	BLOOD	TRIBAL ENROLLMENT		
							Year	County	No.
6172	1 Paxton, Eli	28	First Named	25	M	Full	1896	Wade	10291
6173	2 " Lizzie	29	Wife	26	F	"	1896	"	10292
6174	3 " Missie	8	Dau	5	"	"	1896	"	10293
6175	4 " Lymon	5	Son	1½	M	"			
	5								
	6								
	7								
	8								
	9								
	10								
	11								
	12								
	13								
	14								
	15	ENROLLMENT OF NOS. 1, 2, 3, 4 HEREON APPROVED BY THE SECRETARY OF INTERIOR JAN 17 1903							
	16								
	17								

TRIBAL ENROLLMENT OF PARENTS

Name of Father	Year	County	Name of Mother	Year	County
1 John Paxton	Dead	Gaines		Dead	Gaines
2 Harlnay[sic] Johnico	"	Skullyville	Mary Johnico	"	Skullyville
3	No 1		No 2		
4	No 1		No 2		
5					
6					
7	For child of Nos 1&2 see NB (Mar 3-05) Card #115				
8					
9					
10					
11					
12					
13					
14					
15				Date of Application for Enrollment.	
16				5/30/99	
17					

RESIDENCE: Wade   COUNTY. **Choctaw Nation**   **Choctaw Roll** *(Not Including Freedmen)*   CARD NO. FIELD NO. **2135**

POST OFFICE: Talihina I.T.

Dawes' Roll No.	NAME		Relationship to Person First Named	AGE	SEX	BLOOD	TRIBAL ENROLLMENT		
							Year	County	No.
6176	1 King Adaline	15	First Named	12	F	1/2	1896	Wade	7511
	2								
	3								
	4								
	5								
	6								
	7								
	8								
	9								
	10								
	11								
	12								
	13								
	14								
	15								
	16								
	17								

ENROLLMENT
OF NOS. 1 HEREON
APPROVED BY THE SECRETARY
OF INTERIOR JAN 17 1903

TRIBAL ENROLLMENT OF PARENTS

	Name of Father	Year	County	Name of Mother	Year	County
1	Robert King	1896	Chick Roll	Emma King	Dead	Wade
2						
3						
4						
5						
6						
7						
8						
9						
10						
11						
12						
13						
14					Date of Application for Enrollment.	
15						
16					5/30/99	
17						

Choctaw By Blood Enrollment Cards 1898-1914

RESIDENCE: Wade	COUNTY.							CARD No.
POST OFFICE: Lenox I.T.	**Choctaw Nation**				Choctaw Roll (Not Including Freedmen)			FIELD No. 2136

Dawes' Roll No.	NAME	Relationship to Person First Named	AGE	SEX	BLOOD	TRIBAL ENROLLMENT		
						Year	County	No.
6177	1 Woods Gilbert 21	First Named	18	M	1/8	1896	Wade	13088
	2							
	3							
	4							
	5							
	6							
	7							
	8							
	9							
	10							
	11							
	12							
	13							
	14							
	15	ENROLLMENT OF NOS. 1 HEREON APPROVED BY THE SECRETARY OF INTERIOR JAN 17 1903						
	16							
	17							

TRIBAL ENROLLMENT OF PARENTS

	Name of Father	Year	County	Name of Mother	Year	County
1	B J Woods	1896	Wade	Josephine R Woods	1896	Wade
2						
3						
4						
5	No.1 is now the husband of Lizzie Anderson on Choctaw Card #2146 June 18, 1901					
6	For child of No.1 see NB (March 3, 1905) #1245					
7						
8						
9						
10						
11						
12						
13						
14						
15						Date of Application for Enrollment.
16						5/30/99
17						

36

Choctaw By Blood Enrollment Cards 1898-1914

RESIDENCE: Wade	COUNTY. **Choctaw Nation**			**Choctaw Roll** *(Not Including Freedmen)*	CARD No.	
POST OFFICE: Talihina I.T.					FIELD No. 2137	

Dawes' Roll No.	NAME	Relationship to Person	AGE	SEX	BLOOD	TRIBAL ENROLLMENT		
						Year	County	No.
6178	1 White Louis ²⁶	First Named	23	M	Full	1896	Wade	13060
6179	2 " Elsie ²⁵	Wife	22	F	"	1896	"	9251
6180	3 M°Farland Alexander¹²	S Son	9	M	"	1896	"	9252
	4							
	5							
	6							
	7							
	8							
	9							
	10							
	11							
	12							
	13							
	14							
	15	ENROLLMENT OF NOS. 1, 2, 3 HEREON APPROVED BY THE SECRETARY OF INTERIOR JAN 17 1903						
	16							
	17							

TRIBAL ENROLLMENT OF PARENTS

	Name of Father	Year	County	Name of Mother	Year	County
1	Jerry Whiter	1896	Wade		Ded	Sugar Loaf
2		Ded			"	
3	Easton M°Farland	"	Wade	No 2		
4						
5						
6						
7						
8		No.2 on 1896 roll as Elsie M°Farland				
9						
10						
11						
12						
13						
14					Date of Application for Enrollment	
15						
16					5/30/99	
17						

Choctaw By Blood Enrollment Cards 1898-1914

RESIDENCE: _____ COUNTY.
POST OFFICE: _____

Choctaw Nation

Choctaw Roll (*Not Including Freedmen*)

CARD NO.
FIELD NO. 2138

Dawes' Roll No.	NAME	Relationship to Person First Named	AGE	SEX	BLOOD	TRIBAL ENROLLMENT Year	County	No.
6181	Tasahaya Amos		52	M	Full	1896	Wade	12066
6182	2 " Amaziah 18	Son	15	"	"	1896	"	12067
6183	3 " Emma 12	Dau	9	F	"	1896	"	12068
	4							
	5							
	6							
	7							
	8							
	9							
	10							
	11							
	12							
	13							
	14							
	15	ENROLLMENT OF NOS. 1, 2, 3 HEREON APPROVED BY THE SECRETARY OF INTERIOR JAN 17 1903						
	16							
	17							

TRIBAL ENROLLMENT OF PARENTS

	Name of Father	Year	County	Name of Mother	Year	County
1	Tasahambi	Ded	Nashoba	Onahaoyo	Ded	Nashoba
2	No 1			Listy Tasahaya	"	"
3	No 1			" "	"	"
4						
5						
6	No1 died Sept - 1901: Enrollment cancelled by Department May 2, 1906					
7	No2 is duplicate of Emiziah Bohanan. No3 is duplicate of Emma					
8	Bohanan on Choctaw Card #5622 and #5623 Roll Nos #14838 and					
9	#14839 Enrollment hereon cancelled under Departmental letter					
	of June 7, 1905 (ITD 6366-1905) D.C. 28673-1905					
10	No2 on 1896 roll as Amaziah Tasahaya					
11	No3 " " " " Emeline "					
12						
13						
14						
15						
16				Date of Application for Enrollment.	5/30/99	
17						

38

RESIDENCE: Wade   COUNTY. **Choctaw Nation**   **Choctaw Roll**   CARD NO.

POST OFFICE: Talihina I.T.   *(Not Including Freedmen)*   FIELD NO. 2139

Dawes' Roll No.	NAME	Relationship to Person	AGE	SEX	BLOOD	TRIBAL ENROLLMENT		
						Year	County	No.
6184	1 Willis Chester ²³	First Named	20	M	1/4	1896	Wade	13052
	2							
	3							
	4							
	5							
	6							
	7							
	8							
	9							
	10							
	11							
	12							
	13							
	14							
	15							
	16							
	17							

ENROLLMENT
OF NOS. 1 HEREON
APPROVED BY THE SECRETARY
OF INTERIOR JAN 17 1903

TRIBAL ENROLLMENT OF PARENTS

	Name of Father	Year	County	Name of Mother	Year	County
1	Robert Willis	Ded	Non Citz	Sarah Willis	1896	Wade
2						
3						
4						
5						
6						
7						
8						
9						
10						
11						
12						
13						
14						
15						
16				Date of Application for Enrollment		5/30/99
17						

39

Choctaw By Blood Enrollment Cards 1898-1914

RESIDENCE: Wade   COUNTY. **Choctaw Nation**   **Choctaw Roll** (Not Including Freedmen)   CARD No.
POST OFFICE: Lenox I.T.   FIELD No. 2140

Dawes' Roll No.	NAME	Relationship to Person First Named	AGE	SEX	BLOOD	TRIBAL ENROLLMENT		
						Year	County	No.
6185	1 Woods Wesley 30	Named	27	M	1/8	1896	Wade	13095
	2							
	3							
	4							
	5							
	6							
	7							
	8							
	9							
	10							
	11							
	12							
	13							
	14							
	15	ENROLLMENT OF NOS. 1 HEREON APPROVED BY THE SECRETARY OF INTERIOR JAN 17 1903						
	16							
	17							

TRIBAL ENROLLMENT OF PARENTS

	Name of Father	Year	County	Name of Mother	Year	County
1	Stephen Woods	Ded	Wade	Eliza Woods	Ded	Wade
2						
3						
4						
5						
6	No1 is now the husband of Jane Frazier on Choctaw card #5582					
7						
8						
9						
10						
11						
12						
13						
14						
15						
16					Date of Application for Enrollment.	5/30/99
17						

40

RESIDENCE:	Wade	COUNTY.							CARD No.	
POST OFFICE:	Scott I.T.		**Choctaw Nation**			**Choctaw Roll** *(Not Including Freedmen)*			FIELD No.	2141

Dawes' Roll No.	NAME		Relationship to Person	AGE	SEX	BLOOD	TRIBAL ENROLLMENT		
							Year	County	No.
6186	₁ Tomlis Sibbail	63	First Named	60	F	Full	1896	Wade	12065
	2								
	3								
	4								
	5								
	6								
	7								
	8								
	9								
	10								
	11								
	12								
	13								
	14								
	15	ENROLLMENT OF NOS. 1 HEREON							
	16	APPROVED BY THE SECRETARY							
	17	OF INTERIOR JAN 17 1903							

TRIBAL ENROLLMENT OF PARENTS

Name of Father	Year	County	Name of Mother	Year	County
₁ Alexson Bonn	Ded	Wade	Falamahona	Ded	Wade
2					
3					
4					
5					
6	On 1896 roll as Isabel Tomlis				
7					
8					
9					
10					
11					
12					
13					
14					
15					
16				Date of Application for Enrollment	5/30/99
17					

41

Choctaw By Blood Enrollment Cards 1898-1914

RESIDENCE: Wade   COUNTY. **Choctaw Nation**   **Choctaw Roll** *(Not Including Freedmen)*   CARD NO.

POST OFFICE: Muse I.T.   FIELD NO. 2142

Dawes' Roll No.	NAME		Relationship to Person First Named	AGE	SEX	BLOOD	TRIBAL ENROLLMENT		
							Year	County	No.
6187	1 Billy Maggie	48	First Named	45	F	Full	1896	Wade	1013
6188	2 " Levi	21	Son	18	M	"	1896	"	1015
6189	3 " Sophia	16	Dau	13	F	"	1896	"	1016
	4								
	5								
	6								
	7								
	8								
	9								
	10								
	11								
	12								
	13								
	14								
	15	ENROLLMENT OF NOS. 1, 2, 3 HEREON							
	16	APPROVED BY THE SECRETARY OF INTERIOR JAN 17 1903							
	17								

TRIBAL ENROLLMENT OF PARENTS

	Name of Father	Year	County	Name of Mother	Year	County
1	Alexson Bonn	Ded	Wade	Falamhona[sic]	Ded	Wade
2	James Billy	"	"	No 1		
3	" "	"	"	No 1		
4						
5						
6						
7						
8						
9						
10						
11						
12						
13						
14						
15				Date of Application for Enrollment.		5/30/99
16						
17	P.O. Talihina I.T. 2/25/06					

Choctaw By Blood Enrollment Cards 1898-1914

RESIDENCE: Wade   COUNTY. **Choctaw Nation**   **Choctaw Roll** *(Not Including Freedmen)*   CARD NO.
POST OFFICE: (Scott) I.T.   FIELD NO. 2143

Dawes' Roll No.	NAME	Relationship to Person	AGE	SEX	BLOOD	TRIBAL ENROLLMENT		
	Muse					Year	County	No.
6190	1 McCoy Wisey ⁸³	First Named	80	F	Full	1896	Wade	9238
	2							
	3							
	4							
	5							
	6							
	7							
	8							
	9							
	10							
	11							
	12							
	13							
	14							
	15							
	16							
	17							

ENROLLMENT
OF NOS. 1 HEREON
APPROVED BY THE SECRETARY
OF INTERIOR JAN 17 1903

TRIBAL ENROLLMENT OF PARENTS

	Name of Father	Year	County	Name of Mother	Year	County
1	Alexson Bonn	Ded	Wade	Falamhona	Ded	Wade
2						
3						
4						
5						
6						
7						
8						
9						
10						
11						
12						
13						
14						
15						
16				Date of Application for Enrollment.	5/30/99	
17						

43

Choctaw By Blood Enrollment Cards 1898-1914

| RESIDENCE: | Wade | COUNTY. | | | | | | | | |
| POST OFFICE: | Talihina I.T. | | | | | | | | | |

Choctaw Nation — Choctaw Roll *(Not Including Freedmen)*

CARD No. FIELD No. 2144

Dawes' Roll No.	NAME		Relationship to Person	AGE	SEX	BLOOD	TRIBAL ENROLLMENT		
							Year	County	No.
6191	1 Lewis Silas	24	First Named	21	M	Full	1896	Wade	7887
	2								
	3								
	4								
	5								
	6								
	7								
	8								
	9								
	10								
	11								
	12								
	13								
	14								
	15	ENROLLMENT OF NOS. 1 HEREON							
	16	APPROVED BY THE SECRETARY							
	17	OF INTERIOR JAN 17 1903							

TRIBAL ENROLLMENT OF PARENTS

	Name of Father	Year	County	Name of Mother	Year	County
1	Sampson Lewis	1896	Wade	Leon Lewis	Ded	Wade
2						
3						
4						
5						
6	Child of No1 on NB (Apr 26-06) Card #292					
7	" " " " " (Mar 3-05) " #820					
8						
9						
10						
11						
12						
13						
14						
15						
16				Date of Application for Enrollment:	5/30/99	
17						

44

Choctaw By Blood Enrollment Cards 1898-1914

RESIDENCE: Wade COUNTY. **Choctaw Nation** **Choctaw Roll** CARD No.
POST OFFICE: Tushkahoma[sic] I.T. *(Not Including Freedmen)* FIELD No. 2145

Dawes' Roll No.	NAME	Relationship to Person Named	AGE	SEX	BLOOD	TRIBAL ENROLLMENT		
						Year	County	No.
I.W. 900	1 Bell George W (43)	First Named	40	M	I.W.	1896	Wade	14311
	2							
	3							
	4							
	5	ENROLLMENT						
	6	OF NOS. 1 HEREON APPROVED BY THE SECRETARY						
	7	OF INTERIOR AUG 3 1904						
	8							
	9							
	10							
	11							
	12							
	13							
	14							
	15							
	16							
	17							

TRIBAL ENROLLMENT OF PARENTS

	Name of Father	Year	County	Name of Mother	Year	County
1	G H Bell	Ded	Non Citz	Elizabeth Bell	Ded	Non Citz
2						
3						
4						
5	No1 Claims thru 1st wife Phoebe Bell 1893 Leard Dist Pay Roll Wade Co No 42 [illegible]					
6	See testimony of himself, Davis Anderson					
7	and Allan Anderson as to marriage					
8	No1 is now husband of Amy Cravette on Choctaw card #1914: evidence of marriage filed Dec 15, 1902 on final Roll #546					
9	No1 Evidence of marriage to Phebe McKinney received and filed Aug 17, 1903					
10						
11						
12						
13						
14						
15						
16					Date of Application for Enrollment	5/30/99
17						

45

Choctaw By Blood Enrollment Cards 1898-1914

RESIDENCE: Wade	COUNTY. Choctaw Nation					Choctaw Roll (Not Including Freedmen)	CARD NO.
POST OFFICE: Talihina, I.T.						FIELD NO.	2146

Dawes' Roll No.	NAME	Relationship to Person	AGE	SEX	BLOOD	TRIBAL ENROLLMENT		
						Year	County	No.
6192	1 Anderson, Houston D 44	First Named	41	M	1/2	1896	Wade	151
DEAD	2 " Hester	Wife	19	F	I.W.			
6193	3 " Joshua 19	Son	16	M	3/4	1896	Wade	153
6194	4 Woods, Lizzie E 18	Dau	15	F	3/4	1896	"	154
6195	5 Anderson, Davis 14	Son	11	M	3/4	1896	"	155
6196	6 " James 11	"	8	"	3/4	1896	"	156
6197	7 Woods, Josie Lou 2	Grand dau	6mo	F	7/16			
	8							
	9							
	10 No.2 hereon dismissed under order of							
	11 the Commission to the Five Civilized							
	12 Tribes of March 31, 1905.							
	13							
	14							
	15 ENROLLMENT OF NOS. 1,3,4,5,6,7 HEREON							
	16 APPROVED BY THE SECRETARY OF INTERIOR Jan 17, 1903							
	17							

TRIBAL ENROLLMENT OF PARENTS

	Name of Father	Year	County	Name of Mother	Year	County
1	John Anderson	Ded	Wade	Mary Anderson	Ded	Wade
2	R S Ross	1896	Non Citz	Mary Ross	1896	Non Citz
3	No 1			Lucinda Anderson	Ded	Wade
4	No 1			" "	"	"
5	No 1			" "	"	"
6	No 1			" "	"	"
7	Gilbert Woods	1896	Wade	No 4		
8						
9	For child of No4 see NB (March 3 1905) #1245					
10	For child of No4 see NB (Apr 26 06) Card #869					
11	For children " " 1 " (Mar 3-05) " #484					
12	No4 is now the wife of Gilbert Woods on Choctaw Card #2136 Evidence of marriage filed June 18, 1901					
13	No7 Enrolled June 18 1902					
14	Full maiden name of No4 was Lizzie Edith Anderson See letter of her husband Gilbert W Woods filed this day July 16, 1901				Date of Application for Enrollment.	
15	No2 died Jan'y 19, 1901: Proof of death filed Dec 12 1902					
16	No1 is now husband of Jane Burns Choc #3000				5/30/99	
17						

46

| RESIDENCE: Wade | COUNTY. | | | | | | | | |
| POST OFFICE: Talihina I.T. | **Choctaw Nation** | | | | Choctaw Roll *(Not Including Freedmen)* | | CARD No. FIELD No. 2147 | | |

Dawes' Roll No.	NAME		Relationship to Person	AGE	SEX	BLOOD	TRIBAL ENROLLMENT		
							Year	County	No.
6198	1 Daney Daniel	43	First Named	40	M	Full	1896	Wade	3325
6199	2 " Rebecca	29	Wife	26	F	"	1896	"	3326
6200	3 " Solomon	20	Son	17	M	"	1896	"	3329
6201	4 " Gilbert	15	"	12	"	"	1896	"	3330
6202	5 " Joel	8	"	5	"	"	1896	"	3331
6203	6 " Malinda	6	Dau	3	F	"	1896	"	3332
6204	7 " Benjamin	4	Son	3/4	M	"			
6205	8 " Harris	2	Son	7mo	M	"			
6206	9 " Joseph	1	Son	2mo	M	"			
	10								
	11								
	12								
	13								
	14								
	15	ENROLLMENT OF NOS. 1,2,3,4,5,6,7,8,9 HEREON							
	16	APPROVED BY THE SECRETARY OF INTERIOR JAN 17 1903							
	17								

TRIBAL ENROLLMENT OF PARENTS

	Name of Father	Year	County	Name of Mother	Year	County
1	Solomon Daney	Ded	Wade	Levina Daney	1896	Wade
2	Reny Anderson	"	"	Susie Anderson	Ded	"
3	No 1			Nancy Daney	"	"
4	No 1			" "		
5	No 1			No 2		
6	No 1			No 2		
7	No 1			No 2		
8	No 1			No 2		
9	Nº1			Nº2		
10						
11	No.8 Enrolled April 24, 1901					
12	Nº9 Born July 22, 1901. Enrolled Sept 30, 1902					
13	For child of No3 see NB (March 3 1905) #834					
	" " "Nos1&2 " " " " #835					
14						
15				#1 to 7	Date of Application for Enrollment.	
16			Date of application for enrollment		5/30/99	
17						

Choctaw By Blood Enrollment Cards 1898-1914

RESIDENCE: Wade   COUNTY. **Choctaw Nation**   **Choctaw Roll** *(Not Including Freedmen)*   CARD NO.

POST OFFICE: Talihina I.T   FIELD NO. 2148

Dawes' Roll No.	NAME	Relationship to Person First Named	AGE	SEX	BLOOD	TRIBAL ENROLLMENT Year	TRIBAL ENROLLMENT County	TRIBAL ENROLLMENT No.
DEAD	1 Johnson Mitchell		38	M	Full	1896	Wade	6724
6207	2 " Adeline 31	Wife	28	F	"	1896	"	6725
6208	3 " Ella 5	Dau	2	"	"			
	4							
	5							
	6							
	7							
	8							
	9							
	10							
	11 No. 1 HEREON DISMISSED UNDER ORDER OF THE COMMISSION TO THE FIVE CIVILIZED TRIBES OF MARCH 31, 1905.							
	12							
	13							
	14							
	15 ENROLLMENT OF NOS. 2, 3 HEREON APPROVED BY THE SECRETARY OF INTERIOR JAN 17 1903							
	16							
	17							

TRIBAL ENROLLMENT OF PARENTS

Name of Father	Year	County	Name of Mother	Year	County
1 Tishoamla	Ded	Wade	Aloba	Ded	Wade
2 James Wright	"	"	Lavina Wright	"	"
3 No 1			No 2		
4					
5					
6					
7	No.1 Died April 25, 1900. Evidence of death filed May 11, 1901				
8	No2 on 1896 roll as Adaline Johnson				
9	For child of No2 see NB (Mar 3,05) #834				
10					
11					
12					
13					
14					
15				Date of Application for Enrollment	
16				5/30/99	
17					

Choctaw By Blood Enrollment Cards 1898-1914

RESIDENCE: Wade
POST OFFICE: Talihina I.T.

COUNTY: **Choctaw Nation**

Choctaw Roll (Not Including Freedmen)

CARD NO.
FIELD NO. **2149**

Dawes' Roll No.	NAME		Relationship to Person	AGE	SEX	BLOOD	TRIBAL ENROLLMENT		
							Year	County	No.
6209	1 Benton, Jacob	45	First Named	42	M	Full	1896	Wade	973
6210	2 " Eliza	43	Wife	40	F	"	1896	"	974
Dead	3 Armstrong, Elias DEAD		Neph	17	M	"	1896	"	162
6211	4 " Noel	17	"	14	"	"	1896	"	163
	5								
	6								
	7								
	8								
	9	No. 3 hereon dismissed under order of							
	10	the Commission to the Five Civilized							
	11	Tribes of March 31, 1905.							
	12								
	13	ENROLLMENT							
	14	OF NOS. 1, 2, 4 HEREON APPROVED BY THE SECRETARY							
	15	OF INTERIOR Jan 17, 1903							
	16								
	17								

TRIBAL ENROLLMENT OF PARENTS

	Name of Father	Year	County	Name of Mother	Year	County
1	John Benton	Ded	Wade	Mintihima	Ded	Wade
2	Sidney Dyer	"	"	Susie Dyer	"	"
3	Edwin Armstrong	"	"	Mary Armstrong	"	"
4	"	"	"	"	"	"
5						
6	No 3 Died September 15, 1899 Evidence of death filed April 6, 1901					
7						
8						
9	No 2 Died July 28, 1896 See inhereted[sic] land Sale					
10						
11						
12						
13						
14						
15				Date of Application for Enrollment.		
16				5/30/99		
17						

49

Choctaw By Blood Enrollment Cards 1898-1914

RESIDENCE: Wade   COUNTY. **Choctaw Nation**   **Choctaw Roll** (Not Including Freedmen)   CARD NO.

POST OFFICE: Talihina I.T.   FIELD NO. 2150

Dawes' Roll No.	NAME		Relationship to Person	AGE	SEX	BLOOD	TRIBAL ENROLLMENT		
							Year	County	No.
6212	1 Bohanan Levi W	35	First Named	32	M	3/4	1896	Wade	1036
6213	2 " Harriet	22	Wife	19	F	Full	1896	"	971
	3								
	4								
	5								
	6								
	7								
	8								
	9								
	10								
	11								
	12								
	13								
	14								
	15	ENROLLMENT OF NOS. 1, 2 HEREON							
	16	APPROVED BY THE SECRETARY							
	17	OF INTERIOR JAN 17 1903							

TRIBAL ENROLLMENT OF PARENTS

	Name of Father	Year	County	Name of Mother	Year	County
1	T H Bohanan	1896	Jacks Fork	Margaret Bohanan	1896	Jacks Fork
2	Nelson Bennett	1896	Wade	Phoebe Bennett	1896	Wade
3						
4						
5						
6						
7						
8						
9						
10		No1 on 1896 roll as Levi Bohanan				
11		No2 " " " " Harriett Benton				
12		For child of Nos 1&2 see NB (March 3 1905) #765				
13						
14						Date of Application for Enrollment.
15						
16						5/30/99
17						

RESIDENCE: Nashoba   COUNTY. **Choctaw Nation**   **Choctaw Roll** *(Not Including Freedmen)*

POST OFFICE: Smithville I.T.   CARD NO. FIELD NO. **2151**

Dawes' Roll No.	NAME	Relationship to Person First Named	AGE	SEX	BLOOD	TRIBAL ENROLLMENT Year	County	No.
6214	1 Watson, Podenie 21		18	F	3/4	1896	Nashoba	4776
6215	2 " Mary 4	Dau	6mo	"	1/2			
6216	3 " Isic 2	Son	1yr	M	1/2			
	4							
	5							
	6							
	7							
	8							
	9							
	10							
	11							
	12							
	13							
	14							
	15							
	16							
	17							

ENROLLMENT
OF NOS. 1, 2, 3 HEREON
APPROVED BY THE SECRETARY
OF INTERIOR Jan 17, 1903

TRIBAL ENROLLMENT OF PARENTS

	Name of Father	Year	County	Name of Mother	Year	County
1	Dennis Wilkins	Dead	Nashoba	Mandy Wilkins		Nashoba
2	Thomas Watson		"	No 1		
3	" "		"	No 1		
4						
5			No1 on 1896 Roll as Po Denie Gibson			
6			No1 Affidavit of birth to be supplied			
7			filed Nov 1/99			
8			Husband of No1 Thomas Watson on Card No 5633			
9			No3 Enrolled Dau 14, 1901			
10			For child of No1 see NB (Mar 3-1905) Card No 59			
11						
12						
13						
14						Date of Application for Enrollment.
15						
16						May 30/99
17	P.O. Bethel I.T. 4/6/05					

Choctaw By Blood Enrollment Cards 1898-1914

RESIDENCE: Wade COUNTY. **Choctaw Nation** Choctaw Roll CARD NO.
POST OFFICE: Talihina I.T. (Not Including Freedmen) FIELD NO. 2152

Dawes' Roll No.	NAME		Relationship to Person	AGE	SEX	BLOOD	TRIBAL ENROLLMENT		
							Year	County	No.
6217	1 Beams Seon	35	First Named	32	F	Full	1896	Wade	1021
6218	2 " Lillie	16	Dau	13	F	3/4	1896	"	1022
6219	3 " Susan	5	Dau	18mo	F	3/4			
6220	4 " Carrie Sockey	1	Dau	6mo	F	7/8			
	5								
	6								
	7								
	8								
	9								
	10								
	11								
	12								
	13								
	14								
	15	ENROLLMENT OF NOS. 1, 2, 3, 4 HEREON							
	16	APPROVED BY THE SECRETARY OF INTERIOR JAN 17 1903							
	17								

TRIBAL ENROLLMENT OF PARENTS

Name of Father	Year	County	Name of Mother	Year	County
1 Nott Graham	Dead	Wade	Liney Graham	Dead	Wade
2 Temus Beams	"	"	No 1		
3 " "			No 1		
4 Robert Sockey	1896	"	No 1		
5					
6					
7					
8		No 1 On 1896 roll as Cearn Beams			
9		No2 " " " " Siddie Beams			
10		No.4 born July 14, 1901: Enrolled Jan 9, 1902			
11					
12					
13					
14					#1 to 3
15					Date of Application for Enrollment.
16					5/30/99
17					

Choctaw By Blood Enrollment Cards 1898-1914

RESIDENCE: Wade   COUNTY. **Choctaw Nation**   **Choctaw Roll** *(Not Including Freedmen)*   CARD No. FIELD No. **2153**
POST OFFICE: Muse, I.T.

Dawes' Roll No.	NAME		Relationship to Person First Named	AGE	SEX	BLOOD	TRIBAL ENROLLMENT		
							Year	County	No.
6221	1 James, Patterson	29	First Named	26	M	Full	1896	Wade	6719
6222	2 " Sarah	26	Wife	23	F	"	1896	"	6720
6223	3 " Caroline	7	Dau	4	F	"	1896	"	6721
6224	4 " Ida	4	Dau	4mo	F	"			
6225	5 " Wallace	1	Son	1mo	M	"			
	6								
	7								
	8								
	9								
	10								
	11								
	12								
	13								
	14								
	15	ENROLLMENT OF NOS. 1,2,3,4,5 HEREON APPROVED BY THE SECRETARY OF INTERIOR Jan 17, 1903								
	16								
	17								

TRIBAL ENROLLMENT OF PARENTS

	Name of Father	Year	County	Name of Mother	Year	County
1	Pe-sa-He-ka-be	Dead	Wade	Sally Ann James	1896	Wade
2	Billy Beams	"	"	Hannah Beams	Dead	"
3	No 1			No 2		
4	No 1			No 2		
5	No 1			No 2		
6						
7						
8			No5 Enrolled June 6th 1901			
9						
10			For child of Nos 1&2 see NB (Apr 26-06) Card #676			
11			" " " " " " " (Mar 3-05) " #911			
12						
13						
14						
15						#1 to 4
16				Date of Application for Enrollment.		5/30/99
17						

53

Choctaw By Blood Enrollment Cards 1898-1914

RESIDENCE: Wade   COUNTY. **Choctaw Nation**   **Choctaw Roll** (Not Including Freedmen)   CARD NO.

POST OFFICE: Talihina I.T.   FIELD NO. 2154

Dawes' Roll No.	NAME	Relationship to Person First Named	AGE	SEX	BLOOD	TRIBAL ENROLLMENT		
						Year	County	No.
6226	1 Bacon Ellis 21	First Named	18	M	Full	1896	Wade	1031
	2							
	3							
	4							
	5							
	6							
	7							
	8							
	9							
	10							
	11							
	12							
	13							
	14							
	15							
	16							
	17							

ENROLLMENT OF NOS. 1 HEREON APPROVED BY THE SECRETARY OF INTERIOR JAN 17 1903

TRIBAL ENROLLMENT OF PARENTS

	Name of Father	Year	County	Name of Mother	Year	County
1	Wilson Bacon	Dead	Wade	Luissy Bacon	Dead	Wade
2						
3						
4						
5						
6						
7						
8						
9						
10						
11						
12						
13						
14						
15					Date of Application for Enrollment.	
16						5/30/99
17						

54

Choctaw By Blood Enrollment Cards 1898-1914

RESIDENCE: Wade	COUNTY.				Choctaw Roll	CARD NO.
POST OFFICE: Muse I.T.	Choctaw Nation				(Not Including Freedmen)	FIELD NO. 2155

Dawes' Roll No.	NAME	Relationship to Person	AGE	SEX	BLOOD	TRIBAL ENROLLMENT		
						Year	County	No.
6227 1	Newsom Sophia 32	First Named	29	F	Full	1896	Wade	9625
6228 2	" Martha 10	Dau	7	F	1/2	1896	"	9626
6229 3	" Henry 9	Son	6	M	1/2	1896	"	9627
6230 4	~~" Daphne~~ DIED PRIOR TO SEPTEMBER 25, 1902	Dau	13mo	F	1/2			
6231 5	" Simon L 2	Son	20mo	M	1/2			
6232 6	" Ivey E 1	Son	9mo	M	1/2			
I.W. 714 7	" James 34	Husb	34	M	I.W.			
8		Nos 1 – 2 and 3 all on 1896 roll as Newson						
9								
10								
11	ENROLLMENT							
12	OF NOS. ~~~ 7 ~~~ HEREON APPROVED BY THE SECRETARY							
13	OF INTERIOR MAY -7 1904							
14								
15	ENROLLMENT							
16	OF NOS. 1,2,3,4,5,6 HEREON APPROVED BY THE SECRETARY							
17	OF INTERIOR JAN 17 1903							

TRIBAL ENROLLMENT OF PARENTS

	Name of Father	Year	County	Name of Mother	Year	County
1	Edwin Armstrong	Dead	Wade	Mary Benton	Dead	Wade
2	James Newson	1896	Non Citz	No 1		
3	" "	1896	" "	No 1		
4	" "	1896	" "	No 1		
5	" "		" "	Nº1		
6	" "		" "	Nº1		
7	John W Newsom	Dead	Non Citz	Juliette Newsom	Dead	Non Citz
8						
9	Father James Newson on W.C. No. D186					
10						
11	No4 Affidavit of birth to be supplied					
12	Recd Oct 6/99					
13	Nº5 Born Dec 14, 1900: enrolled Aug 19, 1902					
14	Nº6 Born Nov 16, 1901: enrolled Aug 19, 1902					
	No4 Died Aug 1st 1901: Proof of Death filed Decr 23rd 1902					#1 to 4
15						Date of Application for Enrollment.
16	Nº7 transferred from Choctaw card #D186. See decision of Feby 27, 1904					5/30/99
17	No4 died Aug 1, 1901: Enrollment cancelled by Department [illegible]					

55

Choctaw By Blood Enrollment Cards 1898-1914

RESIDENCE: Wade COUNTY.
POST OFFICE: Lenox I.T.

Choctaw Nation

Choctaw Roll
(Not Including Freedmen)

CARD NO.
FIELD NO. **2156**

Dawes' Roll No.	NAME	Relationship to Person First Named	AGE	SEX	BLOOD	TRIBAL ENROLLMENT Year	County	No.
DEAD	1 Potts Forbes	36	M	Full	1896	Wade	10298
6233	2 Sockey Rhoda ³¹	Wife	28	F	"	1896	"	10299
6234	3 Potts William ¹¹	Son	8	M	"	1896	"	10300
6235	4 " Susanna ⁶	Dau	3	F	"	1896	"	10301
6236	5 " Simon ⁴	Son	5mo	M	"			
6237	6 Sockey, Moses ¹	Son of Nº 2	3mo	M	7/8			
	7							
	8 No.1 hereon dismissed under order							
	9 of the Commissioner to the Five							
	Civilized Tribes of July 18, 1905.							
	10							
	11							
	12 ENROLLMENT							
	13 OF NOS. 2,3,4,5,6 HEREON							
	14 APPROVED BY THE SECRETARY OF INTERIOR Jan 17 1903							
	15							
	16							
	17							

TRIBAL ENROLLMENT OF PARENTS

	Name of Father	Year	County	Name of Mother	Year	County
1	Philip Potts	Dead	Wade	Jinny Potts	Dead	Wade
2	Willis Hampton	"	Sugar Loaf	Charlotta Hampton	"	Sugar Loaf
3	No 1			No 2		
4	No 1			No 2		
5	No 1			No 2		
6	Robert Sakki	1896	Wade	Nº2		
7						
8	No4 On 1896 roll as Susan A Potts					
9	No2 is now the wife of Robert Sakki on Choctaw card #2119 June 14, 1902, evidence of marriage filed 6/14/02					
10	#4 Died 2/4/1901 Proof of death filed Dec 16, 1902 in allotment jacket					
11	Nº6 Born March 23, 1902: enrolled June 14, 1902					
12						
13	No1 died May 14, 1900: proof of death filed Nov 4, 1905					
14	For child of No2 see NB (Apr 26-06) Card #927					
15					1 to 5	
16					Date of Application for Enrollment.	
17	P.O. Talihina, I.T. 5/8/07				5/30/99	

56

Choctaw By Blood Enrollment Cards 1898-1914

RESIDENCE: Wade   COUNTY. **Choctaw Nation**   **Choctaw Roll** CARD NO.
POST OFFICE: Talihina I.T.   *(Not Including Freedmen)*   FIELD NO. 2157

Dawes' Roll No.	NAME	Relationship to Person	AGE	SEX	BLOOD	TRIBAL ENROLLMENT		
						Year	County	No.
6238	1 Bacon Colton ²²	First Named	19	M	Full	1896	Wade	964
	2							
	3							
	4							
	5							
	6							
	7							
	8							
	9							
	10							
	11							
	12							
	13							
	14							
	15							
	16							
	17							

ENROLLMENT
OF NOS. 1 HEREON
APPROVED BY THE SECRETARY
OF INTERIOR JAN 17 1903

TRIBAL ENROLLMENT OF PARENTS

Name of Father	Year	County	Name of Mother	Year	County
1 Reuben Bacon	Dead	Wade	Amanda Bacon	1896	Sugar Loaf
2					
3					
4					
5		On 1896 roll as Colton Bacon			
6					

DATE OF APPLICATION FOR ENROLLMENT. 5/30/99

57

RESIDENCE: Wade	COUNTY.								
POST OFFICE: Talihina, I.T.	**Choctaw Nation**					Choctaw Roll *(Not Including Freedmen)*		CARD NO. FIELD NO.	**2158**

Dawes' Roll No.	NAME	Relationship to Person	AGE	SEX	BLOOD	TRIBAL ENROLLMENT		
						Year	County	No.
6239	1 Anderson, Allen ⁴⁰	First Named	37	M	Full	118961	Wade	176
6240	2 " Levicey ²²	Wife	29	F	"	1896	"	6689
6241	3 " Dixon ¹⁸	Son	15	M	"	1896	"	180
6242	4 " Jincy ¹⁶	Dau	13	F	"	1896	"	178
6243	5 " Nicey ³⁰[sic]	Dau	10	F	"	1896	"	179
~~Dead~~	6 ~~" Israel **DEAD**~~	~~Son~~	~~6~~	~~M~~	"	~~1896~~	~~"~~	~~181~~
6244	7 " Parker ⁶	Son	3	M	"	1896	"	182
~~6245~~	~~8~~ DIED PRIOR TO SEPTEMBER 25, 2902 ~~Bethel~~	Son	9mo	M	"			
6246	9 " Auda ¹	Dau	1mo	F	"			
	10 No.6 hereon dismissed under order of							
	11 the Commission to the Five Civilized							
	12 Tribes of March 31, 1905.							
	13							
	14							
	15 ENROLLMENT							
	16 OF NOS. 1,2,3,4,5 7,8,9 HEREON APPROVED BY THE SECRETARY							
	17 OF INTERIOR Jan 17 1903							

TRIBAL ENROLLMENT OF PARENTS

	Name of Father	Year	County	Name of Mother	Year	County
1	Israel Anderson	Dead	Sugar Loaf	Motsey Anderson	Dead	Jacks Fork
2	Henry Johnson	18961	Wade	Lottie Johnson	1896	Wade
3	No 1			Elsie Anderson	Dead	"
4	No 1			" "	"	"
5	No 1			" "	"	"
6	~~No 1~~			" "	"	"
7	No 1			" "	"	"
8	~~No 1~~			~~No 2~~		
9	No 1			No 2		
10			No2 On 1896 roll as Levicey Johnson			
11			No4 " " " Jancy Anderson			
12			No5 " " " Maggie Anderson			
13			No6 Died July 22 1899. Evidence of death filed May 9, 1901			
14			No3 is not dead See letter of W a Welch filed herein May 9, 1901			
15	No8 died Oct 7 or 8 1901; proof of death filed Dec 16, 1902		No.8 Enrolled July 8, 1901			#1 to 7 inc
16	No8 died Oct 8, 1901: Enrollment cancelled by Department July 8, 1904		No9 Born Sept 5, 1902, enrolled Oct 9, 1902		Date of Application for Enrollment.	
17						5/30/99

Choctaw By Blood Enrollment Cards 1898-1914

RESIDENCE: Wade   COUNTY.   **Choctaw Nation**   **Choctaw Roll** (Not Including Freedmen)   CARD No.
POST OFFICE: Talihini[sic] I.T.   FIELD No. **2159**

Dawes' Roll No.	NAME		Relationship to Person First Named	AGE	SEX	BLOOD	TRIBAL ENROLLMENT		
							Year	County	No.
6247	1 Benton, Nelson	57	First Named	54	M	Full	1896	Wade	969
6248	2 " Phoebe	52	Wife	49	F	"	1896	"	970
6249	3 " Lillie	17	Dau	14	F	"	1896	"	972
	4								
	5								
	6								
	7								
	8								
	9								
	10								
	11								
	12								
	13								
	14								
	15								
	16								
	17								

ENROLLMENT
OF NOS. 1, 2, 3 HEREON
APPROVED BY THE SECRETARY
OF INTERIOR Jan 17 1903

TRIBAL ENROLLMENT OF PARENTS

	Name of Father	Year	County	Name of Mother	Year	County
1	John Benton	Dead	Wade	Min-te-hu-mu	Dead	Wade
2	Tish-o-hom-be	"	"	A-to-ba	"	"
3	No 1			No 2		
4						
5						
6	No3 On 1896 roll as Mollie Benton					
7	For child of No3 see NB (March 3, 1905) #768					
8						
9						
10						
11						
12						
13						
14						
15						
16				Date of Application for Enrollment.	5/30/99	
17						

Choctaw By Blood Enrollment Cards 1898-1914

RESIDENCE:	Wade		COUNTY.						CARD NO.	
POST OFFICE:	Talihina I.T.			**Choctaw Nation**			**Choctaw Roll** *(Not Including Freedmen)*		FIELD NO.	2160

Dawes' Roll No.	NAME		Relationship to Person	AGE	SEX	BLOOD	TRIBAL ENROLLMENT		
							Year	County	No.
6250	₁ Paxton Susan	28	First Named	25	F	Full	1896	Wade	13065
6251	₂ Jones Melvina	9	Dau	6	F	Full	1896	"	6679
6252	₃ Wells Alford	6	Son	3	M	"	1896	"	13066
~~Dead~~	~~₄ Wells Amanda~~		~~Dau~~	~~1~~	~~F~~	~~"~~			
6253	₅ Paxton, Selina	1	Dau	8mo	F	"			
14720	₆ " Norris	3	Son	2½	M	"			
	₇								
	₈								
	₉								
	₁₀ No._4_ HEREON DISMISSED UNDER								
	₁₁ ORDER OF THE COMMISSION TO THE FIVE CIVILIZED TRIBES OF MARCH 31, 1905.								
	₁₂								
	₁₃								
	₁₄								
	₁₅ ENROLLMENT OF NOS. 1, 2, 3, 5 HEREON APPROVED BY THE SECRETARY OF INTERIOR JAN 17 1903			ENROLLMENT OF NOS. 6 HEREON APPROVED BY THE SECRETARY OF INTERIOR MAY 20 1903					
	₁₆								
	₁₇								

TRIBAL ENROLLMENT OF PARENTS

	Name of Father	Year	County	Name of Mother	Year	County
₁	Miluard Wilse[sic]	Dead	Wade	Sophia Willse[sic]	Dead	Wade
₂	Jackson Jones	1896	Sugar Loaf	No 1		
₃	Sylwis Push	1896	Wade	No 1		
₄	" "			No 1		
₅	Gabrial Paxton	1896	Wade	№ 1		
₆	" "	1896	"	№ 1		
₇						
₈						
₉	No2 On 1896 toll as Melvina Jackson					
₁₀	No1 is now the wife of Gabrial Paxton on Choctaw card #2108. Evidence of marriage filed Oct 14, 1902					
₁₁	No5 Born Feby 2, 1902, enrolled Oct 14, 1902					
₁₂	No6 Born March 17, 1900, enrolled Nov 11, 1902					
₁₃	No1 now Susan Pexton[sic] see letter in General Office filed-s #11802 1901 Geo U Benton					
₁₄	No4 Died in July 1899; Proof of death filed Nov 23 1904				#1 to 4	
₁₅					Date of Application for Enrollment.	
₁₆	For child of No1 see NB (Mar 3- 1905) Card No 58				5/30/99	
₁₇						

Choctaw By Blood Enrollment Cards 1898-1914

RESIDENCE: Wade	COUNTY. **Choctaw Nation**			**Choctaw Roll** *(Not Including Freedmen)*	CARD NO.		
POST OFFICE: Lenox I.T.					FIELD NO. 2161		

Dawes' Roll No.	NAME	Relationship to Person	AGE	SEX	BLOOD	TRIBAL ENROLLMENT		
						Year	County	No.
6254	1 Billy Josiah ²⁹	First Named	26	M	Full	1896	Wade	954
6255	2 " Winnie ²⁵	Wife	22	F	1/2	1896	"	955
6256	3 " Nancy ²	Dau	10m	F	3/4			
	4							
	5							
	6							
	7							
	8							
	9							
	10							
	11							
	12							
	13							
	14							
	15	ENROLLMENT OF NOS. 1, 2, 3 HEREON						
	16	APPROVED BY THE SECRETARY						
	17	OF INTERIOR JAN 17 1903						

TRIBAL ENROLLMENT OF PARENTS

	Name of Father	Year	County	Name of Mother	Year	County
1	James Billy	Dead	Wade	Maggie Billy	1896	Wade
2	John Anderson	"	"	Betsy Anderson	Dead	Jacks Fork
3	No 1			No 2		
4						
5						
6						
7	For child of Nos 1&2 see NB (Apr 26,1896) Card No.41					
8	" " " " " " (Mar 3ʳᵈ 1905) " " 116					
9						
10						
11						
12						
13						
14						
15					Date of Application for Enrollment.	
16				Date of application for enrollment 5/30/99		
17						

Choctaw By Blood Enrollment Cards 1898-1914

RESIDENCE: Wade COUNTY. **Choctaw Nation**   Choctaw Roll   CARD No.
POST OFFICE: Albion I.T.   (Not Including Freedmen)   FIELD No. 2162

Dawes' Roll No.	NAME	Relationship to Person	AGE	SEX	BLOOD	TRIBAL ENROLLMENT		
						Year	County	No.
6257	1 Beams Patterson 28	First Named	25	M	Full	1896	Wade	985
6258	2 ~~Nellie~~ DIED PRIOR TO SEPTEMBER 25, 2002	Wife	23	F	"	1896	"	986
6259	3 " Nancy 5	Dau	2	F	"			
	4							
	5							
	6							
	7							
	8							
	9							
	10							
	11							
	12							
	13							
	14							
	15	ENROLLMENT OF NOS. 1, 2, 3 HEREON						
	16	APPROVED BY THE SECRETARY OF INTERIOR JAN 17 1903						
	17							

TRIBAL ENROLLMENT OF PARENTS

	Name of Father	Year	County	Name of Mother	Year	County
1	Willis Beams	Dead	Wade	Sissie Beams	Dead	Wade
2	~~Momba Mcashintubby~~	1896	"	~~Mcha Mcashintubby~~	"	Nashoba
3	No 1			No 2		
4						
5						
6						
7						
8		For child of No1 see NB (Apr 26-06) Card #821				
9						
10		No2 died July 3, 1899; proof of death filed Dec 16, 1902 ~~No.2 died July 3, 1899; Enrollment cancelled by Department July 8, 1904~~				
11						
12						
13						
14						
15					Date of Application for Enrollment.	
16						5/30/99
17						

Choctaw By Blood Enrollment Cards 1898-1914

RESIDENCE: Wade	COUNTY.	CARD NO.
POST OFFICE: Talihina I.T.	**Choctaw Nation** **Choctaw Roll** *(Not Including Freedmen)*	FIELD NO. 2163

Dawes' Roll No.	NAME	Relationship to Person First Named	AGE	SEX	BLOOD	TRIBAL ENROLLMENT		
						Year	County	No.
6260	1 Willis Robert DISMISSED TO SEPTEMBER 25, 2202		19	M	Full	P.R. 1893	Blue	34
	2							
	3							
	4							
	5							
	6							
	7							
	8							
	9							
	10							
	11							
	12							
	13							
	14							
	15	ENROLLMENT OF NOS. 1 HEREON APPROVED BY THE SECRETARY OF INTERIOR JAN 17 1903						
	16							
	17							

TRIBAL ENROLLMENT OF PARENTS

Name of Father	Year	County	Name of Mother	Year	County
1 Thomas Willis	Dead	Wade	Mary Willis	Dead	Wade
2					
3					
4					
5					
6 On 1893 Pay Roll P 119 No 34					
7 No.1 died March 27, 1900: Enrollment cancelled by Department May 2, 1906					
8					
9					
10					
11					
12					
13					
14					
15					
16			Date of Application for Enrollment.	5/30/99	
17					

Choctaw By Blood Enrollment Cards 1898-1914

RESIDENCE:	Wade	COUNTY.				
POST OFFICE:	Talihina I.T.					

Choctaw Nation

Choctaw Roll (Not Including Freedmen)

CARD NO.

FIELD NO. 2164

Dawes' Roll No.	NAME		Relationship to Person First Named	AGE	SEX	BLOOD	TRIBAL ENROLLMENT		
							Year	County	No.
6261	Bishop Sampson			46	M	Full	1896	Wade	1000
6262	" Mary	20	Wife	17	F	3/4	P R 1893	Towson	18
6263	" Berry	3	Son	3 wks	M	7/8			
6264	" Irene Belle	1	Dau	6 mo	F	7/8			
5									
6									
7									
8									
9									
10									
11									
12									
13									
14									
15	ENROLLMENT OF NOS. 1, 2, 3, 4 HEREON APPROVED BY THE SECRETARY OF INTERIOR JAN 17 1903								
16									
17									

DUP PRIOR TO SEPTEMBER 25 1902

TRIBAL ENROLLMENT OF PARENTS

	Name of Father	Year	County	Name of Mother	Year	County
1	William Bishop	Dead	Wade	No-wa-ho-le-ma	Dead	Wade
2	Laymon Roberts	Dead	Kiamatia[sic]	Narriet[sic] Killingsworth	Dead	"
3	No 1			No 2		
4	No 1			No 2		
5						
6						
7						
8	No2 On 1893 Pay Roll Towson Co Page 54 No 18 as Mary Roberts					
9	No4 born April 17, 1901: Enrolled Oct 19, 1901					
10	No.1 died Aug - 1902: Enrollment cancelled by Department July 8, 1904					
11						
12						
13						
14						
15				#1 to 3		
16				Date of Application for Enrollment.	5/30/99	
17						

64

RESIDENCE: Wade   COUNTY. **Choctaw Nation**   **Choctaw Roll** *(Not Including Freedmen)*   CARD No. FIELD No. 2165
POST OFFICE: Albion I.T.

Dawes' Roll No.	NAME		Relationship to Person	AGE	SEX	BLOOD	TRIBAL ENROLLMENT		
							Year	County	No.
6265	1 Potts Davis	55	First Named	52	M	Full	1896	Wade	10282
	2								
	3								
	4								
	5								
	6								
	7								
	8								
	9								
	10								
	11								
	12								
	13								
	14								
	15								
	16								
	17								

ENROLLMENT
OF NOS. 1 HEREON
APPROVED BY THE SECRETARY
OF INTERIOR JAN 17 1903

TRIBAL ENROLLMENT OF PARENTS

	Name of Father	Year	County	Name of Mother	Year	County
1	Ko-ya-be	Dead	Wade	Mollie Ko-ya-be	Dead	Wade
2						
3						
4						
5						
6						
7						
8						
9						
10						
11						
12						
13						
14						
15						
16				Date of Application for Enrollment.	5/30/99	
17						

Choctaw By Blood Enrollment Cards 1898-1914

RESIDENCE:	Sugar Loaf	COUNTY.							
POST OFFICE:	Red Ok I.T.		**Choctaw Nation**				**Choctaw Roll** *(Not Including Freedmen)*	CARD NO. FIELD NO.	2166

Dawes' Roll No.	NAME		Relationship to Person	AGE	SEX	BLOOD	TRIBAL ENROLLMENT		
							Year	County	No.
6266	1 Anderson James	30	First Named	27	M	Full	1896	Sugar Loaf	75
	2								
	3								
	4								
	5								
	6								
	7								
	8								
	9								
	10								
	11								
	12								
	13								
	14								
	15	ENROLLMENT OF NOS. 1 HEREON APPROVED BY THE SECRETARY OF INTERIOR JAN 17 1903							
	16								
	17								

TRIBAL ENROLLMENT OF PARENTS

	Name of Father	Year	County	Name of Mother	Year	County
1	Richard Anderson	Dead	Sugar Loaf	Mary Anna Anderson	Dead	Sugar Loaf
2						
3						
4						
5						
6						
7						
8						
9						
10						
11						
12						
13						
14						
15						Date of Application for Enrollment.
16						5/30/99
17						

Choctaw By Blood Enrollment Cards 1898-1914

RESIDENCE: Wade
POST OFFICE: Talihina I.T.

COUNTY. **Choctaw Nation**

Choctaw Roll (Not Including Freedmen)

CARD NO.
FIELD NO. 2167

Dawes' Roll No.	NAME	Relationship to Person	AGE	SEX	BLOOD	TRIBAL ENROLLMENT		
						Year	County	No.
6267	1 Pitchlynn Ellington P 37	First Named	134	M	Full	1896	Wade	10284
	2							
	3							
	4							
	5							
	6							
	7							
	8							
	9							
	10							
	11							
	12							
	13							
	14							
	15							
	16							
	17							

ENROLLMENT
OF NOS. 1 HEREON
APPROVED BY THE SECRETARY
OF INTERIOR JAN 17 1903

TRIBAL ENROLLMENT OF PARENTS

	Name of Father	Year	County	Name of Mother	Year	County
1	Davis Pitchlynn	Ded	Wade	Malinda Pitchlynn	Ded	Skullyville
2						
3						
4						
5						
6						
7	Nº 1 is now the husband of Agnes Jones on Choctaw card #2117, May 8 1902					
8	Nº 1 states that his full name is Ellington P Pitchlynn. See letter filed herein May 8 1902					
9						
10						
11						
12						
13						
14					Date of Application for Enrollment.	
15						
16					5/30/99	
17						

67

Choctaw By Blood Enrollment Cards 1898-1914

RESIDENCE: Wade COUNTY.
POST OFFICE: Talihina I.T.

Choctaw Nation

Choctaw Roll
(Not Including Freedmen)

CARD No.
FIELD No. 2168

Dawes' Roll No.		NAME		Relationship to Person First Named	AGE	SEX	BLOOD	TRIBAL ENROLLMENT		
								Year	County	No.
6268	1	Campala Julius	32		29	M	Full	1896	Wade	2393
6269	2	" Hannah	26	Wife	23	F	"	1896	"	2394
6270	3	" Jency	10	Dau	7	"	"	1896	"	2395
14721	4	" Hewitt	3	Son	3	M	"			
	5									
	6									
	7									
	8									
	9									
	10									
	11									
	12									
	13									
	14									
	15									
	16									
	17									

ENROLLMENT
OF NOS. 1, 2, 3 HEREON
APPROVED BY THE SECRETARY
OF INTERIOR JAN 17 1903

ENROLLMENT
OF NOS. 4 HEREON
APPROVED BY THE SECRETARY
OF INTERIOR MAY 20 1903

TRIBAL ENROLLMENT OF PARENTS

	Name of Father	Year	County	Name of Mother	Year	County
1	Ben Campala	Ded	Nashoba	Chaligo	Ded	Wade
2	Charlie McCann	"	Sugar Loaf	Silway McCann	"	Sans Bois
3	No 1			No 2		
4	No 1			No 2		
5						
6						
7						
8						
9						
10						
11						
12						
13						
14						
15						
16						
17						

No4 born February 1, 1900: enrolled Dec 13, 1901
For child of Nos 1&2 see NB (Apr 26-06) Card #873

#1 to 3

Date of Application for Enrollment.

5/30/99

Choctaw By Blood Enrollment Cards 1898-1914

RESIDENCE: Wade	COUNTY. **Choctaw Nation**			**Choctaw Roll** *(Not Including Freedmen)*		CARD NO.	
POST OFFICE: Talihina I.T.						FIELD NO. **2169**	

Dawes' Roll No.	NAME		Relationship to Person	AGE	SEX	BLOOD	TRIBAL ENROLLMENT		
							Year	County	No.
6271	1 Foster Wash	29	First Named	26	M	Full	1896	Wade	4067
	2								
	3								
	4								
	5								
	6								
	7								
	8								
	9								
	10								
	11								
	12								
	13								
	14								
	15	ENROLLMENT OF NOS. 1 HEREON APPROVED BY THE SECRETARY OF INTERIOR Jan 17 1903							
	16								
	17								

TRIBAL ENROLLMENT OF PARENTS

	Name of Father	Year	County	Name of Mother	Year	County
1	Billy Foster	Ded	Wade	Jane Foster	Ded	Wade
2						
3						
4						
5						
6			No.1 on 1896 Choctaw roll as Washington Foster			
7						
8						
9						
10						
11						
12						
13						
14						
15						
16				Date of Application for Enrollment.		5/30/99
17						

69

Choctaw By Blood Enrollment Cards 1898-1914

Dawes' Roll No.	NAME	Relationship to Person First Named	AGE	SEX	BLOOD	TRIBAL ENROLLMENT Year	TRIBAL ENROLLMENT County	TRIBAL ENROLLMENT No.
6272	1 Beams Wallace 31	First Named	28	M	Full	1896	Wade	994
6273	2 " Emiline 33	Wife	30	F	"	1896	"	995
6274	3 " Mary 8	Dau	5	"	"	1896	"	996
6275	4 " John 6	Son	3	M	"	1896	"	997
6276	5 Wilmon ~~DIED PRIOR TO SEPTEMBER 25, 1902~~	"	1mo	"	"			
6277	6 Anderson Lizzie 19	S.Dau	16	F	"	1896	"	167
6278	7 Beams Syrena 1	Dau	3mo	F	"			
	8							
	9							
	10							
	11							
	12							
	13							
	14							
	15							
	16							
	17							

ENROLLMENT
OF NOS. 1,2,3,4,5,6,7 HEREON
APPROVED BY THE SECRETARY
OF INTERIOR JAN 17 1903

TRIBAL ENROLLMENT OF PARENTS

	Name of Father	Year	County	Name of Mother	Year	County
1	Johnny Beams	De'd	Wade	Mary Beams	Ded	Wade
2	William Garland	1896	Nashoba	Jimesy Garland	"	"
3	No 1			No 2		
4	No 1			No 2		
5	No 1			No 2		
6	Joe Anderson	Ded	Wade	No 2		
7	Nº1			Nº2		
8						
9						
10	Nº7 Born June 17, 1902, enrolled Sept 29, 1902					
11	No5 died June 8, 1902; proof of death filed Dec 16, 1902					
12	No.5 died June 8, 1902: Enrollment cancelled by Department July 8, 1904					
13						
14						
15					#1 to 6	
16					Date of Application for Enrollment.	
17					5/30/99	

RESIDENCE: Wade   COUNTY. **Choctaw Nation**   **Choctaw Roll** (Not Including Freedmen)   CARD NO.
POST OFFICE: Scott I.T.   FIELD NO. 2171

Dawes' Roll No.	NAME		Relationship to Person	AGE	SEX	BLOOD	TRIBAL ENROLLMENT		
							Year	County	No.
6279	1 Billy Julius	41	First Named	38	M	Full	1896	Wade	1007
6280	2 " Nancy	47	Wife	44	F	"	1896	"	1008
6281	3 " Lymon	13	Son	10	M	"	1896	"	1010
6282	4 " Frances	10	Dau	7	F	"	1896	"	1011
	5								
	6								
	7								
	8								
	9								
	10								
	11								
	12								
	13								
	14								
	15	ENROLLMENT OF NOS. 1, 2, 3, 4 HEREON							
	16	APPROVED BY THE SECRETARY OF INTERIOR JAN 17 1903							
	17								

TRIBAL ENROLLMENT OF PARENTS

	Name of Father	Year	County	Name of Mother	Year	County
1	James Billy	Ded	Wade	Celina Billy	Ded	Atoka
2	Alexson Bonn	"	"	Talimahoma	"	Wade
3	No 1			No 2		
4	No 1			No 2		
5						
6						
7						
8						
9						
10						
11						
12						
13						
14						Date of Application for Enrollment,
15						
16						
17						

71

RESIDENCE: Wade	COUNTY.		CARD No.
POST OFFICE: Talihina I.T.	Choctaw Nation	Choctaw Roll (Not Including Freedmen)	FIELD No. 2172

Dawes' Roll No.	NAME	Relationship to Person First Named	AGE	SEX	BLOOD	TRIBAL ENROLLMENT		
						Year	County	No.
6283	1 James, Payson (DIED PRIOR TO SEPTEMBER 25, 1902)		55	M	Full	1896	Wade	6710
6284	2 " Mary 56	Wife	53	F	"	1896	"	6711
6285	3 " Noel 18	Son	15	M	"	1896	"	6714
6286	4 " Davis 16	"	13	"	"	1896	"	6713
6287	5 " Robinson 14	"	11	"	"	1896	"	6715
6288	6 " Anna 9	Dau	6	F	"	1896	"	6716
6289	7 " Silan 16	Niece	13	"	"	1896	"	6717
6290	8 " Eastman 15	Neph	12	M	"	1896	"	6718
	9							
	10							
	11							
	12	ENROLLMENT OF NOS. 1,2,3,4,5,6,7,8 HEREON APPROVED BY THE SECRETARY OF INTERIOR Jan 17 1903						
	13							
	14							
	15							
	16							
	17							

TRIBAL ENROLLMENT OF PARENTS

Name of Father	Year	County	Name of Mother	Year	County
1 Pisahikabe	Ded	Wade	Aya hona	Ded	Wade
2 Nakichi	"	Sugar Loaf	Kanoye	"	Sugar Loaf
3 No 1			No 2		
4 No 1			No 2		
5 No 1			No 2		
6 No 1			No 2		
7 Charles James	Ded	Wade	Celia James	Ded	Cedar
8 " "	"	"	" "	"	"
9					
10					
11					
12		No5 on 1896 roll as Robertson James			
13		No6 " " " " Annie "			
14		No7 " " " " Sillen "			
15		Not died Dec 1, 1901. proof of death filed Dec 15, 1902 No3 is now husband of Fannie Taylor Choc #2266		Date of Application for Enrollment.	
16	No.1 died Dec 1, 1901: Enrollment cancelled by Department July 8, 1904			5/30/99	
17	For child of No.7 see NB (Mar 3 '05) #492				

Choctaw By Blood Enrollment Cards 1898-1914

RESIDENCE: Wade   COUNTY. **Choctaw Nation**   **Choctaw Roll** *(Not Including Freedmen)*   CARD NO.

POST OFFICE: Albian I.T.   FIELD NO. **2173**

Dawes' Roll No.	NAME		Relationship to Person	AGE	SEX	BLOOD	TRIBAL ENROLLMENT		
							Year	County	No.
15044	1 McKinney, Susan	58	First Named	55	F	Full	1896	Wade	10278
DEAD	2 Pitchlynn, Eastman	21	Son	18	M	"	1896	"	10279
6291	3 " Amy	18	Dau	15	F	"	1896	"	10280
6291	4 " Jincy	11	"	8	"	"	1896	"	10281
14722	5 Frazier Minnie	1	Dau of No 3	5mo	F	"			
	6								
	7								
	8								
	9								
	10								
	11								
	12								
	13								
	14								
	15								
	16								
	17								

No. 2 HEREON DISMISSED UNDER ORDER OF THE COMMISSION TO THE FIVE CIVILIZED TRIBES OF MARCH 31, 1905.

ENROLLMENT OF NOS. 5 HEREON APPROVED BY THE SECRETARY OF INTERIOR MAY 20 1903

ENROLLMENT OF NOS. 3, 4 HEREON APPROVED BY THE SECRETARY OF INTERIOR JAN 17 1903

ENROLLMENT OF NOS. 1 HEREON APPROVED BY THE SECRETARY OF INTERIOR FEB 16 1904

TRIBAL ENROLLMENT OF PARENTS

	Name of Father	Year	County	Name of Mother	Year	County
1	Jacob Smith	Ded	Sans Bois	Sallie Smith	Ded	Cherokee N.
2	Davis Pitchlynn	"	Wade	No 1		
3	" "			No 1		
4	" "			No 1		
5	Loring Frazier			No 3		
6						
7				No3 on 1896 rollas Annie Pitchlynn		
8				No4 " " " " Jane "		
9				No5 born August 20 1902: enrolled Dec 15, 1902		
10	No2 died Oct 3, 1899; proof of death filed Dec 17, 1902					
11	No3 wife of Loren Frazier on Choc card 1365 — Evidence of marriage requested 12/9/02					
12	Nº1 is now the wife of Sweny McKinney Choctaw card #2081 Oct 20.04					
13						
14						#1 to 4
15						Date of Application for Enrollment.
16						5/30/99
17						

Choctaw By Blood Enrollment Cards 1898-1914

RESIDENCE:	Wade		COUNTY.					CARD NO.	
POST OFFICE:	Talihina I.T.		**Choctaw Nation**			Choctaw Roll *(Not Including Freedmen)*		FIELD NO.	2174

Dawes' Roll No.	NAME	Relationship to Person First Named	AGE	SEX	BLOOD	TRIBAL ENROLLMENT		
						Year	County	pNoR
6293	₁ James Laymos	DIED PRIOR TO SEPTEMBER 25 1902	45	M	Full	1893	Wade	275
6294	₂ Jones Morris ¹²	G Son	9	"	"	1896	"	6727
	3							
	4							
	5							
	6							
	7							
	8							
	9							
	10							
	11							
	12							
	13							
	14							
	15	ENROLLMENT OF NOS. 1, 2 HEREON						
	16	APPROVED BY THE SECRETARY OF INTERIOR JAN 17 1903						
	17							

TRIBAL ENROLLMENT OF PARENTS

	Name of Father	Year	County	Name of Mother	Year	County
1	Pisahihabe	Ded	Wade	Ayahona	Ded	Wade
2	Charles Jones	1896	Cedar	Lyda Jones	"	"
3						
4						
5						
6						
7						
8						
9						
10						
11						
12			No2 on 1896 Roll as Maurice Jones			
13			No1 died Feb, 1901; proof of death filed Dec 16, 1902			
14			No.1 died Feb - 1901 Enrollment cancelled by Department July 8, 1904			
15						
16				Date of Application for Enrollment.		5/30/99
17						

Choctaw By Blood Enrollment Cards 1898-1914

RESIDENCE: Nashoba   COUNTY. **Choctaw Nation**   **Choctaw Roll** *(Not Including Freedmen)*   CARD NO. FIELD NO. **2175**

POST OFFICE: Smithville I.T.

Dawes' Roll No.	NAME		Relationship to Person First Named	AGE	SEX	BLOOD	TRIBAL ENROLLMENT		
							Year	County	No.
6295	₁ Nichols Ella	18	First Named	15	F	1/4	1896	Nashoba	9667
6296	₂ " Sam	16	Bro	13	M	1/4	1896	"	9668
6297	₃ " Hampy H	14	"	11	"	1/4	1896	"	9669
	₄								
	₅								
	₆								
	₇								
	₈								
	₉								
	10								
	11								
	12								
	13								
	14								
	15								
	16								
	17								

ENROLLMENT
OF NOS. 1, 2, 3 HEREON
APPROVED BY THE SECRETARY
OF INTERIOR Jan 17 1903

TRIBAL ENROLLMENT OF PARENTS

	Name of Father	Year	County	Name of Mother	Year	County
₁	Mack Nichols	De'd	Jacks Fork	Josie Nichols	Ded	Jacks Fork
₂	" "	"	" "	" "	"	" "
₃	" "	"	" "	" "	"	" "
₄						
₅						
₆			Allen W James Choctaw card #2069 is guardian of			
₇			Nᵒˢ 1 and 3. See papers filed herein Feby 4, 1903			
₈						
₉						
10				All on roll of 96 as Nichols		
11				Enrolled by Judge Dukes		
12						
13						
14						
15				Date of Application for Enrollment.		
16				5/30/99		
17						

75

RESIDENCE:	Wade	COUNTY.							CARD No.	
POST OFFICE:	Talihina I.T.		**Choctaw Nation**				Choctaw Roll *(Not Including Freedmen)*		FIELD No.	2176

Dawes' Roll No.	NAME	Relationship to Person	AGE	SEX	BLOOD	TRIBAL ENROLLMENT		
						Year	County	No.
6298	1 Welch Beatrice R 51	First Named	48	F	1/16	1896	Wade	13074
	2							
	3							
	4							
	5							
	6							
	7							
	8							
	9							
	10							
	11							
	12							
	13							
	14							
	15	ENROLLMENT OF NOS. 1 HEREON APPROVED BY THE SECRETARY OF INTERIOR JAN 17 1903						
	16							
	17							

TRIBAL ENROLLMENT OF PARENTS

	Name of Father	Year	County	Name of Mother	Year	County
1	Joseph Long	De'd	Non Citz	Emeline Long	Ded	Non Citz
2						
3						
4						
5						
6						
7						
8						
9						
10			On roll as BR Welch – Evidence of			
11			marriage of father and mother to			
12			be supplied – The father and mother both lived in Mississippi			
13			and never lived in Choctaw Nation.			
14			Rec'd Aug 9/99			
15	Nº1 is wife of William A Welch Chickasaw card #1197					
16				Date of Application for Enrollment.	5/30/99	
17	P.O. Wister I.T. 12/16/02					

Choctaw By Blood Enrollment Cards 1898-1914

RESIDENCE: Wade   COUNTY. **Choctaw Nation**   **Choctaw Roll** *(Not Including Freedmen)*   CARD NO.

POST OFFICE: Talihina I.T.   FIELD NO. 2177

Dawes' Roll No.	NAME		Relationship to Person	AGE	SEX	BLOOD	TRIBAL ENROLLMENT Year	County	No.
6299	1 White Jerry	72	First Named	69	M	Full	1896	Wade	13058
6300	2 " Delilah	52	Wife	49	F	"	1896	"	13059
6301	3 Anderson Artimussa	22	Dau	20	"	"	1896	"	13061
6302	4 White Benjamin	17	Son	17	M	"	1896	"	13062
6303	5 Anderson Richard Walker	2	Grandson	2mo	M	"			
	6								
	7								

DIED PRIOR TO SEPTEMBER 25, 1902 (rows 3 and 5)

ENROLLMENT OF NOS. 1, 2, 3, 4, 5 HEREON APPROVED BY THE SECRETARY OF INTERIOR JAN 17 1903

TRIBAL ENROLLMENT OF PARENTS

	Name of Father	Year	County	Name of Mother	Year	County
1	Louis White	De'd	Sugar Loaf		Ded	Sugar Loaf
2	Sam Johnson	"	Eagle		"	Eagle
3	No 1			Susan White	"	Sugar Loaf
4	No 1			" "		
5	Rayson Anderson			No 3		

No

Date of Application for Enrollment. 5/30/99

RESIDENCE: Wade	COUNTY.	Choctaw Nation	Choctaw Roll (Not Including Freedmen)	CARD NO.
POST OFFICE: Talihina I.T.				FIELD NO. 2178

Dawes' Roll No.	NAME		Relationship to Person	AGE	SEX	BLOOD	TRIBAL ENROLLMENT		
							Year	County	No.
6304	1 Willis Benjamin	37	First Named	34	M	1/4	1896	Wade	13076
6305	2 " Rosa	23	Wife	20	F	Full	1896	"	10289
6306	3 " Minnie	5	Dau	15mo	F	5/8			
6307	4 " Vicyan DIED PRIOR TO SEPTEMBER 25,1902		"	1mo	F	5/8			
	5								
	6								
	7								
	8								
	9								
	10								
	11								
	12								
	13								
	14								
	15	ENROLLMENT OF NOS. 1, 2, 3, 4 HEREON APPROVED BY THE SECRETARY OF INTERIOR JAN 17 1903							
	16								
	17								

TRIBAL ENROLLMENT OF PARENTS

	Name of Father	Year	County	Name of Mother	Year	County
1	Robert Willis	Dead	Non Citz	Sarah Willis	1896	Wade
2	Charles Potts	"	Wade	Melvina Potts	1896	"
3	No 1			No 2		
4	No 1			No 2		
5						
6						
7			No2 On 1896 Roll as Rosa Potts			
8						
9			For child of Nos 1and 2 see NB (Apr 26'06) card No 224			
10			" " " " " " (Mar 3- 05) " " 67			
11			No.4 died Sept 3, 1899: Enrollment cancelled by Department July 8, 1904			
12						
13						
14						
15				No4 enrolled Nov 24/99		
16				Date of Application for Enrollment. 5/30/99		
17				➤1 to 3		

Choctaw By Blood Enrollment Cards 1898-1914

RESIDENCE: Wade   COUNTY. **Choctaw Nation**   **Choctaw Roll**   CARD NO.
POST OFFICE: Talihina I.T.   *(Not Including Freedmen)*   FIELD NO. 2179

Dawes' Roll No.	NAME	Relationship to Person	AGE	SEX	BLOOD	TRIBAL ENROLLMENT		
						Year	County	No.
6308	1 Willis Sarah ~~DIED PRIOR TO SEPTEMBER 25 6850 2~~	First Named	65	F	1/2	1896	Wade	13051
	2							
	3							
	4							
	5							
	6							
	7							
	8							
	9							
	10							
	11							
	12							
	13							
	14							
	15							
	16							
	17							

ENROLLMENT
OF NOS. 1 HEREON
APPROVED BY THE SECRETARY
OF INTERIOR JAN 17 1903

TRIBAL ENROLLMENT OF PARENTS

	Name of Father	Year	County	Name of Mother	Year	County
1	Horace Woods	Dead	Non Citz	Sarah Woods	Dead	Wade
2						
3						
4						
5						
6	On 1896 roll as Sallie Willis					
7						
8						
9	No1 died March 12, 1900; proof of death filed Dec 12, 1902					
10	No1 died March 12, 1900; Enrollment cancelled by Department July 8, 1904					
11						
12						
13						
14						
15					Date of Application for Enrollment.	
16						5/30/99
17						

Choctaw By Blood Enrollment Cards 1898-1914

RESIDENCE: Wade   COUNTY. **Choctaw Nation**   **Choctaw Roll**   CARD NO.
POST OFFICE: Talihina, I T   *(Not Including Freedmen)*   FIELD NO. 2180

Dawes' Roll No.	NAME		Relationship to Person	AGE	SEX	BLOOD	TRIBAL ENROLLMENT		
							Year	County	No.
6309	1 Harkins Simpson	21	First Named	18	M	Full	1896	Wade	5392
	2								
	3								
	4								
	5								
	6								
	7								
	8								
	9								
	10								
	11								
	12								
	13								
	14								
	15								
	16								
	17								

ENROLLMENT
OF NOS. 1 HEREON
APPROVED BY THE SECRETARY
OF INTERIOR JAN 17 1903

TRIBAL ENROLLMENT OF PARENTS

	Name of Father	Year	County	Name of Mother	Year	County
1	Willis Harkins	Ded	Wade	Lucy Harkins	Ded	Sugar Loaf
2						
3						
4						
5						
6						
7						
8						
9						
10						
11						
12						
13						
14						
15						Date of Application for Enrollment.
16						5/30/99
17						

Choctaw By Blood Enrollment Cards 1898-1914

RESIDENCE: Wade COUNTY.	**Choctaw Nation**	Choctaw Roll	CARD No.
POST OFFICE: Talihina, I.T		(Not Including Freedmen)	FIELD NO. 2181

Dawes' Roll No.	NAME		Relationship to Person First Named	AGE	SEX	BLOOD	TRIBAL ENROLLMENT		
							Year	County	No.
6310	1 Johnson, McGee	28		25	M	Full	1896	Wade	6680
6311	2 " Belle	28	Wife	25	F	"	1896	"	6681
6312	3 " Andrew	9	Son	6	M	"	1896	"	6682
6313	4 " Alfred	5	"	2	"	"			
	5								
	6								
	7								
	8								
	9								
	10								
	11								
	12								
	13								
	14								
	15	ENROLLMENT OF NOS. 1, 2, 3, 4 HEREON APPROVED BY THE SECRETARY OF INTERIOR JAN 17 1903							
	16								
	17								

TRIBAL ENROLLMENT OF PARENTS

	Name of Father	Year	County	Name of Mother	Year	County
1	Joshua Tikbombe	Dead	Eagle	Liley White	1896	Wade
2	Jos Alexander	"	Sugar Loaf	Lotie Alexander	Dead	Sugar Loaf
3	No1			No2		
4	No1			No2		
5						
6						
7						
8	No2 Died prior to September 25, 1902, not [remainder illegible]					
9						
10						
11						
12						
13						
14						
15						
16				Date of Application for Enrollment.	5/30/99	
17						

Choctaw By Blood Enrollment Cards 1898-1914

NAME		Relationship to Person	AGE	SEX	BLOOD	TRIBAL ENROLLMENT		
						Year	County	No.
6314 James, Jefferson	37	First Named	34	M	Full	1896	Wade	6722
" Silina	28	Wife	25	F	"	1896	"	6723
Potts, Jesse	8	S.Son	5	M	"	1896	"	5404
4								
5								
6								
7								
8								
9								
10								
11								
12								
13								
14								

COUNTY. Choctaw Nation — Choctaw Roll *(Not Including Freedmen)* — CARD No. / FIELD No. 2182

ENROLLMENT OF NOS. 1, 2, 3 HEREON APPROVED BY THE SECRETARY OF INTERIOR JAN 17 1903

TRIBAL ENROLLMENT OF PARENTS

	Name of Father	Year	County	Name of Mother	Year	County
1	Pe-sa-ha-cubbee	Dead	Wade	Sillie Tim Bond	1896	Wade
2	Benock Beams	"	"	Cillen Beams	Dead	"
3	Watson Potts			No 2		
4						
5						
6						
7	No 3 on 1896 roll as Jessey Hitcher					
8						
9						
10						
11						
12						
13						
14						
15						
16			Date of Application for Enrollment.	5/30/99		
17						

82

Choctaw By Blood Enrollment Cards 1898-1914

RESIDENCE: Wade	COUNTY.		CARD NO.
POST OFFICE: Lenos I.T.	**Choctaw Nation**	Choctaw Roll (Not Including Freedmen)	FIELD NO. **2183**

Dawes' Roll No.	NAME	Relationship to Person First Named	AGE	SEX	BLOOD	TRIBAL ENROLLMENT		
						Year	County	No.
6317	1 Wright, Joseph *DIED PRIOR TO SEPTEMBER 25, 1902*		34	M	Full	1896	Wade	13107
6318	2 " Ellen 20	Wife	17	F	"	1896	Nashoba	2496
6319	3 " Josephine 3	Dau	1 2/3	F	"			
6320	4 " Amanda *DIED PRIOR TO SEPTEMBER 25, 1902*	"	4mo	F	"			
	5							
	6							
	7							
	8							
	9							
	10							
	11							
	12							
	13							
	14							
	15	ENROLLMENT OF NOS. 1, 2, 3, 4 HEREON						
	16	APPROVED BY THE SECRETARY						
	17	OF INTERIOR Jan 17 1903						

TRIBAL ENROLLMENT OF PARENTS

	Name of Father	Year	County	Name of Mother	Year	County
1	Jacob Wright	Dead	Wade	Istachi Wright	Dead	Wade
2	Levi Colbert	1896	Nashoba		"	Nashoba
3	No.1			No.2		
4	No.1			No.2		
5						
6						
7						
8						
9						
10		No2 on 1896 roll as Ellen Colbert				
11		No.3 Enrolled July 20, 1901				
12		No.4 Enrolled July 20, 1901				
13		No1 died July 20, 1902; No4 died Jan-1902: Enrollment cancelled by Department July 8, 1904				
		No1 died in 1900[sic]: proof of death filed Dec 15, 1902				
14		No.4 is dead Affidavit of death to be supplied. Dec 30, 1902				
15		No2 is now wife of Ned Alexander Choc #1977		Date of Application for Enrollment.		
16				5/30/99		
17						

83

Choctaw By Blood Enrollment Cards 1898-1914

٬CE: Wade		COUNTY.				Choctaw Roll	CARD No.	
OFFICE: Lenox, I.T.		**Choctaw Nation**				(Not Including Freedmen)	FIELD No. 2184	

Dawes' Roll No.	NAME		Relationship to Person	AGE	SEX	BLOOD	TRIBAL ENROLLMENT		
							Year	County	No.
6321	1 Wright, Watson	35	First Named	32	M	Full	1896	Wade	13099
	2								
	3								
	4								
	5								
	6								
	7								
	8								
	9								
	10								
	11								
	12								
	13								
	14								
	15	ENROLLMENT OF NOS. 1 HEREON							
	16	APPROVED BY THE SECRETARY OF INTERIOR JAN 17 1903							
	17								

TRIBAL ENROLLMENT OF PARENTS

	Name of Father	Year	County	Name of Mother	Year	County
1	James Wright	Dead	Wade	Viney Wright	Dead	Wade
2						
3						
4						
5	No 1 has been divorced from Sarah Wright on Choctaw Card #2196					
6						
7	No 1 is now husband of Melvina Jones on Choc card #4563 – Dec 17- 1902					
8						
9						
10						
11						
12						
13						
14					Date of Application for Enrollment.	
15						
16					5/30/99	
17	P.O. Le Flore I.T. 12/18/02					

Choctaw By Blood Enrollment Cards 1898-1914

RESIDENCE: Wade   COUNTY. **Choctaw Nation**   **Choctaw Roll**   CARD NO.
POST OFFICE: Talihina, I.T   *(Not Including Freedmen)*   FIELD NO.   2185

Dawes' Roll No.	NAME	Relationship to Person Named	AGE	SEX	BLOOD	TRIBAL ENROLLMENT		
						Year	County	No.
6322	1 Meashintubby, William	First Named	56	M	Full	1896	Wade	8574
	2							
	3							
	4							
	5							
	6							
	7							
	8							
	9							
	10							
	11							
	12							
	13							
	14							
	15							
	16							
	17							

ENROLLMENT
OF NOS. 1 HEREON
APPROVED BY THE SECRETARY
OF INTERIOR JAN 17 1903

TRIBAL ENROLLMENT OF PARENTS

	Name of Father	Year	County	Name of Mother	Year	County
1	Billie Meashintubby	Dead	Wade	Hi-ya-ka-stuna	Dead	Eagle
2						
3						
4						
5						
6			On 1896 roll as Wm Meashintubby			
7						
8						
9						
10						
11						
12						
13						
14					Date of Application for Enrollment.	
15						
16					5/30/99	
17						

85

Choctaw By Blood Enrollment Cards 1898-1914

| RESIDENCE: Wade | COUNTY. | **Choctaw Nation** | Choctaw Roll | CARD NO. |
| POST OFFICE: Talihina, I.T. 12-22-02 — So McAlester I.T. | | | (Not Including Freedmen) | FIELD NO. 2186 |

Dawes' Roll No.		NAME		Relationship to Person	AGE	SEX	BLOOD	TRIBAL ENROLLMENT		
								Year	County	No.
I.W. 21	1	Matthews, John W	36	First Named	33	M	I.W.	1896	Wade	14818
6323	2	" Rose	24	Wife	21	F	1/2	1896	"	8573
6324	3	" Atha	4	Son	6mo	M	1/4			
6325	4	" Dero	2	Son	2mo	M	1/4			
	5									
	6									
	7									
	8									
	9									
	10									
	11									
	12									
	13									
	14									
	15	ENROLLMENT OF NOS. 2,3,4 HEREON APPROVED BY THE SECRETARY OF INTERIOR JAN 17 1903					ENROLLMENT OF NOS. 1 HEREON APPROVED BY THE SECRETARY OF INTERIOR JUN 13 1903			
	16									
	17									

TRIBAL ENROLLMENT OF PARENTS

	Name of Father	Year	County	Name of Mother	Year	County
1	Nicholas Matthews	Dead	Non Citz	Narcissa Matthews	Dead	Non Citz
2	David Burney	1896	Wade	Eliz Anderson	1896	Wade
3	No 1			No 2		
4	No.1			No2		
5						
6						
7						
8						
9	No2 on 1896 roll as Rosa Matthew					
10	No1 " 1896 " " J Wm Matthews					
11	No3 Affidavit of birth to be supplied Recd June 8/99					
12	No.4 Enrolled April 25, 1901					
13	For child of Nos 1&2 see NB (Apr 26-06) Card #846					
14						#1 to 3
15	For child of Nos 1&2 see NB (Mar 3-05) Card #190				Date of Application for Enrollment.	
16					5/30/99	
17						

RESIDENCE: Wade   COUNTY. **Choctaw Nation**   Choctaw Roll   CARD NO.
POST OFFICE: Talihina, I.T   *(Not Including Freedmen)*   FIELD NO.   2187

Dawes' Roll No.	NAME	Relationship to Person First Named	AGE	SEX	BLOOD	Year	County	No.
6326	1 Killingsworth, Edward 37	First Named	34	M	Full	1896	Wade	7514
6327	2 " Rosanna 35	Wife	32	F	1/4	1896	"	7515
6328	3 " Serena B 4	Dau	4mo	"	5/8			
6330	4 Wilson, Ada 15	S.Dau	12	"	1/8	1896	Wade	13077
6331	5 " Mary J 12	"	9	"	1/8	1896	"	13078
6332	6 Thompson, Robert 10	S.Son	7	M	3/8	1896	"	12058
6329	7 Killingsworth, Elenora 1	Dau	3mo	F	5/8	1896	"	
	8							
	9							
	10							
	11							
	12							
	13							
	14							
	15	ENROLLMENT OF NOS. 1,2,3,4,5,6,7 HEREON APPROVED BY THE SECRETARY OF INTERIOR JAN 17 1903						
	16							
	17							

TRIBAL ENROLLMENT OF PARENTS

Name of Father	Year	County	Name of Mother	Year	County
1 Jesse Boland	Dead	Red River	Susan Bohanan	Dead	Red River
2 Bob Willis	"	Non Citz	Sarah Willis	1896	Wade
3 No1			No2		
4 Abner Wilson	Dead	Non Citz	No2		
5 " "	"	" "	No2		
6 Allen Thompson	1896	Wade	No2		
7 N°1			N°2		
8					
9 No2 on 1896 roll as Rosa A Killingsworth					
10 N°7 Born Jany 26,1902; enrolled April 25, 1902					
11 For child of Nos 1&2 see NB (Apr 26-06) Card #348					
" " " " 4 " " (Mar 3-05) Card #978					
12 " " " " 4 " (Apr 26-06) " #648					
13					
14					
15			#1 to 6		
16			Date of Application for Enrollment.	5/30/99	
17 Lenox I.T. seems to be present P.O.					

Choctaw By Blood Enrollment Cards 1898-1914

RESIDENCE: Wade   COUNTY. **Choctaw Nation**   **Choctaw Roll** *(Not Including Freedmen)*   CARD No.
POST OFFICE: Talihina, I.T   FIELD No. **2188**

Dawes' Roll No.	NAME	Relationship to Person	AGE	SEX	BLOOD	TRIBAL ENROLLMENT Year	TRIBAL ENROLLMENT County	TRIBAL ENROLLMENT No.
I.W. 1105	1 Thomas, Marcus D L ³⁰	First Named	27	M	I.W.	1896	Wade	15101
6333	2 " Susan R ³²	Wife	29	F	1/8	1896	"	12054
6334	3 " Cleo ¹⁴	Dau	11	"	1/16	1896	"	12055
6335	4 " Leo M ¹¹	Son	8	M	1/16	1896	"	12056
6336	5 " De Grace ⁷	Dau	4	F	1/16	1896	"	12057
6337	6 " Florence H ⁵	"	1½	"	1/16			
6338	7 " John Jay Jr ³	Son	4mo	M	1/16			
	8							
	9							
	10							
	11	ENROLLMENT						
	12	OF NOS. ~~~ 1 ~~~ HEREON APPROVED BY THE SECRETARY						
	13	OF INTERIOR NOV 16 1904						
	14							
	15	ENROLLMENT OF NOS. 2,3,4,5,6,7 HEREON						
	16	APPROVED BY THE SECRETARY						
	17	OF INTERIOR JAN 17 1903						

TRIBAL ENROLLMENT OF PARENTS

	Name of Father	Year	County	Name of Mother	Year	County
1	John Thomas	1896	Non Citz	Louisa Thomas	1896	Non Citz
2	Thos H McMurtrey	Dead	" "	Mattie J McMurtrey	1896	Gaines
3	No 1			No 2		
4	No 1			No 2		
5	No 1			No 2		
6	No 1			No 2		
7	No. 1			No. 2		
8						
9						
10						
11	No 1 on 1896 roll as M D L Thomas					
12	No2 " 1896 " " S R "					
13	No3 " 1896 " " Cleo "					
	No4 " 1896 " " Leo "					
14	No 7 Enrolled June 12, 1900					
15					Date of Application for Enrollment.	
16					5/31/99	
17						

RESIDENCE: Gaines						Choctaw Roll		CARD NO.
POST OFFICE: Hartshorne, I.T	COUNTY. **Choctaw Nation**					(Not Including Freedmen)		FIELD NO. 2189

Dawes' Roll No.	NAME	Relationship to Person	AGE	SEX	BLOOD	TRIBAL ENROLLMENT		
						Year	County	No.
6339	1 McMurtrey, Mattie J 68	First Named	65	F	1/4	1896	Gaines	9154
6340	2 Needham Nettie H 22	Dau	19	F	1/8	1896	"	9156
6341	3 McMurtrey Joseph B 19	Son	16	M	1/8	1896	"	9157
I.W. 715	4 Needham Enoch (26)	Husb of N°2	26	M	I.W.			
	5							
	6							
	7							
	8							
	9							
	10							
	11							
	12							
	13							

ENROLLMENT
OF NOS. 1, 2, 3   HEREON
APPROVED BY THE SECRETARY
OF INTERIOR JAN 17 1903

ENROLLMENT
OF NOS. ~~~~ 4 ~~~~ HEREON
APPROVED BY THE SECRETARY
OF INTERIOR MAY -7 1904

TRIBAL ENROLLMENT OF PARENTS

Name of Father	Year	County	Name of Mother	Year	County
1 Wm Lineer	Dead	Non Citz	Susan Lineer	Dead	Skullyville
2 Thos H McMurtrey	"	" "	No 1		
3 " " "	"	" "	No 1		
4 Enoch Needham	"	" "	Mary S Glasscock		non-citz
5					
6					
7					
8	No2 on 1896 roll as Nettie H McMurtrey				
9	No3 " 1896 " " Joe B		"		
10	No.2 is now the wife of Enoch Needham on Choctaw card #D767			July 30, 1902	
11	N°4 transferred from Choctaw Card #D767. See decision of Feby 27, 1904				
12	For child of No.3 see NB (Apr 26-06) No 802				
13	For children of Nos 2&4 see NB (Mar 3-05) No 840				
14	For child of No3 see NB (March 3, 1905) #1345				
15				Date of Application for Enrollment.	
16				5/31/99	
17					

Choctaw By Blood Enrollment Cards 1898-1914

	RESIDENCE: Wade COUNTY. Choctaw Nation Choctaw Roll (Not Including Freedmen)							
	POST OFFICE: Lenox I.T.					CARD NO. FIELD NO. 2190		

Dawes' Roll No.	NAME	Relationship to Person	AGE	SEX	BLOOD	TRIBAL ENROLLMENT		
						Year	County	No.
6342	1 Woods Benjamin J [61]	First Named	58	M	1/2	1896	Wade	13086
6343	2 " Josephine [56]	Wife	53	F	1/2	1896	"	13087
6344	3 " Harriet [19]	Dau	16	"	1/2	1896	"	13089
6345	4 " Nancy B [11]	"	8	"	1/2	1896	"	13090
6346	5 Meashintubby Frances [18]	Ward	15	"	Full	1896	"	8581
	6							
	7							
	8							
	9							
	10							
	11							
	12							
	13							
	14							
	15 ENROLLMENT OF NOS. 1,2,3,4,5 HEREON							
	16 APPROVED BY THE SECRETARY OF INTERIOR Jan 17 1903							
	17							

TRIBAL ENROLLMENT OF PARENTS

	Name of Father	Year	County	Name of Mother	Year	County
1	Horace Woods	Ded	Wade	Nowatima	Ded	Wade
2	Joseph Dukes	"	Towson	Nancy Dukes	"	"
3	No1			No2		
4	No1			No2		
5	Mambe Meashintubby	1896	Wade		Ded	Wade
6						
7						
8						
9			No 1 on 1896 as Benjamin Woods			
10						
11						
12						
13						
14						
15						
16				Date of Application for Enrollment.		5/30/99
17	Albion I.T. 12/12/02					

Choctaw By Blood Enrollment Cards 1898-1914

RESIDENCE: Wade   COUNTY. **Choctaw Nation**   **Choctaw Roll**   CARD NO.
POST OFFICE: Lenox, I.T.   *(Not Including Freedmen)*   FIELD NO. **2191**

Dawes' Roll No.	NAME	Relationship to Person First Named	AGE	SEX	BLOOD	TRIBAL ENROLLMENT Year	County	No.
6347	1 James, Isham DIED PRIOR TO SEPTEMBER 25 1902	Named	29	M	Full	1896	Wade	6728
6348	2 Melvina DIED PRIOR TO SEPTEMBER 25, 1902	Wife	26	F	"	1896	"	6729
6349	3 " Caroline 8	Dau	5	"	"	1896	"	6731
6350	4 Harriet DIED PRIOR TO SEPTEMBER 25, 1902	"	2	"	"			
6351	5 Jefferson, Eliza 14	S.Dau	11	"	"	1896	Wade	6730
	6							
	7							
	8							
	9							
	10							
	11							
	12							
	13							
	14							
	15	ENROLLMENT OF NOS. 1,2,3,4,5 HEREON						
	16	APPROVED BY THE SECRETARY						
	17	OF INTERIOR JAN 17 1903						

TRIBAL ENROLLMENT OF PARENTS

	Name of Father	Year	County	Name of Mother	Year	County
1	Pason James	1896	Wade		Dead	Wade
2	Forbis Williams	Dead	Sugar Loaf	Illean Dwight	1896	Sugar Loaf
3	No1			No2		
4	No1			No2		
5	Watson Jefferson	Dead	Sugar Loaf	No2		
6						
7						
8						
9			No1 on 1896 roll as Isom James			
10			No2 " 1896 " " Florence "			
11			No3 " 1896 " " Melvina "			
			No5 " 1896 " " Eliza "			
12						
13						
14					Date of Application for Enrollment.	
15					5/31/99	
16						
17	No.1 died - - 1899; No.2 died Jan - 1900; No.4 died Feb – 1899; Enrollment [remainder illegible]					

Choctaw By Blood Enrollment Cards 1898-1914

RESIDENCE: Wade COUNTY.
POST OFFICE: Talihina, I.T.

Choctaw Nation

Choctaw Roll
(Not Including Freedmen)

CARD NO.
FIELD NO. **2192**

Dawes' Roll No.	NAME	Relationship to Person First Named	AGE	SEX	BLOOD	TRIBAL ENROLLMENT		
						Year	County	No.
6352	1 Pitchlynn Alexander 42	First Named	39	M	Full	1896	Wade	10307
6353	2 " Malissa 40	Wife	37	F	"	1896	"	10308
6354	3 " Agnes 18	Dau	15	"	"	1896	"	10309
	4							
	5							
	6							
	7							
	8							
	9							
	10							
	11							
	12							
	13							
	14							
	15	ENROLLMENT OF NOS. 1,2,3 HEREON						
	16	APPROVED BY THE SECRETARY						
	17	OF INTERIOR Jan 17 1903						

TRIBAL ENROLLMENT OF PARENTS

	Name of Father	Year	County	Name of Mother	Year	County
1	John Pitchlynn	Dead	Wade	Na-te-we	Dead	Wade
2	Thomas LeFlore	"	"	E-ma-no-le	1896	Nashoba
3	No 1			No 2		
4						
5						
6						
7		No 1 on 1896 roll as Alex Pitchlynn				
8		Nos 2 and 3 – Died prior to September 25, 1902, not entitled to land or money				
9		(See Indian Office letter September 20-1910 D.C. #1288-1900)				
10						
11						
12						
13						
14						
15						
16				Date of Application for Enrollment.	5/31/99	
17						

Choctaw By Blood Enrollment Cards 1898-1914

RESIDENCE: Wade		COUNTY. **Choctaw Nation**				**Choctaw Roll** *(Not Including Freedmen)*		CARD NO.
POST OFFICE: Albion, I.T								FIELD NO. 2193

Dawes' Roll No.	NAME	Relationship to Person Named	AGE	SEX	BLOOD	TRIBAL ENROLLMENT		
						Year	County	No.
6355	₁ Meashintubby, Mambe ⁴⁸ DIED PRIOR TO SEPTEMBER 25 1902	First Named	45	M	Full	1896	Wade	8572
6356	₂ " Susan ⁴⁸	Wife	45	F	"	1896	Nashoba	8629
	3							
	4							
	5							
	6							
	7							
	8							
	9							
	10							
	11							
	12							
	13							
	14							
	15	ENROLLMENT OF NOS. 1, 2 HEREON APPROVED BY THE SECRETARY OF INTERIOR JAN 17 1903						
	16							
	17							

TRIBAL ENROLLMENT OF PARENTS

	Name of Father	Year	County	Name of Mother	Year	County
1	Meashintubby	Dead	Nashoba	Hi-ya-ka-stima	Dead	Eagle
2	Ma-kin-tubby	"	"		"	Nashoba
3						
4						
5						
6		No1 on 1896 roll as Mumby Meashintubby				
7		No2 " 1896 " " Susan Meashintubbi				
8		No1 died April 29, 1902; proof of death filed Dec 16, 1902				
9						
10						
11						
12						
13						
14					Date of Application for Enrollment.	
15					5/31/99	
16						
17	Ludlow, I.T. 12/13/02					

93

Choctaw By Blood Enrollment Cards 1898-1914

RESIDENCE: Wade	COUNTY.					
POST OFFICE: Talihina, I.T	**Choctaw Nation**		Choctaw Roll *(Not Including Freedmen)*	CARD NO. FIELD NO. 2194		

Dawes' Roll No.	NAME	Relationship to Person First Named	AGE	SEX	BLOOD	TRIBAL ENROLLMENT		
						Year	County	No.
6357	1 Thompson, Samuel	DIED PRIOR TO SEPTEMBER 25, 1902	31	M	3/4	1896	Wade	12050
6358	2 " Vina 27	Wife	24	F	Full	1896	"	9242
6359	3 " Mary 11	Dau	8	"	1/2	1896	"	12051
6360	4 " Emiline 8	"	6	"	1/2	1896	"	12052
6361	5 " Susie 6	"	3	"	7/8	1896	"	12053
6362	6 Needles	DIED PRIOR TO SEPTEMBER 25, 1902 Son	1mo	M	7/8			
	7							
	8							
	9							
	10							
	11							
	12							
	13							
	14							
	15 ENROLLMENT OF NOS. 1,2,3,4,5,6 HEREON							
	16 APPROVED BY THE SECRETARY OF INTERIOR JAN 17 1903							
	17							

TRIBAL ENROLLMENT OF PARENTS

	Name of Father	Year	County	Name of Mother	Year	County
1	Jackson Thompson	Dead	Skullyville	Mary Thompson	Dead	Skullyville
2	Brias McCoy	"	"	Betsy McCoy	"	Wade
3	No1			Margaret Thompson	"	"
4	No1			" "	"	"
5	No1			No 2		
6	No1			No 2		
7						
8						
9			No2 on 1896 roll as Vina McCoy			
10			No5 " 1896 " " Infant "			
11	No.1 died Aril 16,1900: No.6 died Dec 8,1900: [Remainder illegible]					
12						
13						
14					Date of Application for Enrollment.	
15						
16			Date of application for enrollment	5/31/99		
17						

94

RESIDENCE: Wade	COUNTY.	Choctaw Nation	Choctaw Roll	CARD NO.
POST OFFICE: Talihina I.T.			(Not Including Freedmen)	FIELD NO. 2195

Dawes' Roll No.	NAME		Relationship to Person First Named	AGE	SEX	BLOOD	TRIBAL ENROLLMENT		
							Year	County	No.
6363	1 Benton Wesley	29	First Named	26	M	Full	1896	Wade	1032
6364	2 " Helen	40	Wife	37	F	"	1896	"	13084
6365	3 " Abner	1	Son	7mo	M	"			
	4								
	5								
	6								
	7								
	8								
	9								
	10								
	11								
	12								
	13								
	14								
	15								
	16								
	17								

ENROLLMENT
OF NOS. 1, 2, 3 HEREON
APPROVED BY THE SECRETARY
OF INTERIOR JAN 17 1903

TRIBAL ENROLLMENT OF PARENTS

	Name of Father	Year	County	Name of Mother	Year	County
1	Edward Benton	Ded	Wade	Malissa Benton	Ded	Wade
2	Nillis Hampton	"	Sugar Loaf	Charity Hampton	"	Sugar Loaf
3	Nº 1			Nº 2		
4						
5						
6						
7						
8	Nº 3 Born Oct 22 1901; enrolled June 2 1902					
9			No 2 on 1896 rolls[sic] as Helen Woods			
10						
11						
12						
13						
14						#1&2
15						Date of Application for Enrollment:
16						5/31/99
17						

Choctaw By Blood Enrollment Cards 1898-1914

RESIDENCE:	Wade	COUNTY.						CARD No.	
POST OFFICE:	Talihina I.T.	**Choctaw Nation**				Choctaw Roll *(Not Including Freedmen)*		FIELD No.	2196

Dawes' Roll No.	NAME		Relationship to Person	AGE	SEX	BLOOD	TRIBAL ENROLLMENT		
							Year	County	No.
6366	₁ Burney Sarah	20	First Named	17	F	1/4	1896	Wade	13069
14892	₂ " Clara May	2	Dau	2	F	3/4			
	₃								
	₄						ENROLLMENT		
	₅						OF NOS. 2 HEREON APPROVED BY THE SECRETARY		
	₆						OF INTERIOR MAY 21 1903		
	₇								
	₈								
	₉								
	₁₀								
	₁₁								
	₁₂								
	₁₃								
	₁₄								
	₁₅	ENROLLMENT OF NOS. 1 HEREON APPROVED BY THE SECRETARY OF INTERIOR JAN 17 1903							
	₁₆								
	₁₇								

TRIBAL ENROLLMENT OF PARENTS

	Name of Father	Year	County	Name of Mother	Year	County
₁	Stephen Woods	Ded	Wade	Winnie James	1896	Non Citz
₂	Alfred Burney	1896	"	Nº1		
₃						
₄						
₅						
₆						
₇						
₈						
₉						
₁₀	For child of No1 see NB (March 3 1905) card #992					
₁₁	For child of No1 see NB (Apr 26-06) Card #612					
	On 1896 rolls[sic] as Sarah Woods					
₁₂	See testimony taken in enrollment of Henry and Ada Woods					
₁₃	as to the marriage of father Stephen Woods and mother Winnie					
	No1 has been divorced from her husband Watson Wright on Choctaw Card					
₁₄	#2184 and is now the wife of Alfred Burney on Choctaw Card #2088 Evidence					
₁₅	of divorce requested. Certificate of marriage filed Sept 26, 1901					
₁₆	Nº2 Born Jany 19 1901. Application received March 8 1901 and					
₁₇	returned for information relative to mother, proof of birth filed Feby 5, 1903					

Date of Application for Enrollment. 5/31/99

Choctaw By Blood Enrollment Cards 1898-1914

RESIDENCE: Wade   COUNTY. **Choctaw Nation**   **Choctaw Roll** *(Not Including Freedmen)*   CARD NO.

POST OFFICE: Talihina, I.T.   FIELD NO.   2197

Dawes' Roll No.	NAME	Relationship to Person	AGE	SEX	BLOOD	TRIBAL ENROLLMENT		
						Year	County	No.
6367	1 Thompson, Charles 24	First Named	21	M	3/4	1896	Wade	12049
6368	2 " Jincy 30	Wife	27	F	Full	1893	"	462
	3							
	4							
	5							
	6							
	7							
	8							
	9							
	10							
	11							
	12							
	13							
	14							
	15	ENROLLMENT OF NOS. 1, 2, HEREON						
	16	APPROVED BY THE SECRETARY OF INTERIOR JAN 17 1903						
	17							

TRIBAL ENROLLMENT OF PARENTS

	Name of Father	Year	County	Name of Mother	Year	County
1	Jack Thompson	Dead	Skullyville	Mary Thompson	Dead	Skullyville
2	Brias McCoy	"	"	Betsy McCoy	"	Wade
3						
4						
5						
6						
7	No2 on 1893 Pay Roll as Jincy Tolbert, Page 60, No 462, Wade Co					
8						
9						
10						
11						
12						
13						
14						
15				Date of Application for Enrollment.		
16					5/31/99	
17						

RESIDENCE: Wade   COUNTY. **Choctaw Nation**   **Choctaw Roll** (Not Including Freedmen)   CARD NO.
POST OFFICE: Talihina, I.T.   FIELD NO. **2198**

Dawes' Roll No.	NAME		Relationship to Person	AGE	SEX	BLOOD	TRIBAL ENROLLMENT		
							Year	County	No.
6369	1 Dukes, Loren D	25	First Named	22	M	1/2	1896	Wade	3336
I.W. 22	2 " Pollie	21	Wife	18	F	I.W.			
6370	3 " Stella	4	Dau	7mo	"	1/4			
6371	4 " J Herbert Hinds	2	Son	6mo	M	1/4			
I.W. 1604	5 Adams, Della		Wife	26	F	I.W			
	6								
	7								
	8								
	9								
	10								
	11								
	12								
	13								
	14								
	15								
	16								
	17								

ENROLLMENT
OF NOS. ~~~ 5 ~~~ HEREON
APPROVED BY THE SECRETARY
OF INTERIOR Feb 12 1907

ENROLLMENT
OF NOS. 1,3,4 HEREON
APPROVED BY THE SECRETARY
OF INTERIOR Jan 17 1903

ENROLLMENT
OF NOS. ~~~ 2 ~~~ HEREON
APPROVED BY THE SECRETARY
OF INTERIOR Jun 13-1903

TRIBAL ENROLLMENT OF PARENTS

	Name of Father	Year	County	Name of Mother	Year	County
1	Charles Dukes	Dead	Wade	Abigail Dukes	Dead	Wade
2	John B Wilson	"	Non Citz	Maria Wilson	1896	Non Citz
3	No1			No2		
4	No1			No2		
5	Jim Maxey	Dead	Non Citz	Ella Maxey	Dead	Non Citz
6						
7						
8	No5 placed hereon under order of the Commission to the Five Civilized Tribes of Nov 16-1896					
9	holding that application was made for her enrollment within the time provided by the					
10	Act of Congress approved April 26-1896					
	No1 on 1896 roll as Loren Dukes					
11						
12	No3 Affidavit of birth to be supplied. Recd June 1/99					
13	No.4 Enrolled March 5th 1901					
	Certified copy of bill of divorce between Loren Dukes and Della Dukes filed Jany 17, 1903					
14	For child of Nos 1&2 see NB (March 3. 1905) #789					
15	#1 to 3					
16	Date of Application for Enrollment. 5/31/99					
17	P.O. No.5 Red Oak I.T. 11/16/06					

Choctaw By Blood Enrollment Cards 1898-1914

RESIDENCE: Wade COUNTY.
POST OFFICE: Talihina, I.T.

Choctaw Nation

Choctaw Roll
(Not Including Freedmen)

CARD NO.
FIELD NO. **2199**

Dawes' Roll No.		NAME		Relationship to Person	AGE	SEX	BLOOD	TRIBAL ENROLLMENT		
								Year	County	No.
6372	1	King, William	30	First Named	27	M	1/2	1896	Wade	7517
I.W. 23	2	" Joanna	27	Wife	24	F	I.W.	1896	"	14727
6373	3	" Lillie	7	Dau	4	"	1/4	1896	"	7518
6374	4	" Charles	6	Son	2	M	1/4			
6375	5	" Emma	4	Dau	5mo	F	1/4			
6376	6	" George William	2	Son	18mo	M	1/4			
	7									
	8									
	9									
	10									
	11									
	12									
	13									
	14									
	15									
	16									
	17									

ENROLLMENT
OF NOS. 1,3,4,5,6 HEREON
APPROVED BY THE SECRETARY
OF INTERIOR Jan 17 1903

ENROLLMENT
OF NOS. ~~ 2 ~~ HEREON
APPROVED BY THE SECRETARY
OF INTERIOR Jun 13 1903

TRIBAL ENROLLMENT OF PARENTS

	Name of Father	Year	County	Name of Mother	Year	County
1	William King	Dead	Jacks Fork	Sophia King	1896	Jacks Fork
2	William Young	1896	Non Citz	Jane Young	1896	Non Citz
3	No 1			No 2		
4	No 1			No 2		
5	No 1			No 2		
6	Nº1			Nº2		
7						
8	No1 on 1896 roll as Willie King					
9						
10	Nº6 Born Oct 29, 1900; enrolled Aug 15, 1902					
11						
12						
13						
14					Date of Application for Enrollment.	
15						
16					5/31/99	
17	P.O. 12/10/02 Tuskahoma					

Choctaw By Blood Enrollment Cards 1898-1914

RESIDENCE: Wade   COUNTY. **Choctaw Nation**   **Choctaw Roll** (Not Including Freedmen)   CARD NO.
POST OFFICE: Lenox, I.T.   FIELD NO. **2200**

Dawes' Roll No.	NAME	Relationship to Person	AGE	SEX	BLOOD	TRIBAL ENROLLMENT		
						Year	County	No.
6377	1 Bohanan, Thomas 41	First Named	38	M	1/2	1896	Wade	990
6378	2 " Lizzie 30	Wife	27	F	Full	1896	"	991
6379	3 " Dave 8	Son	5	M	3/4	1896	"	992
6380	4 " Bertha C 6	Dau	3	F	3/4	1896	"	993
6381	5 " Levina 5	"	1½	F	3/4			
6382	6 " Isabelle 3	"	1½	F	3/4			
	7							
	8							
	9							
	10							
	11							
	12							
	13							
	14	ENROLLMENT OF NOS. 1,2,3,4,5,6 HEREON APPROVED BY THE SECRETARY OF INTERIOR Jan 17 1903						
	15							
	16							
	17							

TRIBAL ENROLLMENT OF PARENTS

	Name of Father	Year	County	Name of Mother	Year	County
1	Sam Bohanan	1896	Jacks Fork	Margaret Bohanan	1896	Jacks Fork
2	James Billy	Dead	Wade	Maggie Billy	1896	Wade
3	No 1			No 2		
4	No 1			No 2		
5	No 1			No 2		
6	No 1			No 2		
7						
8						
9	No.6 Enrolled May 1st, 1901					
10	For child of Nos 1 and 2, see N.B. (Apr 26-06) No.544					
11						
12						
13						
14					Date of Application for Enrollment.	
15					5/31/99	
16						
17	Talihina I.T. 12/11/02					

RESIDENCE: Sugar Loaf
POST OFFICE: Le Flore, I.T.

COUNTY. **Choctaw Nation**

Choctaw Roll
(Not Including Freedmen)

CARD NO.
FIELD NO. **2201**

Dawes' Roll No.	NAME		Relationship to Person First Named	AGE	SEX	BLOOD	TRIBAL ENROLLMENT		
							Year	County	No.
6383	1 Hudson, Charley	24	First Named	21	M	1/4	1896	Sugar Loaf	5245
6384	2 Goen, Jefferson	17	1/2 Bro	14	"	1/2	1896	" "	4677
6385	3 " Jimmie	13	"	10	"	1/2	1896	" "	4678
I.W. 183	4 McFerrin, Margaret		Mother	52	F	I.W.			
I.W. 1667	5 Goen, Cora		Wife of No2	16	F	I.W.			
	6								
	7								
	8	ENROLLMENT							
	9	OF NOS. ~~ 5 ~~ HEREON APPROVED BY THE SECRETARY							
	10	OF INTERIOR Mar 4-1907							
	11								
	12								
	13								
	14	ENROLLMENT		ENROLLMENT					
	15	OF NOS. 1,2,3 HEREON		OF NOS. ~~ 4 ~~ HEREON					
	16	APPROVED BY THE SECRETARY OF INTERIOR Jan 17 1903		APPROVED BY THE SECRETARY OF INTERIOR Jun 13 1903					
	17								

TRIBAL ENROLLMENT OF PARENTS

	Name of Father	Year	County	Name of Mother	Year	County
1	Joel Hudson	Dead	Eagle	Margaret McFerrin	1896	Non Citz
2	Elum Going	"	"	" "	1896	" "
3	" "	"	"	" "	1896	" "
4	Samuel Lewis		non citizen	Manda Lewis	Dead	" "
5	Ben Krems	Dead	" "	Kate Krems	"	" "
6						
7						
8	Mother of above parties on Card No D189					
9	See testimony attached thereto					
10	No4 transferred from Choctaw card #D.189. See decision of April 20, 1903					
	No 5 enrolled by Department 1907					
11						
12						
13						
14					#1 to 3 inc	
					Date of Application for Enrollment.	
15						
16					5/31/99	
17						

Choctaw By Blood Enrollment Cards 1898-1914

RESIDENCE: Sugar Loaf	COUNTY.		
POST OFFICE: Monroe, I.T.	Choctaw Nation	Choctaw Roll *(Not Including Freedmen)*	CARD No. FIELD No. 2202

Dawes' Roll No.	NAME	Relationship to Person	AGE	SEX	BLOOD	TRIBAL ENROLLMENT		
						Year	County	No.
I.W. 242	1 Mathies, Christopher C.[52]	First Named	49	M	I.W.	1896	Sugar Loaf	14808
	2							
	3							
	4							
	5							
	6							
	7 ENROLLMENT							
	8 OF NOS. 1 HEREON APPROVED BY THE SECRETARY							
	9 OF INTERIOR SEP 12 1903							
	10							
	11							
	12							
	13							
	14							
	15							
	16							
	17							

TRIBAL ENROLLMENT OF PARENTS

	Name of Father	Year	County	Name of Mother	Year	County
1	W^m H Mathies	1896	Non Citz	Anna Mathies	1896	Non Citz
2						
3						
4						
5	Further action in connection with allotments No 1 suspended under protest					
6	of Attorneys for Choctaw & Chickasaw Nations Jan 23 1904					
7	Protest overruled by Department March 31, 1904.					
8	On 1896 roll as C C Mathis					
9	Admitted by Dawes Commission as an Intermarried					
10	Citizen Case No 1296. No appeal					
11						
12						
13						
14						
15						
16				Date of Application for Enrollment.	5/31/99	
17						

RESIDENCE: Wade	COUNTY.						CARD No.	
POST OFFICE: Talihina, I.T.	**Choctaw Nation**				**Choctaw Roll** (Not Including Freedmen)		FIELD No. **2203**	

Dawes' Roll No.	NAME		Relationship to Person	AGE	SEX	BLOOD	TRIBAL ENROLLMENT		
							Year	County	No.
6386	1 Dukes, Gilbert W	52	First Named	49	M	1/2	1896	Wade	3333
6387	2 " Isabelle	48	Wife	45	F	1/2	1896	"	3334
6388	3 " Joseph A	29	Son	26	M	11/16	1896	"	3335
6389	4 " Edwin	21	"	18	"	11/16	1896	"	3337
6390	5 " Josephine	16	Dau	13	F	11/16	1896	"	3338
6391	6 " Minerva	12	"	9	"	1/2	1896	"	3339
6392	7 " Leetta E	9	"	6	"	1/2	1896	"	3340
6393	8 " D H	6	Son	2	M	1/2			
6394	9 Sexton, Charles	20	S.Son	17	"	5/8	1896	Wade	11323
	10								
	11								
	12								
	13								
	14								
	15	ENROLLMENT OF NOS. 1,2 3 4 5 6 7 8and9 HEREON							
	16	APPROVED BY THE SECRETARY OF INTERIOR Jan 17 1903							
	17								

TRIBAL ENROLLMENT OF PARENTS

	Name of Father	Year	County	Name of Mother	Year	County
1	Joseph Dukes	Dead	Towson	Nancy Dukes	Dead	Wade
2	Horace Woods	"	Non Citz	No-wa-ho-ke	"	"
3	No 1			Angeline Dukes	"	"
4	No 1			" "	"	"
5	No 1			" "	"	"
6	No 1			No 2		
7	No 1			No 2		
8	No 1			No 2		
9	Alfred Sexton	Dead	Wade	No 2		
10						
11	No1 on 1896 roll as G W Dukes					
12	No3 " 1896 " " Joseph "					
13	No7 " 1896 " " Ella "					
	For child of #3 see NB (Apr 26 '06) Card #273					
14						
15					Date of Application for Enrollment.	
16					5/31/99	
17						

103

Choctaw By Blood Enrollment Cards 1898-1914

RESIDENCE: Wade COUNTY.
POST OFFICE: Talihina, I.T.

Choctaw Nation

Choctaw Roll
(Not Including Freedmen)

CARD NO.
FIELD NO. 2204

Dawes' Roll No.	NAME	Relationship to Person First Named	AGE	SEX	BLOOD	TRIBAL ENROLLMENT		
						Year	County	No.
6395	1 Woods, Martha 63	First Named	60	F	1/2	1896	Wade	13064
	2							
	3							
	4							
	5							
	6							
	7							
	8							
	9							
	10							
	11							
	12							
	13							
	14							
	15	ENROLLMENT OF NOS. 1 HEREON APPROVED BY THE SECRETARY OF INTERIOR JAN 17 1903						
	16							
	17							

TRIBAL ENROLLMENT OF PARENTS

	Name of Father	Year	County	Name of Mother	Year	County
1	Horace Woods	Dead	Towson	No-wa-ho-ke	Dead	Wade
2						
3						
4						
5						
6						
7						
8						
9						
10						
11						
12						
13						
14						
15						
16				Date of Application for Enrollment.	5/31/99	
17						

RESIDENCE: Wade	COUNTY.						CARD NO.	
POST OFFICE: Talihina, I.T.	Choctaw Nation			Choctaw Roll (Not Including Freedmen)			FIELD NO. 2205	

Dawes' Roll No.	NAME	Relationship to Person First Named	AGE	SEX	BLOOD	TRIBAL ENROLLMENT		
						Year	County	No.
6396	1 Beams, Sampson 38	First Named	35	M	Full	1896	Wade	1043
6397	2 " Nancy 12	Dau	9	F	"	1896	"	1040
6398	3 " Sophia 11	"	8	"	"	1896	"	1041
6399	4 " Ephraim 9	Son	6	M	"	1896	"	1042
	5							
	6							
	7							
	8							
	9							
	10							
	11							
	12							
	13							
	14							
	15	ENROLLMENT OF NOS. 1,2,3,4 HEREON APPROVED BY THE SECRETARY OF INTERIOR JAN 17 1903						
	16							
	17							

TRIBAL ENROLLMENT OF PARENTS

	Name of Father	Year	County	Name of Mother	Year	County
1	Thos Beams	Dead	Sans Bois	Lucinda Beams	Dead	Gaines
2	No 1			Miley Beams	"	Wade
3	No 1			" "	"	"
4	No 1			" "	"	"
5						
6						
7	N°1 is now husband of Lena Wilkerson non citizen. Evidence					
8	of marriage filed Jany 21, 1903					
9	For child of No2 see NB (Apr 26-06) Card #832					
10						
11						
12						
13						
14					Date of Application for Enrollment.	
15						
16					6/1/99	
17						

Apr 5-02

RESIDENCE: **Wade** P.O. Iona I.T. COUNTY. **Choctaw Nation** **Choctaw Roll** CARD NO.
POST OFFICE: **Talihina, I.T** (Not Including Freedmen) FIELD NO. **2206**

Dawes' Roll No.	NAME	Relationship to Person First Named	AGE	SEX	BLOOD	TRIBAL ENROLLMENT		
						Year	County	No.
DEAD.	1 Messersmith, Clark	Named	47	M	I.W.	No. 1 HEREON DISMISSED UNDER		
✓ ✓	2 Vanderslice, Laura C	Wife	30	F	1/8	ORDER OF THE COMMISSION TO THE FIVE		
✓DP	3 Messersmith, Agnes	Dau	8mo	"	1/16	CIVILIZED TRIBES OF MARCH 31, 1905.		
D.P.	4 McKinley, Samuel M	S.Son	9	M	1/16			
✓ ✓	5 " Josephine C	S.Dau	6	F	1/16			
✓ ✓	6 " John Leo	S.Son	4	M	1/16			
✓DP	7 Vanderslice, Robert Jackson	Son of N2	2mo	M	1/16			
3 and 7 8	DISMISSED MAY 27 1904					See W Petition #34		
9						Nos 2,4,5 and 6 denied Case #1026		
	Judgement[sic] of U.S. Court admitting Nos2,4,5and6 vacated and							
	set aside by Decree of Choctaw Chickasaw Cit Court Dec' 17 '02.					[on back of card]		
11	Nos 2,4,5and6 now in C.C.C.C. Case #65					No 7 application has also been made for the		
12	#4 DISMISSED FEB 1 1905					enrollment of their child as child of an		
13	2 is now the wife of R.J.Vanderslice on					intermarried citizen of Chickasaw Nation		
14	Chickasaw card #377. Evidence of marriage					under Act of Congress approved April		
	filed April 26, 1902.					26,1896 and his name appears on Chickasaw		
15	7 Born Feby 25, 1902; enrolled April 26, 1902					card [remarks illegible]		
	See Petition "C 132"							
17	See C.132: Duplicate record in Choctaw #4575							

TRIBAL ENROLLMENT OF PARENTS

	Name of Father	Year	County	Name of Mother	Year	County
1	Barney Messersmith	Dead	Non Citz	Nancy Messersmith	Dead	Non Citz
2	Samuel Williams	"	Choctaw	Parlee Williams	"	" "
3	No 1			No 2		
4	John McKinley	Dead	Non Citz	No 2		
5	" "	"	" "	No 2		
6	" "	"	" "	No 2		
7	R J Vanderslice	1897[sic]	Pontotoc	N2		
8	DENIED CITIZENSHIP BY THE CHOCTAW AND					
9	CHICKASAW CITIZENSHIP COURT					
10						
11	No2 was admitted by U.S. Court Central Dist Sept 11/97 Case No62					
12	No4 " " " " " " " 11/97 " " 62					
13	No5 " " " " " " " 11/97 " " 62					
14	No6 " " " " " " " 11/97 " " 62					
15	No2 " " as Laura C McKinley					
16	No1 was married to No2 in August 1897 under U.S. Laws				Date of Application for Enrollment.	
	Remarried under license issued by Choctaw Authorities May 22 1899					
17	No3 Affidavit of birth t be supplied. Recd June 1/99				6/1/99	
	N°1 Died Oct 10, 1899; proof of death filed Oct 15, 1902					

Choctaw By Blood Enrollment Cards 1898-1914

RESIDENCE: Skullyville   COUNTY, **Choctaw Nation**   **Choctaw Roll**   CARD NO.
POST OFFICE: Gurtie[sic], I.T.   *(Not Including Freedmen)*   FIELD NO. **2207**

Dawes' Roll No.	NAME	Relationship to Person	AGE	SEX	BLOOD	TRIBAL ENROLLMENT Year	County	No.
✓ ✓ 1	Johnson, James C ✱	First Named	57	M	1/8			
✓ ✓ 2	" Delilah ✱	Wife	48	F	I.W.			
✓ 3	" Alvin ✱	Son	17	M	1/16			
✓ ✓ 4	" William C ✱	"	14	"	1/16			
✓ ✓ 5	" Jesse B ✱	"	10	"	1/16			
✓ ✓ 6	" Esco ✱	"	8	"	1/16			
✓ 7	" Addie May ✱	Dau	4	F	1/16			

Judgement[sic] of U.S. Court Admitting Nos 1,2,4,5 and 6 vacated and set aside by Decree of Choctaw Chickasaw Citizen Court Decr 17'02 Now in C.C.C.C. Case #65 3/13/03

9

10 No.7: Stricken from card by order of
11 Commission: see evidence and
12 testimony of this date. June 7,1900

13 Letter "B" taken from name of
14 Jesse B, same order:

15

16

17

TRIBAL ENROLLMENT OF PARENTS

	Name of Father	Year	County	Name of Mother	Year	County
1	Carrol Johnson	Dead	Non Citz	Mary A Johnson	Dead	Choctaw
2	Richmond Cole	"	" "	Emily Cole	1896	Non Citz
3	No 1			No 2		
4	No 1			No 2		
5	No 1			No 2		
6	No 1			No 2		
7	No 1			No 2		

8   Nos 1,2,4,5 and 6 denied in 96 case #1026   ⌈ Denied Citizenship by the
9   No2 was admitted by U.S.Court as Delila Johnson   Choctaw and Chickasaw
10   No5 " " " " " " " Jesse B "   Citizenship Court Case #65
   No6 " " " " " " Escoe "   ⌊ April 18 1904
11

12   All admitted by U.S. Court, Central District, September 11/97
13   Case No 62
14   As to residence see testimony of No 1
15   No.3 transferred to Choctaw card 5334
     June 7, 1900   Date of Application for Enrollment.
16 P.O. Mead I.T. 1/19/03   6/1/99
17   See C-132

Duplicate record in Choctaw #4575

107

RESIDENCE: Eagle   COUNTY.

POST OFFICE: Granit, Arkansas

Choctaw Nation

Choctaw Roll
(Not Including Freedmen)

CARD NO.

FIELD NO. 2208

Dawes' Roll No.	NAME	Relationship to Person First Named	AGE	SEX	BLOOD	TRIBAL ENROLLMENT		
						Year	County	No.
✓ ✓	1 Williams, Lena A	First Named	18	F	1/8			
✓ ✓	2 " Samuel C	Bro	14	M	1/8			
	3							
	4							
	5	Nos 1 and 2 denied by Dawes Com in 96 Case #1026						
	6	Judgement (sic) of U.S. Court admitting Nos 1&2 vacated and set						
	7	aside by Choctaw Chickasaw Citizenship Court Oct 17-02						
	8	Both admitted by U.S. Court Central District September 11/97 Case No 62.						
	9							
	10							
	11							
	12							
	13							
	14							
	15							
	16							
	17							

TRIBAL ENROLLMENT OF PARENTS

	Name of Father	Year	County	Name of Mother	Year	County
1	Sam'l Williams	Dead	Choctaw	Parlee Williams	Dead	Non Citz
2	" "	"	"	" "	"	" "
3						
4						
5						
6	As to residence, see testimony of James C. Johnson Card No 2207					
7	No.1 is now the wife of Warren Boggs – a non citizen. Evidence of					
8	Marriage filed Feby 24, 1902.					
	For child of No 1 see (Act Apr 26 '06) NB #1049					
9						
10						
11						
12			Duplicate record in Choctaw #4575			
13			132			
14					Date of Application for Enrollment.	
15						
16					6/1/99	
17						

DENIED CITIZENSHIP BY THE CHOCTAW AND CHICKASAW CITIZENSHIP COURT

Filed April 18, 1907

Choctaw By Blood Enrollment Cards 1898-1914

RESIDENCE: Wade	COUNTY.							CARD NO.	
POST OFFICE: Talihina, I.T.	**Choctaw Nation**					**Choctaw Roll** (*Not Including Freedmen*)		FIELD NO.	**2209**

Dawes' Roll No.	NAME		Relationship to Person Named	AGE	SEX	BLOOD	TRIBAL ENROLLMENT		
							Year	County	No.
6400	1 Dukes, Henry	26	First Named	23	M	1/2	1896	Wade	3341
6401	2 " Le Roy	4	Son	2	"	1/4			
6402	3 DIED PRIOR TO SEPTEMBER 25, 1902 Bud W		"	2mo	"	1/4			
I.W. 1297	4 Dukes, Maud	24	Wife	24	F	I.W.			
	5								
	6								
	7 For child of Nos 1&4 see NB (Apr 26-06) Card #375								
	8								
	9					ENROLLMENT			
	10					OF NOS. 4 HEREON			
	11					APPROVED BY THE SECRETARY OF INTERIOR Mar 14 1905			
	12								
	13								
	14								
	15 ENROLLMENT OF NOS. 1, 2, 3 HEREON								
	16 APPROVED BY THE SECRETARY								
	17 OF INTERIOR Jan 17 1903								

TRIBAL ENROLLMENT OF PARENTS

	Name of Father	Year	County	Name of Mother	Year	County
1	G.W. Dukes	1896	Wade	Angeline Dukes	Dead	Wade
2	No 1			Eva Dukes	1896	Non Citz
3	No 1			" "	1896	" "
4	G.W. Maynor	dead	non citz	L.W. Maynor		non citz
5						
6						
7			No2 Affidavit of birth to be supplied: Filed Nov 1/99			
8						
9			Evidence of marriage to be supplied No3 Died in 1900: Proof of death filed December 20, 1902			
10			Evidence of divorce between No.1 and Eva Dukes filed Jan 6, 1903			
11			Nº1 is now husband of Maud Dukes on Choctaw card #D950			
12	No.3 died - - 1900: Enrollment cancelled by Department July 8, 1904					
13	Nos. 1 and 4 were married June 24, 1902					
14	No.4 originally listed for enrollment on Choctaw card D-950 Dec. 16, 1902 transferred to this card Feb 1, 1905, see decision of Jan 16,1905.				#1&2	
15					Date of Application for Enrollment.	
16					6/1/99	
17	No.4 P.O. Goodwater I.T.			No 3 enrolled Dec 14/99		

RESIDENCE: Wade		COUNTY. Choctaw Nation				Choctaw Roll _(Not Including Freedmen)_		CARD NO.	
POST OFFICE: Lenox, I.T.								FIELD NO. **2210**	

Dawes' Roll No.	NAME		Relationship to Person	AGE	SEX	BLOOD	TRIBAL ENROLLMENT		
							Year	County	No.
6403	1 Durant, John	56	First Named	53	M	Full	1896	Wade	3344
6404	2 " Louisa	40	Wife	37	F	"	1896	"	3345
6405	3 " Lizzie	14	Dau	11	"	"	1896	"	3349
6406	4 " Johnson DIED PRIOR TO SEPTEMBER 25, 1902		Son	5mo	M	"			
6407	5 " Sarah	2	Dau	5mo	F	"			
	6								
	7								
	8								
	9								
	10								
	11								
	12								
	13								
	14								
	15 ENROLLMENT OF NOS. 1,2,3,4,5 HEREON APPROVED BY THE SECRETARY OF INTERIOR Jan 17 1903								
	16								
	17								

TRIBAL ENROLLMENT OF PARENTS

	Name of Father	Year	County	Name of Mother	Year	County
1	Robison Durant	Dead	Red River	Mary Durant	Dead	Nashoba
2	Ta-sa-hi-ya	"	Wade	Leon Tasahiya	"	Wade
3	No 1			No 2		
4	No 1			No 2		
5	No 1			No 2		
6						
7						
8			No2 on 1896 roll as Levicey Durant			
9						
10			No.5 Enrolled May 17, 1901			
11			No.4 died - - 1900. Enrollment cancelled by Department July 8, 1904			
12						
13						
14						
15				#1 to 3 inc.		
16				Date of Application for Enrollment.	6/1/99	
17				No 4 enrolled Nov 1/99		

Choctaw By Blood Enrollment Cards 1898-1914

RESIDENCE: Wade   COUNTY. **Choctaw Nation**   **Choctaw Roll** (Not Including Freedmen)   CARD NO.
POST OFFICE: Lenox I.T.   FIELD NO. 2211

Dawes' Roll No.	NAME		Relationship to Person First Named	AGE	SEX	BLOOD	TRIBAL ENROLLMENT		
							Year	County	No.
6408	1 Willy Joe	24	First Named	21	M	Full	1896	Wade	13073
	2								
	3								
	4								
	5								
	6								
	7								
	8								
	9								
	10								
	11								
	12								
	13								
	14								
	15								
	16								
	17								

ENROLLMENT
OF NOS. 1
APPROVED BY THE SECRETARY HEREON
OF INTERIOR JAN 17 1903

TRIBAL ENROLLMENT OF PARENTS

	Name of Father	Year	County	Name of Mother	Year	County
1		Dead	Tobocksey[sic]	Seliney	Dead	Tobocksey[sic]
2						
3						
4						
5						
6			No 1 on 1896 roll as Joe Willis			
7						
8						
9						
10						
11						
12						
13						
14						
15					Date of Application for Enrollment.	
16					6/1/99	
17						

111

Choctaw By Blood Enrollment Cards 1898-1914

RESIDENCE: **Sugar Loaf**
POST OFFICE: **Wister, I.T.**

COUNTY. **Choctaw Nation**

Choctaw Roll *(Not Including Freedmen)*

CARD No.
FIELD No. **2212**

Dawes' Roll No.	NAME		Relationship to Person	AGE	SEX	BLOOD	TRIBAL ENROLLMENT		
							Year	County	No.
6409	1 James, Austin	25	First Named	22	M	Full	1896	Wade	6712
6410	2 " Plannie	25	Wife	22	F	"	1896	Sugar Loaf	5235
6411	3 " Elie	3	Son	10mo	M	"			
6412	4 " Joshua	1	Son	5mo	M	"			
	5								
	6								
	7								
	8								
	9								
	10								
	11								
	12								
	13								
	14								
	15	ENROLLMENT OF NOS. 1,2,3,4 HEREON							
	16	APPROVED BY THE SECRETARY							
	17	OF INTERIOR Jan 17 1903							

TRIBAL ENROLLMENT OF PARENTS

	Name of Father	Year	County	Name of Mother	Year	County
1	Payson James	1896	Wade	Melinda James	Dead	Wade
2	Coleman Hale	Dead	Sugar Loaf	Ista Hale	1896	Sugar Loaf
3	No 1			No.2		
4	Nº1			No2		
5						
6			No2 on 1896 roll as Plannie Hill			
7			No.3 Enrolled November 14th 1900			
8			Nº4 Born Dec 14, 1901: enrolled May 7, 1902			
9			For child of Nos 1&2 see NB (Mar 3-05) Card #117			
10						
11						
12						
13						
14					#1&2	
15					Date of Application for Enrollment.	
16					6/5/99	
17	P.O. Talihina I.T. 4/7/05					

Choctaw By Blood Enrollment Cards 1898-1914

Choctaw Nation

Choctaw Roll
(Not Including Freedmen)

CARD No.
FIELD No. 2213

Dawes' Roll No.	NAME		Relationship to Person	AGE	SEX	BLOOD	TRIBAL ENROLLMENT		
							Year	County	No.
I.W.901	1 Heavener, Joseph	51	First Named	48	M	I.W.	1896	Sugar Loaf	14603
6413	2 " Tobitha	41	Wife	43	F	1/2	1896	" "	5222
6414	3 " Joseph Jr	13	Son	10	M	1/4	1896	" "	5225
6415	4 " Mary	17	Dau	14	F	1/4	1896	" "	5223
6416	5 " Matthew	15	Son	12	M	1/4	1896	" "	5224
6417	6 Ward, David	21	S.Son	18	M	1/4	1896	" "	12855
	7								
	8								
	9								
	10	ENROLLMENT							
	11	OF NOS. 1 HEREON APPROVED BY THE SECRETARY							
	12	OF INTERIOR AUG 3 1904							
	13								
	14								
	15	ENROLLMENT							
	16	OF NOS. 2,3,4,5,6 HEREON APPROVED BY THE SECRETARY							
	17	OF INTERIOR JAN 17 1903							

TRIBAL ENROLLMENT OF PARENTS

Name of Father	Year	County	Name of Mother	Year	County
1 Jacob Heavener	Dead	Non Citz	Elizabeth Heavener	Dead	Non Citz
2 Samuel Hickman	"	" "	Lucy Hickman	"	Sugar Loaf
3 No1			No2		
4 No1			No2		
5 No1			No2		
6 Zachariah Ward	Ded	Non Citz	No2		
7					

8   No3 on 1896 roll as Joseph Heavener
9   No6 " 1896 " " David Word
10   No5 " 1896 " " Matthew Heavener
   As to marriage of Nos 1-2, see testimony of No1
11   Additional evidence to be supplied
12   Nos1-2: Evidence of marriage filed Dec 20, 1902
   For child of No.4 see NB (Apr 26,06) No. 550
13   " " " " 6 " " " 733
14   " " " " 6 " " (Mar.3,1905) " 846
15   " " " " 4 " " " " 1029

	Date of Application for Enrollment.
16	
	6/5/99

17   Heavener I.T. 12/17/02

113

Choctaw By Blood Enrollment Cards 1898-1914

RESIDENCE: Sugar Loaf	COUNTY.					

RESIDENCE: Sugar Loaf   **COUNTY.**   **Choctaw Nation**   **Choctaw Roll** (Not Including Freedmen)   CARD NO.
POST OFFICE: Wister, I.T.   FIELD NO. **2214**

Dawes' Roll No.	NAME		Relationship to Person First Named	AGE	SEX	BLOOD	TRIBAL ENROLLMENT		
							Year	County	No.
6418	1 Peter, Barnabas	421	First Named	39	M	Full	1896	Sugar Loaf	10121
DEAD.	2 " Louisa DEAD.		Wife	50	F	"	1896	" "	10122
	3								
	4								
	5								
	6								
	7								
	8								
	9								
	10								
	11								
	12								
	13								
	14								
	15								
	16								
	17								

No. 2 HEREON DISMISSED UNDER ORDER OF THE COMMISSION TO THE FIVE CIVILIZED TRIBES OF MARCH 31, 1905.

ENROLLMENT
OF NOS. 1 HEREON
APPROVED BY THE SECRETARY
OF INTERIOR JAN 17 1903

TRIBAL ENROLLMENT OF PARENTS

	Name of Father	Year	County	Name of Mother	Year	County
1	Simon Peter	1896	Sugar Loaf	Na-mi-a-ho-na	Dead	Nashoba
2	James Colbert	Dead	" "		"	Skullyville
3						
4						
5						
6	No 1 on 1896 roll as Barnabas Petter					
7	No 2 " 1896 " " Louizer "					
8	Nº 2 Died Jany 2, 1901, proof of death filed Aug 29, 1902					
9	Nº 1 is now the husband of Emiline Cricklin on Choctaw card #2351 Aug 29, 1902					
10	For child of No 1 see NB (Mar 3-1905) Card 143.					
11						
12						
13						
14						
15						
16				Date of Application for Enrollment.	6/5/99	
17						

114

Choctaw By Blood Enrollment Cards 1898-1914

RESIDENCE: Sugar Loaf COUNTY. **Choctaw Nation** **Choctaw Roll** CARD NO.
POST OFFICE: Heavener, I.T. (Not Including Freedmen) FIELD NO. 2215

Dawes' Roll No.	NAME	Relationship to Person	AGE	SEX	BLOOD	TRIBAL ENROLLMENT		
						Year	County	No.
I.W. 567	1 Shirey, Edmond M ⁴⁰	First Named	39	M	I.W.			
6419	2 " Edmond F ¹²	Son	9	"	1/16	1896	Sugar Loaf	11213
	3							
	4							
	5							
	6							
	7							
	8							
	9							
	10							
	11	ENROLLMENT OF NOS. 1 HEREON APPROVED BY THE SECRETARY OF INTERIOR FEB -8 1904						
	12							
	13							
	14							
	15	ENROLLMENT OF NOS. 2 HEREON APPROVED BY THE SECRETARY OF INTERIOR JAN 17 1903						
	16							
	17							

TRIBAL ENROLLMENT OF PARENTS

	Name of Father	Year	County	Name of Mother	Year	County
1	Edmond L C Shirey	Dead	Non Citz	Mary Shirey	Dead	Non Citz
2	No 1			Ida Shirey	"	Sugar Loaf
3						
4						
5						
6			No2 on 1896 roll as Edward F Shirry			
7						
8						
9						
10						
11						
12						
13						
14						
15						
16				Date of Application for Enrollment.	6/5/99	
17	Stigler I.T. 12/15/02					

115

Choctaw By Blood Enrollment Cards 1898-1914

RESIDENCE: Sugar Loaf COUNTY. **Choctaw Nation** Choctaw Roll CARD NO.
POST OFFICE: Heavener, I.T. (Not Including Freedmen) FIELD NO. 2216

Dawes' Roll No.	NAME		Relationship to Person	AGE	SEX	BLOOD	TRIBAL ENROLLMENT		
							Year	County	No.
6420	1 Nolen, Thomas	72	First Named	69	M	Full	1896	Sugar Loaf	9567
I.W. 902	2 " Rhoda	48	Wife	42	F	I.W.	1896	Sans Bois	14898
	3								
	4								
	5								
	6								
	7	ENROLLMENT OF NOS. 2 HEREON							
	8	APPROVED BY THE SECRETARY							
	9	OF INTERIOR AUG 3 1904							
	10								
	11								
	12								
	13								
	14								
	15	ENROLLMENT OF NOS. 1 HEREON							
	16	APPROVED BY THE SECRETARY							
	17	OF INTERIOR JAN 17 1903							

TRIBAL ENROLLMENT OF PARENTS

	Name of Father	Year	County	Name of Mother	Year	County
1	Lo-ma-tache	Dead	in Mississippi		Dead	in Mississippi
2	Dan Decker	"	Non Citz	Mary Decker	1896	Non Citz
3						
4						
5						
6		No2 on 1896 roll as Rhoda Nolin				
7						
8		As to marriage see testimony of No1				
9		Other evidence to be supplied				
10						
11						
12						
13						
14						
15					Date of Application for Enrollment.	
16					6/5/99	
17						

RESIDENCE: Sugar Loaf   COUNTY. **Choctaw Nation**   **Choctaw Roll** CARD NO.
POST OFFICE: Heavener, I.T.   (Not Including Freedmen)   FIELD NO. 2217

Dawes' Roll No.	NAME	Relationship to Person First Named	AGE	SEX	BLOOD	TRIBAL ENROLLMENT Year	County	No.
DEAD.	1 West, Bettie Jane DEAD.		23	F	1/2	1896	Sugar Loaf	9568
DEAD.	2 " Mary Jane DEAD.	Dau	1 mo	"	1/4			
	3							
	4							
	5							
	6							
	7							
	8 No. 1 and 2 HEREON DISMISSED UNDER							
	9 ORDER OF THE COMMISSION TO THE FIVE CIVILIZED TRIBES OF MARCH 31, 1905							
	10							
	11							
	12							
	13							
	14							
	15							
	16							
	17							

TRIBAL ENROLLMENT OF PARENTS

Name of Father	Year	County	Name of Mother	Year	County
1 Thomas Nolen	1896	Sugar Loaf	Rhoda Nolen	1896	white woman
2 Jesse West	1896	Non Citz	No 1		
3					
4					
5					
6 No 1 on 1896 roll as Janie Nolen					
7 No2 Affidavit of birth to be supplied. Recd June 16/99					
8					
9 As to marriage of parents of No 1, see Card No 2216					
10 No. 1 died January 20, 1900. Proof of death filed Aug 15, 1901					
11 No 2 died February 8, 1900. Proof of death filed Aug 15, 1901					
12					
13					
14					
15					
16			Date of Application for Enrollment.	6/5/99	
17					

117

Choctaw By Blood Enrollment Cards 1898-1914

RESIDENCE: Sugar Loaf COUNTY. **Choctaw Nation** Choctaw Roll CARD No.
POST OFFICE: Gibson, Arkansas *(Not Including Freedmen)* FIELD No. **2218**

Dawes' Roll No.	NAME	Relationship to Person	AGE	SEX	BLOOD	TRIBAL ENROLLMENT		
						Year	County	No.
I.W. 514	1 Loving, Amanda 62	First Named	59	F	I.W.	1896	Sugar Loaf	14746
6421	2 " John D 19	Dau	16	M[sic]	1/8	1896	" "	7772
	3							
	4							
	5							
	6	ENROLLMENT						
	7	OF NOS. 1 HEREON APPROVED BY THE SECRETARY						
	8	OF INTERIOR Dec 24 1903						
	9							
	10							
	11							
	12							
	13							
	14							
	15	ENROLLMENT OF NOS. 2 HEREON						
	16	APPROVED BY THE SECRETARY						
	17	OF INTERIOR Jan 17 1903						

TRIBAL ENROLLMENT OF PARENTS

	Name of Father	Year	County	Name of Mother	Year	County
1	Jonas King	Dead	Non Citz	Jennie King	Dead	Non Citz
2	John Loving	"	Sugar Loaf	No 1		
3						
4						
5						
6	No2 on 1896 roll as Jno. D. Loving					
7						
8	As to marriage of No1 see her testimony and that of Thos Nolen					
9	N°2 is a female. Her correct age is 23. See testimony of					
10	N°s 1 and 2 of May 29, 1903					
11						
12						
13						
14					Date of Application for Enrollment.	
15						
16					6/5/99	
17	12/18/02 P.O. Godman Ark.					

118

Choctaw By Blood Enrollment Cards 1898-1914

RESIDENCE: Sugar Loaf COUNTY. **Choctaw Nation** Choctaw Roll CARD NO.
POST OFFICE: Gibson, Arkansas *(Not Including Freedmen)* FIELD NO. **2219**

Dawes' Roll No.	NAME		Relationship to Person First Named	AGE	SEX	BLOOD	TRIBAL ENROLLMENT		
							Year	County	No.
6422	1 Fox, John R	37	First Named	34	M	1/2	1896	Chick Dist	4581
I.W. 24	2 " Mollie	28	Wife	25	F	I.W.			
6423	3 " Edie M J	3	Son	4mo	M	1/4			
6424	4 " Emry Lee	1	Son	2wks	M	1/4			
	5								
	6								
	7								
	8								
	9								
	10								
	11								
	12								
	13								
	14								
	15								
	16								
	17								

ENROLLMENT OF NOS. 1, 3, 4 HEREON APPROVED BY THE SECRETARY OF INTERIOR Jan 17 1903

ENROLLMENT OF NOS. ~ 2 ~ HEREON APPROVED BY THE SECRETARY OF INTERIOR Jun 13 1903

TRIBAL ENROLLMENT OF PARENTS

	Name of Father	Year	County	Name of Mother	Year	County
1	Jackson Fox	Dead	Sugar Loaf	Ellen Fox	Dead	Non Citz
2	Marion Canady	"	Non Citz	Lou Canady	1896	" "
3	No 1			No 2		
4	No 1			No 2		
5						
6						
7						
8						
9	No1 on 1896 roll John Fox					
10						
11	As to marriage of parents of No1 and of his marriage to No2 see testimony of Amanda Loving Card No 2218					
12	Additional evidence to be supplied Recd June 16/99					
13	No4 Born July 31, 1902: enrolled Aug 16, 1902					
14						
15	For child of Nos 1&2 see NB (Apr 26 '06) Card#193			#1&2		
16				Date of Application for Enrollment	6/5/99	
17	Page I.T. 12/18/02			No3 enrolled Nov 1/99		

119

Choctaw By Blood Enrollment Cards 1898-1914

RESIDENCE:	Sugar Loaf	COUNTY.					
POST OFFICE:	Gibson, Arkansas						

Choctaw Nation

Choctaw Roll *(Not Including Freedmen)*

CARD NO. FIELD NO. **2220**

Dawes' Roll No.	NAME	Relationship to Person	AGE	SEX	BLOOD	TRIBAL ENROLLMENT Year	County	No.
6425	1 Norman, Sarah J ³⁷	First Named	34	F	1/4	1896	Sugar Loaf	9577
6426	2 Justice, Bettie M ¹⁶	Dau	13	"	1/8	1896	" "	6522
6427	3 " Lela V ¹³	"	10	"	1/8	1896	" "	6523
6428	4 Norman, Lue M ⁶	"	2	"	1/8			
6429	5 " Arzena ²	Dau	1mo	"	1/8			
	6							
	7							
	8							
	9							
	10							
	11							
	12							
	13							
	14							
	15	ENROLLMENT OF NOS. 1,2,3,4,5 HEREON APPROVED BY THE SECRETARY OF INTERIOR JAN 17 1903						
	16							
	17							

TRIBAL ENROLLMENT OF PARENTS

	Name of Father	Year	County	Name of Mother	Year	County
1	John Loving	Dead	Sugar Loaf	Amanda Loving	1896	white woman
2	Irvin Justice	"	Non Citz	No 1		
3	" "	"	" "	No 1		
4	Reuben Norman	1896	" "	No 1		
5	" " "		" "	No.1		
6						
7			For child of No1 see NB (Mar 3 '05) #450			
8			" children" " 2 " " " " #461			
9			No3 on 1896 roll as Lela M Justice			
10			No4 Affidavit of birth to be supplied. Recd June 5/99			
11			As to evidence of marriage of No1 see Card No 2218.			
12						
13			No.5 Enrolled Aug. 27, 1900.			
14					#1 to 4	
15					Date of Application for Enrollment.	
16					6/5/99	
17						

120

Choctaw By Blood Enrollment Cards 1898-1914

RESIDENCE: Sugar Loaf   COUNTY. **Choctaw Nation**   **Choctaw Roll**   CARD No.
POST OFFICE: Heavener, I.T.   *(Not Including Freedmen)*   FIELD No. 2221

Dawes' Roll No.	NAME		Relationship to Person	AGE	SEX	BLOOD	TRIBAL ENROLLMENT		
							Year	County	No.
6430	1 Rail, Mary	21	First Named	18	F	1/2	1896	Sugar Loaf	9569
DEAD.	2 " Thomas I	DEAD.	Son	1mo	M	1/4			
6431	3 " William S	2	Son	3mo	M	1/4			
6432	4 " Fannie	1	Dau	7wks	F	1/4			
	5								
	6								
	7								
	8								
	9								
	10								
	11								
	12	No. 2 HEREON DISMISSED UNDER ORDER OF THE COMMISSION TO THE FIVE CIVILIZED TRIBES OF MARCH 31, 1905.								
	13								
	14								
	15	ENROLLMENT OF NOS. 1, 3, 4 HEREON APPROVED BY THE SECRETARY OF INTERIOR JAN 17 1903								
	16								
	17								

TRIBAL ENROLLMENT OF PARENTS

	Name of Father	Year	County	Name of Mother	Year	County
1	Thomas Nolen	1896	Sugar Loaf	Rhoda Nolen	1896	white woman
2	William Rail	1896	Non Citz	No 1		
3	" " "	"	" " "	No.1		
4	" " "	"	" " "	No 1		
5						
6						
7						
8	No1 on 1896 roll as Mary Nolen					
9	No2 Affidavit of birth to be supplied Recd Jun3 16/99					
10	As to evidence of marriage of parents of					
11	No1 see testimony of Thomas Nolen					
12						
13	No.3 Enrolled Aug 18th 1900					
14	No.2 died June 11, 1899. Proof of death filed Aug 15, 1901					
15	Nº4 Born July 26, 1902; enrolled Sept 4, 1902					
16	For child of No1 see NB (March 3, 1905) #1316					
17	P.O. Guertie I.T. 2/20/03			Date of Application for Enrollment.	6/5/99	

Choctaw By Blood Enrollment Cards 1898-1914

RESIDENCE: Sugar Loaf COUNTY. **Choctaw Nation** **Choctaw Roll** CARD NO.
POST OFFICE: Wister, I.T. *(Not Including Freedmen)* FIELD NO. **2222**

Dawes' Roll No.	NAME		Relationship to Person	AGE	SEX	BLOOD	TRIBAL ENROLLMENT		
							Year	County	No.
6433	1 White, Amy	59	First Named	56	F	Full	1896	Sugar Loaf	12878
6434	2 " Cane	30	Son	27	M	"	1896	" "	12879
	3								
	4								
	5								
	6								
	7								
	8								
	9								
	10								
	11								
	12								
	13								
	14	ENROLLMENT OF NOS. 1 – 2 HEREON APPROVED BY THE SECRETARY OF INTERIOR							
	15								
	16								
	17								

TRIBAL ENROLLMENT OF PARENTS

	Name of Father	Year	County	Name of Mother	Year	County
1	Ma-hau-tubbee	Dead	in Mississippi	Betsy	Dead	in Mississippi
2	Charley White	"	" "	No 1		
3						
4						
5						
6	No1 on 1896 roll as Annie White					
7	No2 " 1896 " " Can "					
8						
9	#2 Died Aug 18, 1904					
10						
11						
12						
13						
14						
15				Date of Application for Enrollment		
16				6/5/99		
17						

122

RESIDENCE: Sugar Loaf	COUNTY.	CARD NO.
POST OFFICE: Wister, I.T.	**Choctaw Nation** **Choctaw Roll** *(Not Including Freedmen)*	FIELD NO. 2223

Dawes' Roll No.	NAME		Relationship to Person	AGE	SEX	BLOOD	TRIBAL ENROLLMENT		
							Year	County	No.
6435	1 Lewis Seas	32	First Named	29	F	Full	1896	Sugar Loaf	8508
6436	2 Martin Bennett	7	Son	4	M	"	1896	" "	8509
6437	3 Lewis, Dixon	2	Son	20mo	M	"			
	4								
	5								
	6								
	7								
	8								
	9								
	10								
	11								
	12								
	13								
	14								
	15	ENROLLMENT OF NOS. 1, 2, 3 HEREON APPROVED BY THE SECRETARY OF INTERIOR JAN 17 1903							
	16								
	17								

TRIBAL ENROLLMENT OF PARENTS

	Name of Father	Year	County	Name of Mother	Year	County
1	Charley White	Dead	in Mississippi	Amy White	1896	Sugar Loaf
2	William Martin	"	Sugar Loaf	No 1		
3	Cyrus Lewis	1896	"	Nº1		
4						
5						
6						
7	No1 on 1896 roll as Sisce Martin					
8	No2 " 1896 " " Bannett "					
9	Nº3 Born Dec 12 1900: enrolled Sept. 6. 1902					
10	Nº1 is now the wife of Cyrus Lewis on Choctaw card #3020. Evidence of marriage requested Sept. 6, 1902.					
11						
12						
13						
14						
15				#1&2		
16				Date of Application for Enrollment.	6/5/99	
17	P.O. Lodi I.T. 2/19/04					

Choctaw By Blood Enrollment Cards 1898-1914

RESIDENCE: Sugar Loaf	COUNTY.	**Choctaw Nation**	Choctaw Roll	CARD No.
POST OFFICE: Wister, I.T.			*(Not Including Freedmen)*	FIELD No. 2224

Dawes' Roll No.	NAME		Relationship to Person First Named	AGE	SEX	BLOOD	TRIBAL ENROLLMENT		
							Year	County	No.
6438	1 Folsom, Jerry	50	First Named	47	M	1/2	1896	Sugar Loaf	3974
6439	2 " Amanda	25	Wife	22	F	Full	1893	Gaines	570
6440	3 " Peter	18	Son	15	M	3/4	1896	Sugar Loaf	3976
6441	4 " Mand	12	Dau	9	F	1/2	1896	" "	3978
6442	5 " Dora	11	"	8	"	1/2	1896	Sans Bois	3903
6443	6 " Davis	4	Son	1	M	3/4			
6444	7 " Eugene	2	Son	3mo	M	3/4			
	8								
	9								
	10								
	11								
	12								
	13								
	14								
	15	ENROLLMENT OF NOS. 1,2,3,4,5,6,7 HEREON							
	16	APPROVED BY THE SECRETARY OF INTERIOR JAN 17 1903							
	17								

TRIBAL ENROLLMENT OF PARENTS

	Name of Father	Year	County	Name of Mother	Year	County
1	Peter Folsom	Dead	Sans Bois	Ellen Folsom	Dead	Sans
2	Aaron Williams	1896	Sugar Loaf	Asen Williams	"	Gaines
3	No 1			Nancy Folson	"	Sans B
4	No 1			Ellen Folson	1896	Jacks F
5	No 1			" "	1896	"
6	No 1			No 2		
7	No.1			No.2		
8	No 4 on 1896 roll as Manda Folsom also on 1896 roll , Page 97					
9	No.3991 as Mardie Folson, Gaines Co.					
10	No 2 on 1893 Pay roll as Mary William Page 61, No 570, Gaines Co					
	No 7 Enrolled May 22, 1901					
11	Nº 1 is father of Jackson L Folsom Choctaw card #2230					
12	Nº 3 is husband of Rachel Perryman Choctaw card #2443, Dec 15, 1902					
13	For child of Nos 1 and 2 see NB (April 26, 1896) No. 532					
	" " " No.3 " " " " No 460					
14						#1 to 6
15						Date of Application for Enrollment.
16						6/5/99
17	McCurtain I.T. 1/5/03					

124

Choctaw By Blood Enrollment Cards 1898-1914

RESIDENCE: Sugar Loaf   COUNTY. **Choctaw Nation**   **Choctaw Roll** *(Not Including Freedmen)*   CARD NO.
POST OFFICE: Kennedy I.T.   FIELD NO. **2225**

Dawes' Roll No.	NAME	Relationship to Person First Named	AGE	SEX	BLOOD	TRIBAL ENROLLMENT Year	County	No.
6445	1 McAlvain, Polk 54	First Named	51	M	1/2	1896	Sugar Loaf	9110
IW 100	2 " Louisa 39	Wife	36	F	I.W.	1896	" "	14860
6446	3 " Stonewall J 25	Son	22	M	1/2	1893	" "	567
6447	4 " Robert 23	"	20	"	1/2	1896	" "	9111
6448	5 " Louis Riley 21	"	18	"	1/4	1896	" "	9112
6449	6 " John W 19	"	16	"	1/4	1896	" "	9113
6450	7 " William R 15	"	12	"	1/4	1896	" "	9114
6451	8 " Thomas J 13	"	10	"	1/4	1896	" "	9115
6452	9 " Florence 10	Dau	7	F	1/4	1896	" "	9116
6453	10 " David W 8	Son	5	M	1/4	1896	" "	9117
6454	11 " Andy C 4	"	1	"	1/4			
14723	12 " Orin Earle 1	Gr.Son	3wks	"	1/4			
6455	13 " Odus 1	Gr.Son	2mo	M	1/4			

(Right margin, vertical) For child of No5 see No4 NB(Apr26 '06) Card #293 #28

ENROLLMENT OF NOS. 1,3,4,5,6,7,8,9,10,11,13 HEREON APPROVED BY THE SECRETARY OF INTERIOR Jan 17 1903

14 Wife of No4 is on Choctaw card #5748 3/17/04   No1 on 1896 Roll as Polk McAlvane
15 No9 on 1896 Roll as Florence McAlvane   No5 " 1896 " Righly "
   No10 " " " " David   No6 " 1896 " John "
16 No3 " 1893 Pay Roll Page 59   No7 " 1896 " Richard "
17 No567 as Stonewall J McLevin   No8 " 1896 " Jay Bird "

Evidence of marriage of parents of No12 filed Oct 24,1902

Sugar Loaf County   TRIBAL ENROLLMENT OF PARENTS   For child of No6 see NB (Apr26-06)Card#293

	Name of Father	Year	County	Name of Mother	Year	County
1	Benjamin McAlvain	Dead	Non Citz	Mary McAlvain	Dead	Sugar Loaf
2	John Bowers	"	" "	Mary Bowers	"	Non Citz
3	No 1			Mary McAlvain	"	Sugar Loaf
4	No 1			" "	"	" "
5	No 1			" "	"	" "
6	No 1			No 2		
7	No 1			No 2		
8	No 1			No 2		
9	No 1			No 2		
10	No 1			No 2		
11	No 1			No 2		
12	No 5			Bell McAlvain		Non Citz
13	No 4			Mollie B McAlvain		intermarried

ENROLLMENT OF NOS. 2 ~~~ HEREON APPROVED BY THE SECRETARY OF INTERIOR Jun 13, 1903

ENROLLMENT OF NOS ~~~ 12 ~~~ HEREON APPROVED BY THE SECRETARY OF INTERIOR May 20, 1903

14 No.11 Aff of birth to [sic] supplied Recd June 8, 1899   No5 is husband of No1 on Choctaw card 5958
15 No.4 is now the husband of Mollie Belle McAlvain
   on Choctaw card #D632 May 18, 1901   #1 to 11 inc
16 No.12 Born Aug 26,1902, enrolled Sept 17, 1902
17 No.13 Born July 31, 1902; enrolled Oct 15, 1902   Date of Application for Enrollment. 6/5/99

No5 P.O. Wister IT 6/14/05

RESIDENCE: Gaines	COUNTY.	Choctaw Nation		Choctaw Roll	CARD NO.	
POST OFFICE: Wilburton I.T.				(Not Including Freedmen)	FIELD NO. 2226	

Dawes' Roll No.	NAME	Relationship to Person	AGE	SEX	BLOOD	TRIBAL ENROLLMENT		
						Year	County	No.
I.W. 25	1 Kennady James F 60	First Named	57	M	I.W.	1896	Sugar Loaf	14717
6456	2 " Mary 33	Wife	39	F	Full	1896	" "	7464
	3							
	4							
	5							
	6							
	7							
	8							
	9							
	10							
	11							
	12							
	13							
	14							
	15	ENROLLMENT OF NOS. 2 HEREON APPROVED BY THE SECRETARY OF INTERIOR JAN 17 1903				ENROLLMENT OF NOS. ~~ 1 ~~ HEREON APPROVED BY THE SECRETARY OF INTERIOR JUN 13 1903		
	16							
	17							

TRIBAL ENROLLMENT OF PARENTS

	Name of Father	Year	County	Name of Mother	Year	County
1	Benjamin T Kennady	Dead	Non Citz	Naney Kennady	Dead	Non Citz
2	Robert Benton	1896	Sugar Loaf	Jane Benton	1896	Sugar Loaf
3						
4						
5						
6	No1 On 1896 roll as J.F. Kennedy and admitted by Dawes					
7	Commission as intermarried citizen as J.F. Kennedy #1207					
8	No2 On 1896 roll as Mary Kennedy					
9	Certified copy of divorce proceedings between Nº1 and his former wife filed Feby 21, 1903.					
10						
11						
12						
13						
14						
15						
16			DATE OF APPLICATION FOR ENROLLMENT. 6/5/99			
17						

126

Choctaw By Blood Enrollment Cards 1898-1914

RESIDENCE: Chickasaw Nation ~~COUNTY.~~   **Choctaw Nation**   Choctaw Roll   CARD No.

POST OFFICE: Lebanon, I.T.   *(Not Including Freedmen)*   FIELD No.   2227

Dawes' Roll No.	NAME		Relationship to Person	AGE	SEX	BLOOD	TRIBAL ENROLLMENT		
							Year	County	No.
6457	1 Willis, Brit	33	First Named	30	M	1/8	1893	Chick Dist	623
	2								
	3								
	4								
	5								
	6								
	7								
	8								
	9								
	10								
	11								
	12								
	13								
	14								
	15								
	16								
	17								

ENROLLMENT OF NOS. 1 HEREON APPROVED BY THE SECRETARY OF INTERIOR JAN 17 1903

TRIBAL ENROLLMENT OF PARENTS

	Name of Father	Year	County	Name of Mother	Year	County
1	Jim P Willis	Dead	Non Citz	Elizabeth Willis	Dead	Towson
2						
3						
4						
5	On 1893 Pay Roll, Page 67, No 623, Chickasaw District					
6	Is insane					
7						
8						
9						
10						
11						
12						
13						
14						
15				Date of Application for Enrollment.		
16				6/5/99		
17						

Choctaw By Blood Enrollment Cards 1898-1914

RESIDENCE: Skullyville COUNTY. **Choctaw Nation** **Choctaw Roll** CARD NO.
POST OFFICE: Shady Point, I.T. (Not Including Freedmen) FIELD NO. 2228

Dawes' Roll No.	NAME	Relationship to Person First Named	AGE	SEX	BLOOD	TRIBAL ENROLLMENT Year	County	No.
✓ ✗	1 Shepherd, Henry		9	M	1/16			
	2							
	3							
	4							
	5							
	6							
	7							
	8							
	9							
	10							
	11							
	12							
	13							
	14							
	15							
	16							
	17							

TRIBAL ENROLLMENT OF PARENTS

	Name of Father	Year	County	Name of Mother	Year	County
1	D.W. Wilson	1896	Non Citz	Louie Wilson	Dead	Choctaw
2						
3						
4						
5						
6	No1 Denied by Dawes Com in 96 Chic Cit Case #598					
7	Admitted by U.S. Court Central District, Aug 24/97					
8	Case No 944					
9	See testimony of Dock W Shepherd					
10	Judgement[sic] of US Court C D admitting No1 vacated and set aside by Decree of					
11	Choctaw-Chickasaw Citizenship Court Dec' 17 '02					
12						
13						
14						
15						
16			Date of Application for Enrollment.	6/5/99		
17						

RESIDENCE:	Sugar Loaf	COUNTY.							CARD NO.	
POST OFFICE:	Wister, I.T.		**Choctaw Nation**				**Choctaw Roll** *(Not Including Freedmen)*		FIELD NO.	2229

Dawes' Roll No.		NAME		Relationship to Person First Named	AGE	SEX	BLOOD	TRIBAL ENROLLMENT		
								Year	County	No.
6458	1	Collin, Stephen	30	First Named	27	M	Full	1896	Sugar Loaf	2247
Dead	2	" Malinda		Dau	4	F	"	1896	" "	2249
6459	3	" Noah	14	Bro	11	M	"	1896	" "	2251
6460	4	DIED PRIOR TO SEPTEMBER 25 1902 " Simon		"	7	"	"	1896	" "	2252
	5									
	6									
	7									
	8	No. 2 HEREON DISMISSED UNDER								
	9	ORDER OF THE COMMISSION TO THE FIVE								
	10	CIVILIZED TRIBES OF MARCH 31, 1905.								
	11									
	12									
	13									
	14									
	15	ENROLLMENT OF NOS. 1, 3, 4 HEREON								
	16	APPROVED BY THE SECRETARY								
	17	OF INTERIOR JAN 17 1903								

TRIBAL ENROLLMENT OF PARENTS

	Name of Father	Year	County	Name of Mother	Year	County	
1	David Collin	Dead	Sugar Loaf	Melissa Collin	Dead	Sugar Loaf	
2	No 1			Silway Collin	"	" "	
3	David Collin	Dead	Sugar Loaf	Ellen Collin	"	" "	
4	" "	"	" "	" "	"	" "	
5							
6							
7							
8	No.2 Died July 14, 1898. Evidence of death filed March 20, 1901.						
9	No.4 Died November 30th 1901: Proof of Death filed December 20th 1902						
10	Nº 1 is husband of Malinda Bell Choctaw Card #2354, Jany 21, 1903						
11	No.4 died Nov 30, 1902: Enrollment cancelled by Department July 8, 1904						
12							
13							
14							
15					Date of Application for Enrollment.		
16					June 5/99a		
17							

Choctaw By Blood Enrollment Cards 1898-1914

RESIDENCE:	Sugar Loaf	COUNTY.							CARD No.	
POST OFFICE:	Wister, I.T.		**Choctaw Nation**				Choctaw Roll (Not Including Freedmen)		FIELD No.	2230

Dawes' Roll No.	NAME		Relationship to Person	AGE	SEX	BLOOD	TRIBAL ENROLLMENT		
							Year	County	No.
6461	1 Folsom Jackson L	23	First Named	20	M	3/4	1893	Sans Bois	P R 255
	2								
	3								
	4								
	5								
	6								
	7								
	8								
	9								
	10								
	11								
	12								
	13								
	14								
	15	ENROLLMENT OF NOS. 1 HEREON APPROVED BY THE SECRETARY OF INTERIOR JAN 17 1903							
	16								
	17								

TRIBAL ENROLLMENT OF PARENTS

	Name of Father	Year	County	Name of Mother	Year	County
1	Jerry Folsom	1896	Sugar Loaf	Nancy Folsom	1896	Sans Bois
2						
3						
4						
5	On 1893 pay roll, Page 26 #255 Sans Bois Co as Jack Folsom					
6						
7						
8						
9						
10						
11						
12						
13						
14						Date of Application for Enrollment.
15						
16						6/5/99
17						

Choctaw By Blood Enrollment Cards 1898-1914

RESIDENCE: Suglar[sic] Loaf COUNTY.
POST OFFICE: Kully Chaha I.T.

Choctaw Nation

Choctaw Roll
(Not Including Freedmen)

CARD NO.
FIELD NO. 2231

Dawes' Roll No.	NAME	Relationship to Person First Named	AGE	SEX	BLOOD	TRIBAL ENROLLMENT		
						Year	County	No.
14724	1 Garrett Leroy B 6	First Named	3	M	1/4	1896	Sugar Loaf	4680
	2							
	3							
	4							
	5	ENROLLMENT OF NOS. 1 HEREON APPROVED BY THE SECRETARY OF INTERIOR MAY 20 1903						
	6							
	7							
	8							
	9							
	10							
	11							
	12							
	13							
	14							
	15							
	16							
	17							

TRIBAL ENROLLMENT OF PARENTS

	Name of Father	Year	County	Name of Mother	Year	County
1	Calvin Garret[sic]	1896	Non Citz	Belle Garret	Dead	Sugar Loaf
2						
3						
4						
5						
6						
7						
8						
9						
10						
11						
12						
13						
14						
15						
16					Date of Application for Enrollment.	6/5/99
17						

131

Choctaw By Blood Enrollment Cards 1898-1914

RESI... Sugar Loaf COUNTY. **Choctaw Nation** Choctaw Roll CARD NO.
POST... Kennady[sic] I.T. (Not Including Freedmen) FIELD NO. **2232**

Da...		NAME		Relationship to Person	AGE	SEX	BLOOD	TRIBAL ENROLLMENT		
								Year	County	No.
		Simon	DEAD	First Named	79	M	Full	1896	Sugar Loaf	10117
		r Sambray	47	Wife	44	F	I.W.			
6462	3	Peter Ollie	12	Dau	9	F	1/2	1896	Sugar Loaf	10118
6463	4	" Lela	9	Dau	6	F	1/2	1896	" "	10119
6464	5	" James	6	Son	3	M	1/2	1896	" "	10120
	6									
	7									
	8									
	9									
	10									
	11									
	12									
	13									
	14									
	15									
	16									
	17									

No. 1 HEREON DISMISSED UNDER ORDER OF THE COMMISSION TO THE FIVE CIVILIZED TRIBES OF MARCH 31, 1905.

ENROLLMENT
OF NOS. ~ 2 ~ HEREON
APPROVED BY THE SECRETARY
OF INTERIOR DEC 13 1904

ENROLLMENT
OF NOS. 3, 4, 5 HEREON
APPROVED BY THE SECRETARY
OF INTERIOR JAN 17 1903

No. 1 HEREON DISMISSED UNDER ORDER OF THE COMMISSION TO THE FIVE CIVILIZED TRIBES OF MARCH 31, 1905.

TRIBAL ENROLLMENT OF PARENTS

	Name of Father	Year	County	Name of Mother	Year	County
1	No-pav-ok-cha-ya	Dead	Mississippi	Kav-key	1896	Skullyville
2	N N Frizzell	Dead	Non Citz	Fannie Frizzell	Dead	Non Citz
3	No 1			No 2		
4	No 1			No 2		
5	No 1			No 2		
6						
7						
8	No1 On 1896 roll as Simon Petter					
9	No2 See testimony of Simon Peter and Barnabas Peter as to marriage					
10	No3 On 1896 roll as Allie Petter					
	No4 " " " " Lula Petter					
11	No5 " " " " James Petter					
12	No1 Died December 29, 1899. Proof of death filed February 1, 1901					
13						
14						
15					Date of Application for Enrollment.	
16					6/5/99	
17						

Choctaw By Blood Enrollment Cards 1898-1914

RESIDENCE: Sugar Loaf   COUNTY. **Choctaw Nation**   **Choctaw Roll**   CARD NO.
POST OFFICE: Heavener, I.T.   *(Not Including Freedmen)*   FIELD NO. **2233**

Dawes' Roll No.	NAME	Relationship to Person First Named	AGE	SEX	BLOOD	TRIBAL ENROLLMENT Year	County	No.
6465	1 Kinslow, Gertrude ~~DIED PRIOR TO SEPTEMBER 25 1902~~		24	F	1/4	1896	Sugar Loaf	7465
6466	2 " Jenison T [11]	Son	8	M	1/8	1896	" "	7466
6467	3 " Magnettie [9]	Dau	6	F	1/8	1896	" "	7467
6468	4 " Nellie [6]	"	3	"	1/8	1896	" "	7468
6469	5 " Levergie [5]	"	2	"	1/8			
	6							
	7							
	8							
	9							
	10							
	11							
	12							
	13							
	14							
	15	ENROLLMENT OF NOS. 1,2,3,4,5 HEREON APPROVED BY THE SECRETARY						
	16	OF INTERIOR Jan 17 1903						
	17							

TRIBAL ENROLLMENT OF PARENTS

	Name of Father	Year	County	Name of Mother	Year	County
1	John Loving	Dead	Sugar Loaf	Amanda Loving		white woman
2	Bert Kinslow		Non Citz	No 1		
3	" "		" "	No 1		
4	" "		" "	No 1		
5	" "		" "	No 1		
6						
7						
8						
9						
10						
11	No2 on 1896 Roll as Jamison T Kinslow					
12	No5 Affidavit of birth to be supplied. Recd June 16/99					
13						
14	As to marriage of parents of No1 see card					
15	of her mother, Amanda Loving, No 2218					Date of Application for Enrollment.
16	~~No1 died Nov 10 1900: Proof of death filed Dec 20-1902~~ No. 1 died Nov 10, 1900: Enrollment cancelled by Department July 8, 1904					June 5/99
17	Goldman Ark					

133

Choctaw By Blood Enrollment Cards 1898-1914

RESIDENCE: Sugar Loaf   COUNTY. **Choctaw Nation**   **Choctaw Roll** *(Not Including Freedmen)*   CARD NO.

POST OFFICE: Heavener, I.T.   FIELD NO. 2234

Dawes' Roll No.	NAME		Relationship to Person	AGE	SEX	BLOOD	TRIBAL ENROLLMENT		
							Year	County	No.
I.W.1402	1 Camp, Mary	41	First Named	38	F	I.W.	1896	Sugar Loaf	14383
6470	2 " Richard T	13	Son	10	M	1/2	1896	" "	2213
6471	3 " Josephine	10	Dau	7	F	1/2	1896	" "	2214
6472	4 " William R	8	Son	5	M	1/2	1896	" "	2215
	5								
	6								
	7	ENROLLMENT OF NOS. 1 HEREON APPROVED BY THE SECRETARY OF INTERIOR JUN 12 1905							
	8								
	9								
	10								
	11								
	12								
	13								
	14								
	15	ENROLLMENT OF NOS. 2, 3, 4 HEREON APPROVED BY THE SECRETARY OF INTERIOR JAN 17 1903							
	16								
	17								

TRIBAL ENROLLMENT OF PARENTS

	Name of Father	Year	County	Name of Mother	Year	County
1	Daniel Decker	Dead	Non Citz	Mary Decker		Non Citz
2	Isom Canip	"	Sugar Loaf	No 1		
3	" "	"	" "	No 1		
4	" "	"	" "	No 1		
5						
6						
7			No1 formerly wife of Isom Canip, 1893 Sugar Loaf, No 110,			
8			and who died in 1898			
9			No2 on 1896 Roll as Richard Camp			
10			No3 " 1896 " " Josie "			
			No4 " 1896 " " William "			
11						
12			As to marriage of No1, see her testimony			
13						
14						
15				Date of Application for Enrollment.		
16				June 5/99		
17						

Choctaw By Blood Enrollment Cards 1898-1914

RESIDENCE: Sugar Loaf   COUNTY. **Choctaw Nation**   Choctaw Roll   CARD NO.
POST OFFICE: Poteau, I.T.   *(Not Including Freedmen)*   FIELD NO. 2235

Dawes' Roll No.	NAME		Relationship to Person First Named	AGE	SEX	BLOOD	TRIBAL ENROLLMENT		
							Year	County	No.
DEAD.	₁ Beard, John G	DEAD.	First Named	73	M	I.W.	1896	Sugar Loaf	14293
6473	₂ " Julia Ann	54	Wife	51	F	1/32	1896	" "	758
6474	₃ " Ada M	17	Dau	14	"	1/64	1896	" "	759
6475	₄ " Buchanan	16	Son	13	M	1/64	1896	" "	760
6476	₅ " Amos S	14	"	11	"	1/64	1896	" "	761
6477	₆ " Matthew	11	"	8	"	1/64	1896	" "	762
6478	₇ James, Isadora	23	S.Dau	20	F	1/64	1896	" "	6496
	₈								
	₉								
	₁₀ No. 1 HEREON DISMISSED UNDER								
	ORDER OF THE COMMISSION TO THE FIVE								
	₁₁ CIVILIZED TRIBES OF MARCH 31, 1905.								
	₁₂								
	₁₃								
	₁₄								
	₁₅ ENROLLMENT OF NOS. 2,3,4,5,6,7 HEREON								
	APPROVED BY THE SECRETARY								
	₁₆ OF INTERIOR JAN 17 1903								
	₁₇								

TRIBAL ENROLLMENT OF PARENTS

	Name of Father	Year	County	Name of Mother	Year	County
₁	Littleton Beard	Dead	Non Citz	Elizabeth Beard	Dead	Non Citz
₂	Wᵐ Merryman	"	" "	Anna Merryman	"	Skullyville
₃	No1			No2		
₄	No1			No2		
₅	No1			No2		
₆	No1			No2		
₇	Martin James	Dead	Chick Roll	No2		
₈						
₉						
₁₀	No5 on 1896 roll as A.S. Beard					
₁₁	No1 " 1896 " " Jno G "					
₁₂	Certificate of marriage to be supplied. Recd June 6/99					
₁₃	No.1 Died March 26" 1900. Proof of Death filed Decʳ 20ᵗʰ 1902					
₁₄						
₁₅				Date of Application for Enrollment.		
₁₆				6/5/99		
₁₇						

Choctaw By Blood Enrollment Cards 1898-1914

RESIDENCE: Sugar Loaf
POST OFFICE: Poteau, I.T.

COUNTY. **Choctaw Nation**

Choctaw Roll
(Not Including Freedmen)

CARD NO.
FIELD NO. 2236

Dawes' Roll No.	NAME		Relationship to Person	AGE	SEX	BLOOD	TRIBAL ENROLLMENT		
							Year	County	No.
I.W. 101	1 Hill, Cornelius D	38	First Named	35	M	I.W.	1896	Sugar Loaf	14601
6479	2 " Izora	34	Wife	31	F	1/32	1896	" "	5195
6480	3 " Horace C	14	Son	11	M	1/64	1896	" "	5196
6481	4 " Orval Q	12	"	9	"	1/64	1896	" "	5197
6482	5 " Elba N	10	Dau	7	F	1/64	1896	" "	5198
6483	6 " Louis A	4	Son	1mo	M	1/64			
	7								
	8								
	9								
	10								
	11								
	12	ENROLLMENT OF NOS. ~~~ 1 ~~~ HEREON APPROVED BY THE SECRETARY OF INTERIOR JUN 13 1903							
	13								
	14								
	15	ENROLLMENT OF NOS. 2,3,4,5,6 HEREON APPROVED BY THE SECRETARY OF INTERIOR JAN 17 1903							
	16								
	17								

TRIBAL ENROLLMENT OF PARENTS

	Name of Father	Year	County	Name of Mother	Year	County
1	A.T. Hill	Dead	Non Citz	Neoma Hill	Dead	Non Citz
2	Martin V James	"	Chick Roll	Julia A James	1896	Sugar Loaf
3	No1			No2		
4	No1			No2		
5	No1			No2		
6	No1			No2		
7						
8						
9	No1 on 1896 roll as C.D. Hill					
10	No3 " 1896 " " H.C. "					
11	No4 " 1896 " " O.Y. "					
12	No5 " 1896 " " E.N. "					
	For child of Nos 1and2 see NB (Mar 3'05) #451					
13						
14					Date of Application for Enrollment.	
15						
16					6/5/99	
17						

136

Choctaw By Blood Enrollment Cards 1898-1914

| RESIDENCE: Sugar Loaf | COUNTY. | Choctaw Nation | Choctaw Roll | CARD No. |
| POST OFFICE: Howe, I.T. | | | *(Not Including Freedmen)* | FIELD No. **2237** |

Dawes' Roll No.	NAME	Relationship to Person First Named	AGE	SEX	BLOOD	TRIBAL ENROLLMENT Year	County	No.
6484	1 Folsom, Loring S	40	M	1/2	1896	Sugar Loaf	3927
6485	2 " Jincy ³⁹	Wife	36	F	1/2	1896	" "	3948
6486	3 " Maud ¹⁸	Dau	15	"	1/2	1896	" "	3949
6487	4 " Emma ¹²	"	9	"	1/2	1896	" "	3950
6488	5 " Pearl M ¹⁰	"	7	"	1/2	1896	" "	3951
6489	6 " Sidney L ⁶	Son	2	M	1/2			
6490	7 Slaughter, Florence ⁹	Ward	6	F	3/4	1896	Sugar Loaf	11186
6491	8 " John ⁷	"	4	M	3/4	1896	" "	11187
6492	9 Folsom, Ruth ³	Dau	1mo	F	1/2			
	10							
	11 Ruth Folsom, daughter of Nos1&2							
	12 born Nov 24/99 on Card No D-546							
	No9 born November 24, 1899;							
	13 transferred to this card May 24, 1902							
	14							
	15 ENROLLMENT							
	OF NOS. 1,2,3,5,6,7,8,9 HEREON							
	16 APPROVED BY THE SECRETARY							
	OF INTERIOR Jan 17 1903							
	17							

TRIBAL ENROLLMENT OF PARENTS

Name of Father	Year	County	Name of Mother	Year	County
1 Ellis Folsom	Dead	Sugar Loaf	Selina Folsom	Dead	Sugar Loaf
2 Adam Morris	"	Non Citz	E-la-ho-to-na	"	" "
3 No1			No2		
4 No1			No2		
5 No1			No2		
6 No1			No2		
7 John Slaughter	Dead	Sugar Loaf	Tobitha Slaughter	Dead	Sugar Loaf
8 " "	"	" " "	" "	"	" " "
9 No1			No2		
10					
11					
12 No1 on 1896 roll as Loring Folsom					
13 No4 " 1896 " " Annie "					
No5 " 1896 " " Pearl "					
14 No8 " 1896 " " Jno Slaughter Jr				#1 to 8 inc
15 For child of No.3 see NB (Apr 26,06) No 547				Date of Application for Enrollment.
16 No.6 Affidavit of birth to be supplied:				6/5/99
Recd Oct 6/99				
17 No1 Died Jan 24th 1900 Proof of death filed Dec 20 1902				

No.1 died Jan 24, 1900: Enrollment cancelled by Department July 8, 1904

Choctaw By Blood Enrollment Cards 1898-1914

RESIDENCE: Skullyville	COUNTY.								
POST OFFICE: Cameron I.T.		**Choctaw Nation**			Choctaw Roll (Not Including Freedmen)		CARD NO. FIELD NO. **2238**		

Dawes' Roll No.	NAME	Relationship to Person	AGE	SEX	BLOOD	TRIBAL ENROLLMENT		
						Year	County	No.
✓ * 1	London Julia	First Named	36	F	1/4			
✓ * 2	" Jessie	Dau	13	F	1/8			
✓ * 3	" Dillard	Dau	8	F	1/8			
4								
5								
6								
7								
8	Nos 1,2 and 3 denied by Com in 96 Case #1258.							
9	No 1 as to residence see testimony of Mr John London							
10	Admitted by U.S. Court Sept 1st 1897 Case #241							
	John London father of Jessie and Dillard on W.C. No D 199							
11								
12								
13								
14								
15								
16								
17								

TRIBAL ENROLLMENT OF PARENTS

	Name of Father	Year	County	Name of Mother	Year	County
1	James C Bruner	Dead	Non Citz	Elizabeth Bruner	Dead	Choctaw
2	John London			No 1		
3	" "			No 1		
4						
5						
6						
7						
8	Judgement[sic] of U.S. Court admitting Nos 1,2 and 3 vacated and set aside by Decree of					
9	Choctaw-Chickasaw Cit Crt Decr 17,02					
10	☞ Nos 1,2 and 3 now in C.C.C.C. Case #55 3/12/03					
11	* ☞ Nos 1,2 and 3 denied by C.C.C.C. Case #55 March 14 '04					
12						
13	Denied citizenship by Choctaw and Chickasaw Citizenship Court March 14 '04					
14						
15	August 27, 1896 Motion for rehearing received June 27, 1896 forwarded Dept					
16	December 8, 1906 " " " Denied by the Dept	Date of Application for Enrollment.			6/5/99	
17	Dec 28-1906 – Parties in interest notified.					

No

Choctaw By Blood Enrollment Cards 1898-1914

RESIDENCE: Sugar Loaf   COUNTY. **Choctaw Nation**   **Choctaw Roll**   CARD No.

POST OFFICE: Howe, I.T.   *(Not Including Freedmen)*   FIELD No. 2239

Dawes' Roll No.	NAME	Relationship to Person	AGE	SEX	BLOOD	TRIBAL ENROLLMENT		
						Year	County	No.
6492	1 Ishtilaihona DIED PRIOR TO SEPTEMBER 25, 6692	First Named	63	F	Full	1896	Sugar Loaf	6254
	2							
	3							
	4							
	5							
	6							
	7							
	8							
	9							
	10							
	11							
	12							
	13							
	14							
	15							
	16							
	17							

ENROLLMENT
OF NOS. 1 HEREON
APPROVED BY THE SECRETARY
OF INTERIOR JAN 17 1903

TRIBAL ENROLLMENT OF PARENTS

	Name of Father	Year	County	Name of Mother	Year	County
1	Ah-le-moh-tubbee	Dead	in Mississippi	Ok-cha-le-ho-na	Dead	Choctaw
2						
3						
4						
5						
6			On 1896 roll as Ishtilayotima			
7			No1 Died in March 1901. Proof of death filed Dec 20th , 1902			
8			No.1 died March - 1901. Enrollment cancelled by Department July 8, 1904			
9						
10						
11						
12						
13						
14						
15						
16				Date of Application for Enrollment.	6/5/99	
17						

Choctaw By Blood Enrollment Cards 1898-1914

RESIDENCE: Sugar Loaf   COUNTY. **Choctaw Nation**   **Choctaw Roll**   CARD NO.
POST OFFICE: Conser I.T.   *(Not Including Freedmen)*   FIELD NO.   2240

Dawes' Roll No.	NAME		Relationship to Person	AGE	SEX	BLOOD	TRIBAL ENROLLMENT		
							Year	County	No.
6494	1 Wade Nicholas	29	First Named	26	M	Full	1896	Tobucksy	13044
	2								
	3								
	4								
	5								
	6								
	7								
	8								
	9								
	10								
	11								
	12								
	13								
	14								
	15	ENROLLMENT OF NOS. 1 HEREON APPROVED BY THE SECRETARY OF INTERIOR JAN 17 1903							
	16								
	17								

TRIBAL ENROLLMENT OF PARENTS

	Name of Father	Year	County	Name of Mother	Year	County
1	Henry Wade	De'd	Sugar Loaf	Lucy Wade	Ded	Sugar Loaf
2						
3						
4						
5						
6						
7						
8						
9						
10						
11						
12						
13						
14						
15						
16				DATE OF APPLICATION FOR ENROLLMENT.	6/5/99	
17	Richart[sic] I.T. 12/18/02					

140

Choctaw By Blood Enrollment Cards 1898-1914

RESIDENCE: Sugar Loaf COUNTY.		Choctaw Nation			Choctaw Roll (Not Including Freedmen)		CARD No.
POST OFFICE: Kully Chaha, I.T.							FIELD No. 2241

Dawes' Roll No.	NAME	Relationship to Person First Named	AGE	SEX	BLOOD	TRIBAL ENROLLMENT		
						Year	County	No.
6495	1 Garland, Samuel A 48	First Named	45	M	1/2	1896	Sans Bois	4650
I.W. 515	2 " Mandy C 47	Wife	44	F	I.W.	1896	Skullyville	14563
6496	3 " Gilbert W 18	Son	15	M	1/4	1896	Sans Bois	4651
6497	4 " Jackson 15	"	13	"	1/4	1896	" "	4652
6498	5 " Della M 7	Dau	4	F	1/4	1896	" "	4653
	6							
	7							
	8							
	9							
	10	ENROLLMENT OF NOS. 2 HEREON APPROVED BY THE SECRETARY OF INTERIOR DEC 24 1903						
	11							
	12							
	13							
	14							
	15	ENROLLMENT OF NOS. 1,3,4,5 HEREON APPROVED BY THE SECRETARY OF INTERIOR JAN 17 1903						
	16							
	17							

TRIBAL ENROLLMENT OF PARENTS

	Name of Father	Year	County	Name of Mother	Year	County
1	Cornelius Garland	Ded	Towson	Emily Garland	Ded	Towson
2	Daniel Brown	"	Non Citz	Jane E Brown	1896	Non Citz
3	No 1			No 2		
4	No 1			No 2		
5	No 1			No 2		
6						
7						
8						
9						
10						
11						
12			No1 on 1896 roll as Sam Garland			
13			No3 " " " " Gilbert "			
14			No5 " " " " Della "			
15			As to evidence of marriage see testimony of No1 – Other		Date of Application for Enrollment.
16			evidence to be supplied		6/5/99
17	Affidavits of Wm Brown and S F Brown as to marriage between Nos 1 and 2 filed Feby 21, 1903					

141

Choctaw By Blood Enrollment Cards 1898-1914

RESIDENCE:	Sugar Loaf	COUNTY.						
POST OFFICE:	Heavener I.T.							

Choctaw Nation

Choctaw Roll (Not Including Freedmen)

CARD NO.
FIELD NO. 2242

Dawes' Roll No.	NAME	Relationship to Person First Named	AGE	SEX	BLOOD	TRIBAL ENROLLMENT		
						Year	County	No.
6499	1 Williams Ada 23		20	F	1/4	1896	Sugar Loaf	12874
6500	2 " Elsie 6	Dau	3	"	1/8	1896	" "	12875
6501	3 " John 4	Son	1	M	1/8			
	4							
	5							
	6							
	7							
	8							
	9							
	10							
	11							
	12							
	13							
	14							
	15	ENROLLMENT OF NOS. 1, 2, 3 HEREON						
	16	APPROVED BY THE SECRETARY						
	17	OF INTERIOR JAN 17 1903						

TRIBAL ENROLLMENT OF PARENTS

Name of Father	Year	County	Name of Mother	Year	County
1 John Loving	Ded	Sugar Loaf	Amandy Loving	1896	Sugar Loaf
2 Lum Williams	1896	Non Citz	No 1		
3 " "			No 1		
4					
5					
6					
7					
8	For child of No 1 see NB (Mar 3 '05) #452				
9					
10					
11					
12					
13					
14					
15				Date of Application for Enrollment.	
16				6/5/99	
17					

142

Choctaw By Blood Enrollment Cards 1898-1914

RESIDENCE: Sugar Loaf	COUNTY.	CARD No.
POST OFFICE: Heavener I.T.	**Choctaw Nation**	**Choctaw Roll** *(Not Including Freedmen)* FIELD No. 2243

Dawes' Roll No.	NAME	Relationship to Person First Named	AGE	SEX	BLOOD	TRIBAL ENROLLMENT Year	County	No.
6502	1 West Rhoda ²⁰		17	F	1/4	1896	Sugar Loaf	2212
6503	2 " Kenneth Fevirson ³	Son	3mo	M	1/8			
6504	3 " Orvil Fitzroy ¹	Son	2mo	M	1/8			
	4							
	5							
	6							
	7							
	8							
	9							
	10							
	11							
	12							
	13							
	14							
	15	ENROLLMENT OF NOS. 1, 2, 3 HEREON APPROVED BY THE SECRETARY OF INTERIOR JAN 17 1903						
	16							
	17							

TRIBAL ENROLLMENT OF PARENTS

	Name of Father	Year	County	Name of Mother	Year	County
1	Isom Camp	1896	Sugar Loaf	Mary Camp	1896	Non Citz
2	George West		Non-citizen	No 1		
3	" "		" "	No 1		
4						
5						
6						
7						
8	For child of No1 see NB (Mar 3ʳᵈ 1905) Card #118					
9						
10	On 1896 roll as Rhoda Camp. As to marriage					
11	of father and mother see testimony					
12	of mother, Mary Camp					
13	No2 Enrolled June 26, 1900 No3 Enrolled Aug 15, 1901					
14						
15						
16				Date of Application for Enrollment.		6/5/99
17						

143

Choctaw By Blood Enrollment Cards 1898-1914

RESIDENCE: Sugar Loaf COUNTY. **Choctaw Nation** **Choctaw Roll** CARD NO.
POST OFFICE: Howe I.T. *(Not Including Freedmen)* FIELD NO. 2244

Dawes' Roll No.	NAME		Relationship to Person	AGE	SEX	BLOOD	TRIBAL ENROLLMENT		
							Year	County	No.
6505	1 Folsom Sidney J	30	First Named	27	M	1/2	1896	Sugar Loaf	3963
I.W.26	2 " Hattie	29	Wife	26	F	I.W.			
6506	3 " Porter R	4	Son	5/6	M	1/4			
6507	4 " Loren L W	2	Son	1mo	M	1/4			
	5								
	6								
	7								
	8								
	9								
	10								
	11								
	12								
	13								
	14								
	15								
	16								
	17								

ENROLLMENT OF NOS. 1, 3, 4 HEREON APPROVED BY THE SECRETARY OF INTERIOR JAN 17 1903

ENROLLMENT OF NOS. 2 HEREON APPROVED BY THE SECRETARY OF INTERIOR JUN 13 1903

TRIBAL ENROLLMENT OF PARENTS

	Name of Father	Year	County	Name of Mother	Year	County
1	E W Folsom	Ded	Tobucksy	Silna Folsom	Ded	Sugar Loaf
2	J P Hall	1896	Non Citz	Palistine Hall	1896	Non Citz
3	No 1			No 2		
4	No 1			No 2		
5						
6						
7						
8	For child of Nos 1&2 see NB (Apr 26 1906) Card No 264					
9	" " " " " " " (Mar 3 1905) " " 119					
10						
11	No 1 on 1896 roll as Sidney Folsom					
12						
13						
14	No.4 Enrolled May 24, 1900					
15						Date of Application for Enrollment.
16						6/5/99
17	Heavener I.T.					

144

RESIDENCE: Skullyville   COUNTY.   **Choctaw Nation**   **Choctaw Roll** *(Not Including Freedmen)*   CARD NO.
POST OFFICE: Sparrow I.T. (Spiro)   FIELD NO. 2245

Dawes' Roll No.	NAME	Relationship to Person	AGE	SEX	BLOOD	TRIBAL ENROLLMENT		
						Year	County	No.
✓ * 1	Gibson Rosa L	First Named	17	F	1/8			
✓SP 2	" Della L	Dau	2mo	"	1/16			
3								
4								
Nº2	DISMISSED							
6	MAY 23 1904							
7								
8								
9 *	No 1 Denied by Dawes Com in 96 Choc Cit Case #598 as Rosa Lee Biddie							
10	* Judgement[sic] admitting No1 by US Court CD vacated and set aside by Decree of Choctaw-Chickasaw Citizenship Court Dec 17 02							
11	* Not denied by Choctaw and Chickasaw Court Feb 1 1904 Case #13							
12								
13								
14								
15								
16								
17								

TRIBAL ENROLLMENT OF PARENTS

	Name of Father	Year	County	Name of Mother	Year	County
1	James F Biddie	1896	Sugar Loaf	Adaline Gibson	Ded	Non Citz
2	George Gibson		Non Citz	No 1		
3						
4						
5						
6						
7	No. 1 DENIED CITIZENSHIP BY THE CHOCTAW AND					
8	CHICKASAW CITIZENSHIP COURT					
9						
10			Admitted by US. Court at South McAlester			
11			Aug 24 1897 #94 as Rosa L. Biddie			
12						
13						
14					Date of Application for Enrollment.	
15						
16	Wrote her at Spiro and Poteau 9/27/02				6/5/99	
17					No2 enrolled Oct 6/99	

RESIDENCE: Sugar Loaf   P.O. Stigler IT   COUNTY. **Choctaw Nation**   **Choctaw Roll** (Not Including Freedmen)   CARD NO.
POST OFFICE: Poteau I.T.   FIELD NO. 2246

Dawes' Roll No.	NAME	Relationship to Person	AGE	SEX	BLOOD	TRIBAL ENROLLMENT		
						Year	County	No.
✓ *	1 Biddie James F	First Named	49	M	1/4			
✓	2 " Nancy A	Wife	17	F	I.W.			
✓ *	3 " James	Son	14	M	1/8			
✓ *	4 " Francis	"	11	"	1/8			
✓	5 " Tony M	"	1/3yr	"	1/8			
✓	6 " Ira Iris	"	3mo	"	1/8			
✓	7 " Osaola	Dau	11mo	F	1/8			
1,3,4	8							
	9	DENIED CITIZENSHIP BY THE CHOCTAW AND						
	10	CHICKASAW CITIZENSHIP COURT						
	11							
No 2	12	DISMISSED MAY 7 1904						
	13							
#5-6 and 7	14	DISMISSED MAY 23 1904						
	15							
	16							
	17							

TRIBAL ENROLLMENT OF PARENTS

	Name of Father	Year	County	Name of Mother	Year	County
1	J J Biddie	1896	Skullyville	Mary J Biddie	1896	Non Citz
2	Statham	1896	Non Citz	Statham	Ded	" "
3	No 1			Adaline Biddie	"	" "
4	No 1			" "		
5	No 1			No 2		
6	No 1			No.2		
7	No 1			No 2		
8				As to residence and marriage see his testimony.		
9				Nos 1,3-4 Admitted by U.S. Court South McAlester		
10				Aug 24 1897 Case #94		
11				No.6 Enrolled June 23d, 1900		
12				No7 Born Aug 5" 1901: Enrolled July 3rd 1901		
13	Judgement[sic] by U.S. Court CD Admitting Nos 1,3-4 vacated and set aside by Decree of					
14	Choctaw-Chickasaw Citizenship Court Dec 17 '02					
15	Nos1,3-4 denied by Choctaw-Chickasaw Citizenship Court Feb 1 1904 Case # 13.					
16						
17						

Choctaw By Blood Enrollment Cards 1898-1914

RESIDENCE: Sugar Loaf   COUNTY. **Choctaw Nation**   **Choctaw Roll** *(Not Including Freedmen)*   CARD No.
POST OFFICE: Howe, I.T.   FIELD No. 2247

Dawes' Roll No.		NAME		Relationship to Person	AGE	SEX	BLOOD	TRIBAL ENROLLMENT		
								Year	County	No.
6508	1	Britton Mary	28	First Named	25	F	1/4	1896	Sugar Loaf	789
6509	2	" Samuel	11	Son	8	M	1/8	1896	" "	790
6510	3	" Margaret	9	Dau	6	F	1/8	1896	" "	791
6511	4	" James	8	Son	5	M	1/8	1896	" "	792
6512	5	" Effie	DIED PRIOR TO SEPTEMBER 25, 1902	Dau	3	F	1/8	1896	" "	793
6513	6	" Myrtle	4	"	5mo	"	1/8			
6514	7	" Owen Columbus	1	Son	5wks	M	1/8			
	8									
	9									
	10									
	11									
	12									
	13									
	14									
	15									
	16									
	17									

ENROLLMENT
OF NOS. 1,2,3,4,5,6,7 HEREON
APPROVED BY THE SECRETARY
OF INTERIOR JAN 17 1903

TRIBAL ENROLLMENT OF PARENTS

	Name of Father	Year	County	Name of Mother	Year	County
1	Sam Hickman	1896	Non Citz	Margaret Hickman	Ded	Sugar Loaf
2	Samuel Britton	1896	" "	No 1		
3	" "			No 1		
4	" "			No 1		
5	" "			No 1		
6	" "			No 1		
7	" "			No 1		
8						
9						
10						
11				Affidavits to be supplied. Rec'd June 8/99		
12				No.7 born Nov. 28, 1901; Enrolled Jan 6, 1902.		
13				No.5 Died March 18th 1901; Proof of Death filed Dec 20th, 1902		
14						
15				#1 to 6		
16				Date of Application for Enrollment.		6/5/99
17						

147

Choctaw By Blood Enrollment Cards 1898-1914

RESIDENCE: Sugar Loaf   COUNTY.   **Choctaw Nation**   Choctaw Roll   CARD No.
POST OFFICE: Wister I.T.   (Not Including Freedmen)   FIELD No. 2248

Dawes' Roll No.	NAME	Relationship to Person	AGE	SEX	BLOOD	TRIBAL ENROLLMENT		
						Year	County	No.
6515	1 Benton Robert 60	First Named	57	M	Full	1896	Sugar Loaf	816
6516	2 " Jane 54	Wife	51	F	1/2	1896	" "	817
6517	3 DIED PRIOR TO SEPTEMBER 25 1902 John C Neph	20	M	Full	1896	" "	2263
	4							
	5							
	6							
	7							
	8							
	9							
	10							
	11							
	12							
	13							
	14							
	15	ENROLLMENT						
	16	OF NOS. 1, 2, 3 HEREON APPROVED BY THE SECRETARY						
	17	OF INTERIOR JAN 17 1903						

TRIBAL ENROLLMENT OF PARENTS

	Name of Father	Year	County	Name of Mother	Year	County
1	Wa-ka-tombi	Dead	Sugar Loaf	Sha-ka-pa-ho-ma	Dead	Atoka
2	A-pa-san-ta-be	"	Sans Bois	Rhoda Perry	"	Sugar Loaf
3	John Parshall	"	Sugar Loaf	No-yo-ho-ko	"	" "
4						
5						
6						
7		No3 On 1896 roll as John Parshall				
8	No3 died before [illegible] Department May 2, 1906					
9						
10						
11						
12						
13						
14						
15				DATE OF APPLICATION		
16				FOR ENROLLMENT.	6/5/99	
17						

Choctaw By Blood Enrollment Cards 1898-1914

RESIDENCE: Gaines   COUNTY.   **Choctaw Nation**   **Choctaw Roll**   CARD NO.
POST OFFICE: Wilburton I.T.   *(Not Including Freedmen)*   FIELD NO.   2249

Dawes' Roll No.	NAME		Relationship to Person First Named	AGE	SEX	BLOOD	TRIBAL ENROLLMENT		
							Year	County	No.
6518	1 Collin Annie	27	First Named	24	F	Full	1896	Gaines	2298
6519	2 " Kagin	6	Son	3	M	"	1896	"	2299
	3								
	4								
	5								
	6								
	7								
	8								
	9								
	10								
	11								
	12								
	13								
	14								
	15								
	16								
	17								

ENROLLMENT
OF NOS. 1, 2 HEREON
APPROVED BY THE SECRETARY
OF INTERIOR JAN 17 1903

TRIBAL ENROLLMENT OF PARENTS

	Name of Father	Year	County	Name of Mother	Year	County
1	Jackson Collin	Dead	Gaines	E-ya-tema	Dead	Gaines
2				No 2		
3						
4						
5						
6	No1 On 1896 roll as Annie Collins					
7	No2 On 1896 roll as Hagin Collins					
8	No 1 par on Choc card #1099 is child of No 1 She died Mch 12 1901					
9						
10						
11						
12						
13						
14					Date of Application for Enrollment.	
15						
16					6/5/99	
17						

149

Choctaw By Blood Enrollment Cards 1898-1914

RESIDENCE:	Sugar Loaf
POST OFFICE:	Wister I.T.

COUNTY. **Choctaw Nation**

Choctaw Roll (Not Including Freedmen)

CARD NO. FIELD NO. **2250**

Dawes' Roll No.	NAME	Relationship to Person	AGE	SEX	BLOOD	TRIBAL ENROLLMENT Year	County	No.
6520	₁ Jones Charley ²⁴	First Named	21	M	Full	1896	Sugar Loaf	6510
14725	₂ " Elsie ³³	Wife	30	F	"	1896	" "	9574
14726	₃ Noel Luena ¹⁴	Step Dau	11	F	"	1896	" "	9475
15420	₄ Jones Mary ¹	Dau	1½	F				
	₅							
	₆							
	₇							
	₈							
	₉							
	₁₀							
	₁₁							
	₁₂							
	₁₃							
	₁₄							
	₁₅							
	₁₆							
	₁₇							

ENROLLMENT
OF NOS. ~~~ 4 ~~~ HEREON
APPROVED BY THE SECRETARY
OF INTERIOR May 9 1904

ENROLLMENT
OF NOS. 1 HEREON
APPROVED BY THE SECRETARY
OF INTERIOR Jan 17 1903

ENROLLMENT
OF NOS. 2 and 3 HEREON
APPROVED BY THE SECRETARY
OF INTERIOR May 20 1903

TRIBAL ENROLLMENT OF PARENTS

	Name of Father	Year	County	Name of Mother	Year	County
₁	Joseph Jones	1896	Sugar Loaf	Betsy Ushta	Dead	Skullyville
₂	Jacob Going	Dead	Sugar Loaf	Wisey	"	Sugar Loaf
₃	Sim Noel	"	" "	No 2		
₄	No 1			No 2		
₅						
₆						
₇						
₈						
₉						
₁₀	No2 on 1896 roll as Elphie Noel					
₁₁	No3 " " " " Lauana Noel					
₁₂	No1 and 2 are divorced and No1 is now husband of No3 on this card. Evidence of divorce filed Feby 14 1903					
₁₃	No4 Application for enrollment first received Sept 24, 1902 and returned for information as to mother. N°4 Enrolled Dec 23, 1903					
₁₄	For child of Nos 1&3 see NB (Mar 3, 1905) #560 #1 to 3 inc					
₁₅					Date of Application for Enrollment.	
₁₆					6/5/99	
₁₇						

150

Choctaw By Blood Enrollment Cards 1898-1914

RESIDENCE:	Sugar Loaf
POST OFFICE:	Poteau I.T.

COUNTY. **Choctaw Nation**

Choctaw Roll *(Not Including Freedmen)*

CARD NO.

FIELD NO. **2251**

Dawes' Roll No.	NAME		Relationship to Person	AGE	SEX	BLOOD	TRIBAL ENROLLMENT		
							Year	County	No.
I.W. 995	1 Sage James W	68	First Named	65	M	I.W.	1896	Sugar Loaf	115026
6521	2 " Jane F	54	Wife	51	F	1/32	1896	" "	11162
	3								
	4								
	5								
	6								
	7								
	8								
	9								
	10	ENROLLMENT							
	11	OF NOS. 1 HEREON APPROVED BY THE SECRETARY OF INTERIOR Oct 21 1904							
	12								
	13								
	14								
	15	ENROLLMENT OF NOS. 2 HEREON							
	16	APPROVED BY THE SECRETARY OF INTERIOR Jan 17 1903							
	17								

TRIBAL ENROLLMENT OF PARENTS

	Name of Father	Year	County	Name of Mother	Year	County
1	Morgan Sage	Dead	Non Citz	Caroline Sage	Dead	Non Citz
2	W.P. Merriman	"	Skullyville Co	Anna Merriman	"	Skullyville Xo
3						
4						
5						
6			No 1 On 1896 roll as J.W. Sage			
7			No 2 " " " " Frances Sage			
8						
9						
10						
11						
12						
13						
14						
15						
16				Date of Application for Enrollment.	6/5/99	
17	P.O. Tamala I.T. 3/5/03					

151

Choctaw By Blood Enrollment Cards 1898-1914

RESIDENCE: Skullyville, I.T. COUNTY. **Choctaw Nation** Choctaw Roll CARD NO.
POST OFFICE: Pocola, I.T. *(Not Including Freedmen)* FIELD NO. 2252

Dawes' Roll No.	NAME	Relationship to Person	AGE	SEX	BLOOD	TRIBAL ENROLLMENT Year	County	No.
6522	1 LaForce, Monte ²⁹	First Named	26	M	1/4	1896	Skullyville	7765
	2							
	3							
	4							
	5							
	6							
	7							
	8							
	9							
	10							
	11							
	12							
	13							
	14							
	15							
	16							
	17							

ENROLLMENT
OF NOS. 1 HEREON
APPROVED BY THE SECRETARY
OF INTERIOR JAN 17 1903

TRIBAL ENROLLMENT OF PARENTS

	Name of Father	Year	County	Name of Mother	Year	County
1	Perry LaForce	1896	Non Citz	Weslan LaForce	Dead	Skullyville
2						
3						
4						
5						
6				No.1 in San Quinton, Cl. Penetentiary[sic]	12/18 '02	
7						
8						
9						
10						
11						
12						
13						
14						
15						
16				Date of Application for Enrollment.	6/5/99	
17						

Choctaw By Blood Enrollment Cards 1898-1914

RESIDENCE: Sugar Loaf COUNTY. **Choctaw Nation** Choctaw Roll CARD NO.
POST OFFICE: Fanshaw, I.T. (Not Including Freedmen) FIELD NO. 2253

Dawes' Roll No.	NAME		Relationship to Person First Named	AGE	SEX	BLOOD	TRIBAL ENROLLMENT		
							Year	County	No.
6523	1 Collin, Jesse	48	First Named	45	M	Full	1896	Sugar Loaf	2245
6524	2 " Martha	68	Wife	65	F	"	1896	" "	2246
	3								
	4								
	5								
	6								
	7								
	8								
	9								
	10								
	11								
	12								
	13								
	14								
	15								
	16								
	17								

ENROLLMENT
OF NOS. 1, 2 HEREON
APPROVED BY THE SECRETARY
OF INTERIOR JAN 17 1903

TRIBAL ENROLLMENT OF PARENTS

	Name of Father	Year	County	Name of Mother	Year	County
1		Dead	Sugar Loaf	A-le-ha-ma	Dead	Sugar Loaf
2	Sho-tubbee	"	" " "		"	" " "
3						
4						
5						
6						
7						
8						
9						
10						
11						
12						
13						
14						
15						
16				Date of Application for Enrollment.	6/5/99	
17						

153

Choctaw By Blood Enrollment Cards 1898-1914

RESIDENCE: Gaines COUNTY.
POST OFFICE: Hartshorne, I.T

Choctaw Nation

Choctaw Roll
(Not Including Freedmen)

CARD NO.
FIELD NO. 2254

Dawes' Roll No.	NAME	Relationship to Person First Named	AGE	SEX	BLOOD	TRIBAL ENROLLMENT Year	TRIBAL ENROLLMENT County	TRIBAL ENROLLMENT No.
6525	1 Webster, Milsie	DIED PRIOR TO SEPTEMBER 25 1902	40	F	Full	1896	Gaines	12948
6526	2 Kincade, Mary 20	Dau	17	"	"	1896	"	7475
6527	3 Webster, Shingo 16	Son	13	M	"	1896	"	12949
	4							
	5							
	6							
	7							
	8							
	9							
	10							
	11							
	12							
	13							
	14							
	15	ENROLLMENT OF NOS. 1, 2, 3, HEREON APPROVED BY THE SECRETARY OF INTERIOR JAN 17 1903						
	16							
	17							

TRIBAL ENROLLMENT OF PARENTS

	Name of Father	Year	County	Name of Mother	Year	County
1	Ish-ko-lih-cha	Dead	Sugar Loaf	Sibyl	1896	Sugar Loaf
2	Willis Kincade	"	" "	No 1		
3	Isom Webster	"	Gaines	No 1		
4						
5						
6						
7						
8		No 1 died Nov 17 1901; Enrollment (remainder illegible) Dec 24, 1901				
9						
10		For child of No2 see NB (Mar 3rd 1905) Card #120.				
11						
12						
13						
14						
15						
16				Date of Application for Enrollment.	6/5/99	
17						

Choctaw By Blood Enrollment Cards 1898-1914

RESIDENCE: Sugar Loaf   COUNTY. **Choctaw Nation**   **Choctaw Roll** CARD NO.
POST OFFICE: Poteau I.T.   *(Not Including Freedmen)* FIELD NO. 2255

Dawes' Roll No.	NAME		Relationship to Person First Named	AGE	SEX	BLOOD	TRIBAL ENROLLMENT		
							Year	County	No.
6528	1 Page, Robert	44	First Named	41	M	3/4	1896	Sugar Loaf	10130
I.W. 27	2 " Montie S	42	Wife	39	F	I.W.			
6529	3 " Edward E	6	Son	3	M	3/8	1896	Sugar Loaf	10132
6530	4 " Robert N	4	"	3mo	"	3/8			
	5								
	6								
	7								
	8								
	9								
	10								
	11								
	12								
	13								
	14								
	15	ENROLLMENT OF NOS. 1, 3, 4, HEREON APPROVED BY THE SECRETARY OF INTERIOR JAN 17 1903			ENROLLMENT OF NOS. 2 HEREON APPROVED BY THE SECRETARY OF INTERIOR JUN 13 1903					
	16								
	17								

TRIBAL ENROLLMENT OF PARENTS

	Name of Father	Year	County	Name of Mother	Year	County
1	John Page	Ded	Skullyville	Jane Page	1896	Skullyville
2	Wᵐ Davis	1896	Non Citz	Hester Davis	Ded	Non Citz
3	No 1			No 2		
4	No 1			No 2		
5						
6						
7						
8						
9						
10						
11						
12	No 3 on 1896 roll as Edward Page					
13						
14						
15					Date of Application for Enrollment.	
16					6/5/99	
17						

Choctaw By Blood Enrollment Cards 1898-1914

| | RESIDENCE: Skullyville COUNTY. | POST OFFICE: Cameron I.T. | | | **Choctaw Nation** | | Choctaw Roll (Not Including Freedmen) | CARD No. FIELD No. 2256 | |

Dawes' Roll No.	NAME	Relationship to Person	AGE	SEX	BLOOD	TRIBAL ENROLLMENT		
						Year	County	No.
6531	1 Sexton Thomas J 31	First Named	28	M	1/4	1896	Skullyville	11145
I.W. 29	2 " Fannie M 31	Wife	28	F	IW.	1896	"	15023
6532	3 " Ralph H 6	Son	3	M	1/8	1896	"	11146
6533	4 " Roberta 4	Dau	7mo	F	1/8			
6534	5 " William Earl 2	Son	2w	M	1/8			
	6							
	7							
	8							
	9							
	10							
	11							
	12							
	13							
	14							
	15	ENROLLMENT OF NOS. 1,3,4,5 HEREON APPROVED BY THE SECRETARY OF INTERIOR JAN 17 1903				ENROLLMENT OF NOS 2 HEREON APPROVED BY THE SECRETARY OF INTERIOR JUN 13 1903		
	16							
	17							

TRIBAL ENROLLMENT OF PARENTS

	Name of Father	Year	County	Name of Mother	Year	County
1	T D Sexton	1896	Sugar Loaf	Ruth Sexton	Ded	Non Citz
2	Robert Docking	1896	Non Citz	Martha Docking	1896	" "
3	No 1			No 2		
4	No 1			No 2		
5	No 1			No 2		
6						
7	No1 is guardian of minor children of Thompson D Sexton, deceased, on					
8	Choctaw card #3016					
9						
10			No3 on 1896 roll as Ralph H Sexton			
11			As to fathers and mothers marriage			
12			see testimony of Mrs. Margaret Wade.			
13			No1 on 1896 roll as Thompson J. Sexton			
			No.5 Enrolled January 25, 1901.			
14						
15						Date of Application for Enrollment.
16	For child of Nos1&2 see NB (Mar 3rd 1905) Card #121					
	" " " " " " (Apr 26-1906) " #227					6/5/99
17	P.O. [Illegible] IT 3/20/05					

156

Choctaw By Blood Enrollment Cards 1898-1914

RESIDENCE: Sugar Loaf   COUNTY. **Choctaw Nation**   **Choctaw Roll**   CARD No.
POST OFFICE: Wister I.T.   *(Not Including Freedmen)*   FIELD No. **2257**

Dawes' Roll No.	NAME		Relationship to Person	AGE	SEX	BLOOD	TRIBAL ENROLLMENT		
							Year	County	No.
6535	1 Bond Johnson	72	First Named	69	M	Full	1896	Sugar Loaf	786
6536	2 " Sarbale	69	Wife	66	F	"	1896	" "	787
	3								
	4								
	5								
	6								
	7								
	8								
	9								
	10								
	11								
	12								
	13								
	14								
	15	ENROLLMENT OF NOS. 1, 2 HEREON APPROVED BY THE SECRETARY OF INTERIOR JAN 17 1903							
	16								
	17								

TRIBAL ENROLLMENT OF PARENTS

	Name of Father	Year	County	Name of Mother	Year	County
1	Dead	Mississippi	A-chito-na		Dead	Sugar Loaf
2	"	"			"	" "
3						
4						
5						
6						
7						
8						
9						
10						
11						
12						
13						
14						
15						
16				Date of Application for Enrollment.		6/5/99
17						

** Nos 1&2 "Died prior to Sept 25, 1902; not entitled to land or money"
See I.O. Letter No. 1016-1911

157

Choctaw By Blood Enrollment Cards 1898-1914

RESIDENCE: Sugar Loaf   COUNTY, **Choctaw Nation**   **Choctaw Roll**   CARD NO.
POST OFFICE: Richard, I.T.   *(Not Including Freedmen)*   FIELD NO. 2258

Dawes' Roll No.	NAME		Relationship to Person	AGE	SEX	BLOOD	TRIBAL ENROLLMENT		
							Year	County	No.
6537	1 McElroy, Jeff J	42	First Named	39	M	Full	1896	Sugar Loaf	9142
6538	2 " Malinda	42	Wife	39	F	3/4	1896	" "	9143
~~6539~~	3 DIED PRIOR TO SEPTEMBER 25 1902 ~~Emma~~		~~Dau~~	~~19~~	"	~~7/8~~	~~1896~~	" "	~~9144~~
6540	4 " Alice	13	"	10	"	7/8	1896	" "	9145
6541	5 Bohanan, Jackson	19	Nephew	16	M	3/4	1896	Skullyville	715
6542	6 " Samuel	17	"	14	"	3/4	1896	"	716
6543	7 " Fannie	15	Niece	13	F	3/4	1896	"	717
	8								
	9								
	10								
	11								
	12								
	13								
	14								
	15								
	16								
	17								

ENROLLMENT
OF NOS. 1,2,3,4,5,6,7, HEREON
APPROVED BY THE SECRETARY
OF INTERIOR JAN 17 1903

TRIBAL ENROLLMENT OF PARENTS

	Name of Father	Year	County	Name of Mother	Year	County
1	Joseph McElroy	Dead	Wade	Lucy McElroy	Dead	Nashoba
2	Dixon Anderson	"	"		"	Wade
3	No 1			No 2		
4	No 1			No 2		
5	Lymon Bohanan	Dead	Skullyville	Celie Bohanan	Dead	Skullyville
6	" "	"	"	" "	"	"
7	" "	"	"	" "	"	"
8						
9			No5 on 1896 roll as Jack Bohanan			
10			No6 " 1896 " " Sam "			
11			No3 Died March 8th 1902	Proof of Death filed Decr 23 1902		
12			No3 died March 2, 1902. Enrollment [remainder illegible] July 8, 1904			
13			For child of No7 see NB (Apr 26-06) Card #645			
14						
15				Date of Application for Enrollment.		
16				6/5/99		
17	P.O. Chickasha I.T. 5/5/0[?]					

Choctaw By Blood Enrollment Cards 1898-1914

Dawes' Roll No.	NAME		Relationship to Person First Named	AGE	SEX	BLOOD	TRIBAL ENROLLMENT		
							Year	County	No.
6544	1 Mackey, Forbis	33	First Named	30	M	Full	1896	Sugar Loaf	9091
6545	DIED PRIOR TO SEPTEMBER 25, 24 1902 Sukey		Wife	21	F	"	1896	" "	9092
6546	3 " Eli	6	Son	3	M	"	1896	" "	9094
	4								
	5								
	6								
	7								
	8								
	9								
	10								
	11								
	12								
	13								
	14								
	15								
	16								
	17								

RESIDENCE: Sugar Loaf **COUNTY.**
POST OFFICE: Fanshaw, I.T

Choctaw Nation

Choctaw Roll *(Not Including Freedmen)*

CARD No.
FIELD No. 2259

ENROLLMENT
OF NOS. 1, 2, 3, HEREON
APPROVED BY THE SECRETARY
OF INTERIOR JAN 17 1903

TRIBAL ENROLLMENT OF PARENTS

Name of Father	Year	County	Name of Mother	Year	County
1 Ellis Mackey	Dead	Sugar Loaf	Te-ma-ho-ke	Dead	Sugar Loaf
2 Columbus Thompson	"	" "	Nicey Pevey	1896	" "
3 No 1			No 2		
4					
5					
6					
7		No1 on 1896 roll as Forbes McKey			
8		No2 " 1896 " " Sokey "			
9		No3 " 1896 " " Elie "			
10		No.2 Died November 25" 1899: Proof of death filed December 20th 1902 No.2 died Nov 25 1899: Enrollment cancelled by Department July 8, 1904			
11					
12					
13					
14					
15			Date of Application for Enrollment.		
16			6/5/99		
17	P.O. Wister, I.T. 12/16 '02				

RESIDENCE: Sugar Loaf   COUNTY.
POST OFFICE: Howe, I.T.

Choctaw Nation

Choctaw Roll
(Not Including Freedmen)

CARD NO.
FIELD NO.   2260

Dawes' Roll No.	NAME	Relationship to Person	AGE	SEX	BLOOD	TRIBAL ENROLLMENT		
						Year	County	No.
6547	1 McCasson, Samuel ⁶²	First Named	59	M	Full	1896	Sugar Loaf	9097
6548	2 DIED PRIOR TO SEPTEMBER 25 1902 Eliza J	Wife	51	F	1/4	1896	" "	9098
6549	3 " Enos F ²²	Son	19	M	5/8	1896	" "	9099
6550	4 Blake Lillie A ¹⁷	Dau	14	F	5/8	1896	" "	9100
6551	5 McCasson Sam R ¹⁴	Son	11	M	5/8	1896	" "	9101
6552	6 Blake, Robert W ¹	Grandson	1mo	M	5/16			
	7							
	8							
	9							
	10							
	11							
	12							
	13							
	14							
	15	ENROLLMENT OF NOS. 1,2,3,4,5,6 HEREON						
	16	APPROVED BY THE SECRETARY OF INTERIOR JAN 17 1903						
	17							

TRIBAL ENROLLMENT OF PARENTS

	Name of Father	Year	County	Name of Mother	Year	County
1	Pe-sa-te-cubbee	Dead	Nashoba	He-ya-he-na	Dead	Sugar Loaf
2	Jim Morris	"	Non Citz	Martha Morris	"	" " "
3	No1			No2		
4	No1			No2		
5	No1			No2		
6	Wᵐ P Blake		non-citizen	No 4		
7						
8	No2 on 1896 roll as Eliz J McCasson					
9	No.4 is now the wife of William P. Blake a non-citizen Nov 20, 1901.					
10	No.6 born Oct 31, 1901: Enrolled Nov 20, 1901 No2 Died July 2ⁿᵈ 1901. Proof of death filed Dec 20ᵗʰ 1902					
11	Nº3 is the husband of Nancy M Hickman on Choctaw Card #2263					
12	No.2 died July 2. 1902. Enrollment cancelled by Department July 8, 1904					
13						
14	For children of No4 see NB (Mar 3-1905) Card #122				#1to5	
15					Date of Application for Enrollment.	
16	No.4 P.O. Haileyville, I.T. 12/18 '02				6/5/99	
17						

Choctaw By Blood Enrollment Cards 1898-1914

RESIDENCE: Sugar Loaf   COUNTY. **Choctaw Nation**   **Choctaw Roll**   CARD No.
POST OFFICE: Wister I.T.   *(Not Including Freedmen)*   FIELD No.   2261

Dawes' Roll No.	NAME		Relationship to Person	AGE	SEX	BLOOD	TRIBAL ENROLLMENT		
							Year	County	No.
6553	1 Hamlin Israel	45	First Named	42	M	Full	1896	Sugar Loaf	5239
6554	2 " Sallie	42	Wife	39	F	Full	1896	" "	5240
Dead	3 " Hannah		Dau	5 days	F	"			
	4								
	5								
	6								
	7								
	8								
	9								
	10								
	11	No. 3 HEREON DISMISSED UNDER ORDER OF THE COMMISSION TO THE FIVE							
	12	CIVILIZED TRIBES OF MARCH 31, 1905.							
	13								
	14								
	15	ENROLLMENT OF NOS. 1, 2, HEREON							
	16	APPROVED BY THE SECRETARY OF INTERIOR JAN 17 1903							
	17								

TRIBAL ENROLLMENT OF PARENTS

	Name of Father	Year	County	Name of Mother	Year	County
1	E-ya-kattabe	Dead	Sugar Loaf		Dead	Sugar Loaf
2	Amos Washington	"	" "	Mary Washington	1896	Wade
3	No 1			No 2		
4						
5						
6						
7	No1 On 1896 roll as Israel Hamplin					
8	No2 " " " " Silly "					
9	No.3 Died August 10, 1899. Evidence of death filed March 20, 1901					
10	For child of Nos 1&2 see NB (Mar 3, 1905) #558					
11						
12						
13						
14						
15						
16				Date of Application for Enrollment.		6/5/99
17						

Choctaw By Blood Enrollment Cards 1898-1914

	RESIDENCE: Sugar Loaf	COUNTY.					

RESIDENCE: Sugar Loaf
POST OFFICE: Conser I.T.
COUNTY. Choctaw Nation
Choctaw Roll *(Not Including Freedmen)*
CARD NO.
FIELD NO. 2262

Dawes' Roll No.	NAME		Relationship to Person	AGE	SEX	BLOOD	TRIBAL ENROLLMENT		
							Year	County	No.
6555	1 Wade Stanford	36	First Named	33	M	3/4	1896	Skullyville	12757
I.W. 28	2 " Eliza J	32	Wife	29	F	I.W.	1896	"	15150
6556	3 " Viola	14	Dau	11	"	3/8	1896	"	12758
6557	4 " William	12	Son	9	M	3/8	1896	"	12759
6558	5 " Sarah	10	Dau	7	F	3/8	1896	"	12760
6559	6 " Noah	7	Son	4	M	3/8	1896	"	12761
6560	7 " Charles H	5	"	13mo	"	3/8			
	8								
	9								
	10								
	11								
	12								
	13								
	14								
	15								
	16								
	17								

ENROLLMENT
OF NOS. 1,3,4,5,6,7 HEREON
APPROVED BY THE SECRETARY
OF INTERIOR Jan 17 1903

ENROLLMENT
OF NOS. ~~ 2 ~~ HEREON
APPROVED BY THE SECRETARY
OF INTERIOR Jun 13 1903

TRIBAL ENROLLMENT OF PARENTS

	Name of Father	Year	County	Name of Mother	Year	County
1	Henry Wade	Ded	Sugar Loaf	Lucy Wade	1896	Sugar Loaf
2	Charlie Cagle	"	Non Citz	Sarah Cagle	1896	Non Citz
3	No 1			No 2		
4	No 1			No 2		
5	No 1			No 2		
6	No 1			No 2		
7	No 1			No 2		
8						
9						
10			No2 on 1896 roll as Eliza Wade			
11			Evidence of marriage to be sup-			
12			plied. Rec'd June 16/99			
13						
14					Date of Application for Enrollment.	
15						
16					6/5/99	
17	P.O. Heavener, I.T. 12/18 '02					

Choctaw By Blood Enrollment Cards 1898-1914

RESIDENCE: Sugar Loaf   COUNTY. **Choctaw Nation**   **Choctaw Roll**   CARD NO.
POST OFFICE: Heavener I.T.   *(Not Including Freedmen)*   FIELD NO. **2263**

Dawes' Roll No.	NAME	Relationship to Person	AGE	SEX	BLOOD	TRIBAL ENROLLMENT		
						Year	County	No.
6561	1 Hickman Joshua	First Named	43	M	1/2	1896	Sugar Loaf	5226
6562	2 " Betsy 48	Wife	45	F	3/4	1896	" "	5227
6563	3 " Nancy M 15	Dau	12	"	5/8	1896	" "	5228
6564	4 " Atchison 8	Son	5	M	5/8	1896	" "	5229
6565	5 " Samuel 6	"	2	"	5/8			
6566	6 " William P	"	2mo	"	5/8			
	7							
	8							
	9							
	10							
	11							
	12							
	13							
	14							
	15							
	16							
	17							

(DIED PRIOR TO SEPTEMBER 25, 1902 — noted on rows 1 and 6)

ENROLLMENT
OF NOS. 1,2,3,4,5,6
APPROVED BY THE SECRETARY HEREON
OF INTERIOR Jan 17 1903

TRIBAL ENROLLMENT OF PARENTS

	Name of Father	Year	County	Name of Mother	Year	County
1	Samuel Hickman	De'd	Skullyville		Ded	Sugar Loaf
2	Tom Camp	Ded	Sugar Loaf	Camp	"	" "
3	No 1			No 2		
4	No 1			No 2		
5	No 1			No 2		
6	No 1			No 2		
7						
8	No.1 Died June 5 1901: Proof of death filed Dec 23 1902					
9	No.1 died June 5, 1901 No.6 died Nov – 1899: Enrollment cancelled by Department July 8, 1904					
10	No.3 on 1896 roll as Narcy Hickman					
11	No 4 " " " " Etcherson "					
12	No.3 is wife of Enos F. McCasson, on Choc Card #2260					
13						
14						
15					Date of Application for Enrollment.	
16					6/5/99	
17				No6 ~~enrolled~~ Nov 1/99		

163

Choctaw By Blood Enrollment Cards 1898-1914

RESIDENCE: Sugar Loaf   COUNTY. **Choctaw Nation**   **Choctaw Roll** CARD NO.
POST OFFICE: Howe I.T.   *(Not Including Freedmen)*   FIELD NO.   2264

Dawes' Roll No.	NAME	Relationship to Person	AGE	SEX	BLOOD	TRIBAL ENROLLMENT		
						Year	County	No.
6567	1 Hickman Austin ²⁰	First Named	17	M	1/4	1896	Sugar Loaf	5231
	2							
	3							
	4							
	5							
	6							
	7							
	8							
	9							
	10							
	11							
	12							
	13							
	14							
	15	ENROLLMENT OF NOS. 1 HEREON						
	16	APPROVED BY THE SECRETARY OF INTERIOR JAN 17 1903						
	17							

TRIBAL ENROLLMENT OF PARENTS

	Name of Father	Year	County	Name of Mother	Year	County
1	Samuel Hickman	1896	Sugar Loaf	Margaret Hickman	Ded	Sugar Loaf
2						
3						
4						
5						
6						
7						
8						
9						
10						
11						
12						
13						
14						
15						
16				Date of Application for Enrollment.		6/5/99
17						

164

Choctaw By Blood Enrollment Cards 1898-1914

RESIDENCE: Sugar Loaf   COUNTY. **Choctaw Nation**   **Choctaw Roll** *(Not Including Freedmen)*   CARD NO.

POST OFFICE: Howe I.T.   FIELD NO. 2265

Dawes' Roll No.	NAME		Relationship to Person	AGE	SEX	BLOOD	TRIBAL ENROLLMENT		
							Year	County	No.
6568	1 Folsom Noel	45	First Named	42	M	3/4	1893	Sans Bois	P.R. 260
6569	2 " Sarah	40	Wife	37	F	3/4	1893	" "	261
6570	3 " Moses	14	Son	11	M	3/4	1893	" "	263
	4								
	5								
	6								
	7								
	8								
	9								
	10								
	11								
	12								
	13								
	14								
	15								
	16								
	17								

ENROLLMENT
OF NOS. 1, 2, 3, HEREON
APPROVED BY THE SECRETARY
OF INTERIOR JAN 17 1903

TRIBAL ENROLLMENT OF PARENTS

	Name of Father	Year	County	Name of Mother	Year	County
1	Alech Folsom	Ded	Sans Bois	Hannah Folsom	Ded	Sans Bois
2	Daniel Carney	"	Skullyville	Wiley Carney	"	" "
3	No 1			No 2		
4						
5						
6						
7						
8						
9						
10						
11						
12						
13						
14						
15						Date of Application for Enrollment.
16						6-5-99
17						

Choctaw By Blood Enrollment Cards 1898-1914

RESIDENCE: Sugar Loaf   COUNTY. **Choctaw Nation**   **Choctaw Roll**   CARD NO.
POST OFFICE: Wister, I.T   (Not Including Freedmen)   FIELD NO. 2266

Dawes' Roll No.	NAME	Relationship to Person	AGE	SEX	BLOOD	TRIBAL ENROLLMENT		
						Year	County	No.
6571	₁ Thompson Simpson ³¹	First Named	28	M	Full	1896	Sugar Loaf	11969
DEAD.	₂ " Jincy DEAD.	Wife	42	F	"	1896	" "	11970
6572	₃ Lewis, Carrie ¹²	S.Dau	9	"	"	1896	" "	773
6573	₄ Taylor, Fannie ¹⁹	Ware	16	"	"	1896	" "	11949
14727	₅ James Aaron ¹	Son of No 4	7mo	M	"			
	₆							
	₇							
	₈							
	₉							
	₁₀							
	₁₁							
	₁₂							
	₁₃							
	₁₄							
	₁₅							
	₁₆							
	₁₇							

NO. 2 HEREON DISMISSED UNDER ORDER OF THE COMMISSION TO THE FIVE CIVILIZED TRIBES OF MARCH 31, 1905.

ENROLLMENT OF NOS. 1, 3, 4, HEREON APPROVED BY THE SECRETARY OF INTERIOR JAN 17 1903

ENROLLMENT OF NOS. 5 HEREON APPROVED BY THE SECRETARY OF INTERIOR MAY 20 1903

TRIBAL ENROLLMENT OF PARENTS

	Name of Father	Year	County	Name of Mother	Year	County
₁	Isaac Thompson	Dead	Sugar Loaf	Betsy Thompson	Dead	Sugar Loaf
₂	Lohn	"	" " "	A-ho-te-ma	"	" " "
₃	Ben Lewis	"	" " "	No 2		
₄	Solomon Taylor	"	" " "	Sinie Durant	Dead	Sugar Loaf
₅	Noel James		Choctaw Roll	No 4		
₆						
₇						
₈	No4 on 1896 roll as Finie Taylor					
₉	No2 Died May 18ᵗʰ 1900; Evidence of Death filed June 25ᵗʰ 1902					
₁₀	No5 born May 4, 1902: enrolled Dec 15, 1902					
₁₁	Nº4 is now wife of Noel James, Choc Care #2172					
₁₂						
₁₃						
₁₄	For child of No1 see NB (Apr 26-06) Card #313					
₁₅	" " " " 4 " " "		" #1156	#1 to 4		
₁₆				Date of Application for Enrollment.	6/5/99	
₁₇	P.O. Talihina I.T.					

166

Choctaw By Blood Enrollment Cards 1898-1914

RESIDENCE:	Sugar Loaf	COUNTY.					CARD No.	
POST OFFICE:	Heavener, I.T	**Choctaw Nation**		Choctaw Roll (Not Including Freedmen)			FIELD No.	2267

Dawes' Roll No.	NAME	Relationship to Person First Named	AGE	SEX	BLOOD	TRIBAL ENROLLMENT		
						Year	County	No.
6574	1 Quincy, Robert	Named	25	M	Full	1896	Sugar Loaf	10652
	2							
	3							
	4							
	5							
	6							
	7							
	8							
	9							
	10							
	11							
	12							
	13							
	14							
	15	ENROLLMENT OF NOS. 1 HEREON						
	16	APPROVED BY THE SECRETARY OF INTERIOR JAN 17 1903						
	17							

DIED PRIOR TO SEPTEMBER 25, 2892

TRIBAL ENROLLMENT OF PARENTS

	Name of Father	Year	County	Name of Mother	Year	County
1	Joe Quincy	Dead	Sugar Loaf	Lena Quincy	Dead	Sugar Loaf
2						
3						
4						
5						
6		On 1896 roll as Robert Quinsy				
7		No1 Died in September 1899: Proof of death filed Dec 23rd 1902				
8		No 1 died Sept - 1899 Enrollment cancelled by Department July 8, 1904				
9						
10						
11						
12						
13						
14						
15						
16				Date of Application for Enrollment.	6/5/99	
17						

Choctaw By Blood Enrollment Cards 1898-1914

RESIDENCE: Sugar Loaf   COUNTY. **Choctaw Nation**   **Choctaw Roll** CARD No.
POST OFFICE: Wister, I.T   *(Not Including Freedmen)* FIELD No. 2268

Dawes' Roll No.	NAME	Relationship to Person	AGE	SEX	BLOOD	TRIBAL ENROLLMENT		
						Year	County	No.
6575	1 Thompson, Benjamin 23	First Named	20	M	Full	1896	Sugar Loaf	11976
	2							
	3							
	4							
	5							
	6							
	7							
	8							
	9							
	10							
	11							
	12							
	13							
	14							
	15							
	16							
	17							

ENROLLMENT
OF NOS. 1 HEREON
APPROVED BY THE SECRETARY
OF INTERIOR JAN 17 1903

TRIBAL ENROLLMENT OF PARENTS

	Name of Father	Year	County	Name of Mother	Year	County
1	Isom Thompson	Dead	Sugar Loaf	Betsy Thompson	Dead	Sugar Loaf
2						
3						
4						
5						
6						
7						
8						
9						
10						
11						
12						
13						
14						
15						
16				Date of Application for Enrollment.	6/5/99	
17	P.O. Bacons, I.T. 12/18 '02					

RESIDENCE: Sugar Loaf	COUNTY.	Choctaw Nation	Choctaw Roll	CARD No.	
POST OFFICE: Heavener, I.T.			(Not Including Freedmen)	FIELD No. **2269**	

Dawes' Roll No.	NAME		Relationship to Person	AGE	SEX	BLOOD	TRIBAL ENROLLMENT		
							Year	County	No.
6576	₁ Quincy, Jefferson	26	First Named	23	M	Full	1896	Sugar Loaf	10653
I.W. 102	₂ " Allie	21	Wife	18	F	I.W.			
6577	₃ " Robert Lee	2	Son	7mo	M	1/2			
	4								
	5								
	6								
	7								
	8								
	9								
	10								
	11								
	12								
	13								
	14								
	15								
	16								
	17								

ENROLLMENT
OF NOS. 1, 3 HEREON
APPROVED BY THE SECRETARY
OF INTERIOR Jan 17 1903

ENROLLMENT
OF NOS. 2 HEREON
APPROVED BY THE SECRETARY
OF INTERIOR Jun 13 1903

TRIBAL ENROLLMENT OF PARENTS

	Name of Father	Year	County	Name of Mother	Year	County
₁	John Quincy	Dead	Sugar Loaf	Lena Quincy	Dead	Sugar Loaf
₂	Marion Kennedy	"	Non Citz	Lou Kennedy	1896	Non Citz
₃	No 1			No 2		
4						
5						
6						
7	No1 on 1896 roll as Jefferson Quinsy					
8						
9	Evidence of marriage to be supplied. Recd June 16/99					
10	No3 Enrolled July 10, 1901					
11						
12	For child of Nos 1&2 see NB (Mar 3rd 1905) Card #123					
13						
14						
15					Date of Application for Enrollment.	
16					6/5/99	
17						

169

RESIDENCE: Sugar Loaf
POST OFFICE: Heavener, I.T

COUNTY. **Choctaw Nation**

Choctaw Roll
(Not Including Freedmen)

CARD NO.

FIELD NO. 2270

Dawes' Roll No.	NAME		Relationship to Person	AGE	SEX	BLOOD	TRIBAL ENROLLMENT		
							Year	County	No.
6578	1 Smith, Emma	25	First Named	22	F	1/2	1896	Sugar Loaf	11188
6579	2 " Willy	6	Dau	3	"	1/4	1896	" "	11189
6580	3 " Fred	5	Son	1½	M	1/4			
6581	4 " Theodore	4	"	7mo	"	1/4			
14728	5 " Alen	1	"	1	"	1/4			
	6								
	7								
	8								
	9								
	10								
	11								
	12								
	13								
	14								
	15								
	16								
	17								

ENROLLMENT
OF NOS. 1, 2, 3, 4, HEREON
APPROVED BY THE SECRETARY
OF INTERIOR JAN 17 1903

ENROLLMENT
OF NOS. 5 HEREON
APPROVED BY THE SECRETARY
OF INTERIOR MAY 20 1903

TRIBAL ENROLLMENT OF PARENTS

	Name of Father	Year	County	Name of Mother	Year	County
1	Joshua Hickman	1896	Sugar Loaf	Betsy Hickman	1896	Sugar Loaf
2	John C. Smith	1896	" "	No 1		
3	" " "	1896	" "	No 1		
4	" " "	1896	" "	No 1		
5	" " "	1896	" "	No 1		
6						
7						
8						
9			For child of No.1 see NB (Apr 26, 1906) Card No 22			
10			No1 on 1896 roll as Ammy Smith			
11						
12			Nos 3-4 Affidavits of birth to be supplied Recd June 16/99			
13			No5 Born Aug 23, 1901: enrolled Decr 23, 1902			
14						
15				#1 to 4 inc		
16				Date of Application for Enrollment.	6/5/99	
17	P.O. Howe, I.T.		For children of No.1 see NB #22 (Act of Apr 26-06)			

RESIDENCE: Skullyville	COUNTY.					CARD No.
POST OFFICE: Braden, I.T.	**Choctaw Nation**				**Choctaw Roll** *(Not Including Freedmen)*	FIELD No. 2271

Dawes' Roll No.	NAME	Relationship to Person First Named	AGE	SEX	BLOOD	TRIBAL ENROLLMENT		
						Year	County	No.
✓ * 1	Broome, Charles U	Named	38	M	1/4			
✓ * 2	" Annie	Wife	38	F	I.W.			
✓ DP 3	" Julia E	Dau	5mo	"	1/8			
✓ DP 4	" Lillard S	Dau	8mo	F	1/8			
5								
6	DISMISSED							
7	MAY 23 1904							
8								
9	DENIED CITIZENSHIP BY THE CHOCTAW AND							
10	CHICKASAW CITIZENSHIP COURT							
11								
12								
13								
14								
15	ENROLLMENT OF NOS. HEREON							
16	APPROVED BY THE SECRETARY OF INTERIOR							
17								

TRIBAL ENROLLMENT OF PARENTS

Name of Father	Year	County	Name of Mother	Year	County
1 J C Broome	Dead	Non Citz	Mary E Broome	Dead	Choctaw
2 U.T. Morrow	"	" "		"	Non Citz
3 No 1			No 2		
4 No 1			No 2		
5					
6	Nos 1and2 denied by Com in '96 case #1258				
7	Nos 1&2 Admitted by U.S. Court, Central District, Sept 1/97				
8	Case No 241				
9	No 1 admitted as Chas U. Brown				
10					
11	As to residence see testimony of No 1				
12	No.4 born Feby 28, 1901 and enrolled Oct 16th 1901				
13	Judgement of US Court admitting Nos 1and 2 vacated and try free under ideath				
14	Nos 1 & 2 denied by C.C.C. decision as to remainder illegible				
15					
16				Date of Application for Enrollment.	6/5/99
17					

RESIDENCE:	Sugar Loaf	COUNTY.							
POST OFFICE:	Murrow, I.T.		**Choctaw Nation**		Choctaw Roll (Not Including Freedmen)			CARD NO. FIELD NO.	**2272**

Dawes' Roll No.		NAME		Relationship to Person	AGE	SEX	BLOOD	TRIBAL ENROLLMENT		
								Year	County	No.
6582	1	Harris, Abel	57	First Named	54	M	Full	1896	Sugar Loaf	5204
IW243	2	" Susan G	43	Wife	40	F	I.W.	1896	" "	14602
6583	3	" Henry	22	Son	19	M	1/2	1896	" "	5205
6584	4	" William	20	"	17	"	1/2	1896	" "	5206
6585	5	McCurtain Ruthie	18	Dau	15	F	1/2	1896	" "	5207
6586	6	Harris Thomas	13	Son	10	M	1/2	1896	" "	5209
6587	7	" Zado	9	Dau	6	F	1/2	1896	" "	5210
6588	8	" James	6	Son	2	M	1/2			
6589	9	" Elizabeth	3	Dau	4mo	F	1/2			
6590	10	" Everette J	1	Gr.Son	4mo	M	1/4			
6591	11	McCurtain, Ada	1	Gr.Dau	1mo	F	2/8			
	12	ENROLLMENT								
	13	OF NOS. 2 HEREON APPROVED BY THE SECRETARY								
	14	OF INTERIOR Sept 12 1903							›1 to 8 inc	
	15	No10 Born Jany 8, 1901. Enrolled May 22, 1902							6/5/99	
	16	ENROLLMENT OF NOS. 1,3,4,5,6,7,8,9,10,11 HEREON								
	17	APPROVED BY THE SECRETARY OF INTERIOR Jan 17 1903								

TRIBAL ENROLLMENT OF PARENTS

	Name of Father	Year	County	Name of Mother	Year	County
1	Gilly Harris	Dead	Sugar Loaf	Susan Harris	Dead	Sugar Loaf
2	Wm Maxey	"	Non Citz	Ruthie Maxey	"	Non Citz
3	No 1			No 2		
4	No 1			No 2		
5	No 1			No 2		
6	No 1			No 2		
7	No 1			No 2		
8	No 1			No 2		
9	No.1			No.2		
10	No3			Francis Harris		non citizen
11	Elum McCurtain	1896	Sugar Loaf	No5		
12			As to evidence of marriage see evidence of No1			
13			For child of No.4 see NB (March 3, 1905) #949 No8 Affidavit of birth to be supplied. Recd June 6/99			
14	No5 is now the wife of Elum McCurtain on Choctaw card #2374 evidence of marriage filed Oct 6,1902					
15	No.9 Enrolled June 7,1900 No11 Born Aug 31, 1902 enrolled Oct 6,1902					
16	No3 is now the husband of Frances Harris-non citizen: Evidence of marriage filed May 22, 1902 7-5961					
17	P.O. Houston IT 12/16/02 For child of No.3 see NB (March 3, 1905) #1428					

Choctaw By Blood Enrollment Cards 1898-1914

RESIDENCE: Sugar Loaf   COUNTY.   **Choctaw Nation**   Choctaw Roll   CARD NO.
POST OFFICE: Wister, I.T.   (Not Including Freedmen)   FIELD NO. 2273

Dawes' Roll No.	NAME	Relationship to Person First Named	AGE	SEX	BLOOD	TRIBAL ENROLLMENT Year	County	No.
6592	1 Perry, Robinson 59		56	M	Full	1896	Sugar Loaf	10140
6593	2 " Larsin 59	Wife	56	F	"	1896	" "	10141
	3							
	4							
	5							
	6							
	7							
	8							
	9							
	10							
	11							
	12							
	13							
	14							
	15							
	16							
	17							

ENROLLMENT
OF NOS. 1, 2, HEREON
APPROVED BY THE SECRETARY
OF INTERIOR JAN 17 1903

TRIBAL ENROLLMENT OF PARENTS

	Name of Father	Year	County	Name of Mother	Year	County
1	Sandy Perry	Dead	Skullyville	Sarah Perry	Dead	Sugar Loaf
2	Ea-ka-tabbe	"	Sugar Loaf	Ta-ho-na	"	" "
3						
4						
5						
6						
7						
8						
9						
10						
11						
12						
13						
14						
15						
16				Date of Application for Enrollment.	6/5/99	
17						

173

Choctaw By Blood Enrollment Cards 1898-1914

RESIDENCE: Sugar Loaf   COUNTY. **Choctaw Nation**   **Choctaw Roll** *(Not Including Freedmen)*   CARD No.
POST OFFICE: Wister, I.T.   FIELD No. **2274**

Dawes' Roll No.	NAME	Relationship to Person	AGE	SEX	BLOOD	TRIBAL ENROLLMENT		
						Year	County	No.
6594	₁ Milton, Mita ³⁰	First Named	27	F	Full	1896	Sugar Loaf	8491
6595	₂ Billy, Rosie ⁸	Dau	5	F	"	1896	" "	796
6596	₃ Milton, Mary ⁴	"	1	"	"			
	4							
	5							
	6							
	7							
	8							
	9							
	10							
	11							
	12							
	13							
	14							
	15	ENROLLMENT OF NOS. 1, 2, 3, HEREON						
	16	APPROVED BY THE SECRETARY						
	17	OF INTERIOR JAN 17 1903						

TRIBAL ENROLLMENT OF PARENTS

	Name of Father	Year	County	Name of Mother	Year	County
1	Amos Milton	1896	Wade	Larsin Perry	1896	Sugar Loaf
2	Forbis Mackey	1896	Sugar Loaf	No 1		
3	Eastman Billy	Dead	" "	No 1		
4						
5						
6						
7						
8		No1 on 1896 roll as Mary Milton				
9						
10		No3 Affidavit of birth to be supplied. Recd June 7/99				
11		For child of No1 see NB (March 3, 1905) #1094				
12						
13						
14					Date of Application for Enrollment.	
15						
16					6/5/99	
17						

174

Choctaw By Blood Enrollment Cards 1898-1914

RESIDENCE:	Sugar Loaf	COUNTY.						
POST OFFICE:	Howe I.T.	**Choctaw Nation**		Choctaw Roll *(Not Including Freedmen)*		CARD NO. FIELD NO.	2275	

Dawes' Roll No.	NAME		Relationship to Person	AGE	SEX	BLOOD	TRIBAL ENROLLMENT		
							Year	County	No.
6597	1 Folsom Ben	24	First Named	21	M	3/4	P R 1893	Sans Bois	262
	2								
	3								
	4								
	5								
	6								
	7								
	8								
	9								
	10								
	11								
	12								
	13								
	14								
	15	ENROLLMENT OF NOS. 1 HEREON APPROVED BY THE SECRETARY							
	16	OF INTERIOR JAN 17 1903							
	17								

TRIBAL ENROLLMENT OF PARENTS

	Name of Father	Year	County	Name of Mother	Year	County
1	Noah Folsom	1896	Sugar Loaf	Martha Folsom	Dead	Sans Bois
2						
3						
4						
5						
6	On Page 26 No 262, 1893 Pay Roll Sans Bois Co.					
7						
8						
9						
10						
11						
12						
13						
14						
15				Date of Application for Enrollment.		
16					6/5/99	
17						

175

Choctaw By Blood Enrollment Cards 1898-1914

Dawes' Roll No.	NAME	Relationship to Person	AGE	SEX	BLOOD	TRIBAL ENROLLMENT		
						Year	County	No.
6598	1 McCurtain Edmond ²³	First Named	20	M	Full	1896	Sugar Loaf	9087
	2							
	3							
	4							
	5							
	6							
	7							
	8							
	9							
	10							
	11							
	12							
	13							
	14							
	15							
	16							
	17							

ENROLLMENT
OF NOS. 1 HEREON
APPROVED BY THE SECRETARY
OF INTERIOR JAN 17 1903

TRIBAL ENROLLMENT OF PARENTS

	Name of Father	Year	County	Name of Mother	Year	County
1	Cornelius McCurtain	Dead	Sugar Loaf	Louisa McCurtain	Dead	Sugar Loaf
2						
3						
4						
5						
6						
7						
8						
9						
10						
11						
12						
13						
14						
15						
16				Date of Application for Enrollment.		6/5/99
17						

Choctaw By Blood Enrollment Cards 1898-1914

RESIDENCE: Sugar Loaf
POST OFFICE: Wister I.T.

COUNTY. **Choctaw Nation**

Choctaw Roll
(Not Including Freedmen)

CARD No.
FIELD No. **2277**

Dawes' Roll No.		NAME		Relationship to Person First Named	AGE	SEX	BLOOD	TRIBAL ENROLLMENT		
								Year	County	No.
6599	1	Harrison Thomas	21	First Named	18	M	Full	1896	Sugar Loaf	2252
15421	2	" Cillin	23	Wife	23	F	"	1893	Tobucksy	98/820
15422	3	" Susan	1	Dau	9mo	F	"			
	4									
	5									
	6									
	7									
	8									
	9									
	10									
	11		ENROLLMENT OF NOS. 2 3 HEREON APPROVED BY THE SECRETARY OF INTERIOR May 9 1904							
	12									
	13									
	14									
	15		ENROLLMENT OF NOS. 1 HEREON APPROVED BY THE SECRETARY OF INTERIOR Jan 17 1903							
	16									
	17									

TRIBAL ENROLLMENT OF PARENTS

	Name of Father	Year	County	Name of Mother	Year	County
1	Dave Harrison	Ded	Kiamatia[sic]	Silin Tobley	Ded	Kiamatia[sic]
2	Unknown	Dead	Miss Choc	Nannie ---------	Dead	Choc in Miss
3	N° 1			N° 2		
4						
5						
6	No3 Born March 22, 1902. Enrolled Dec 17, 1902					
7	N°2 on 1893 Leased Dist pay roll Tobucksy Co as Cillin Willis					
8	No1 is husband of Sillin Harrison on Choctaw Card #D951					
9	Nos 2 and 3 transferred from Choctaw card #D951, March 19, 1904					
10						
11						
12						
13						
14						
15					#1	
16				Date of Application for Enrollment	6/5/99	
17	P.O. No2 LeFlore 3/16/04					

177

RESIDENCE:	Sugar Loaf	COUNTY.	**Choctaw Nation**		**Choctaw Roll**	CARD No.	
POST OFFICE:	Cavanal, I.T.				*(Not Including Freedmen)*	FIELD No.	2278

Dawes' Roll No.	NAME		Relationship to Person	AGE	SEX	BLOOD	TRIBAL ENROLLMENT		
							Year	County	No.
6600	1 Morris, Robert	41	First Named	38	M	1/2	1896	Sugar Loaf	8525
I.W. 103	2 " Corinne S M	41	Wife	38	F	I.W.	1896	" "	14809
6601	3 " William G	19	Son	16	M	1/4	1896	" "	8526
6602	4 " Robert A	17	"	14	"	1/4	1896	" "	8527
	5								
	6								
	7								
	8								
	9								
	10								
	11								
	12								
	13								
	14								
	15	ENROLLMENT OF NOS. 1, 3, 4, HEREON APPROVED BY THE SECRETARY OF INTERIOR JAN 17 1903		ENROLLMENT OF NOS. ~~ 2 ~~ HEREON APPROVED BY THE SECRETARY OF INTERIOR JUN 13 1903					
	16								
	17								

TRIBAL ENROLLMENT OF PARENTS

	Name of Father	Year	County	Name of Mother	Year	County
1	A.G. Morris	Dead	Sugar Loaf	Ho-to-na	Dead	Sugar Loaf
2	Jim Carter	"	Non Citz	Rebecca Carter		Non Citz
3	No 1			No 2		
4	No 1			No 2		
5						
6						
7						
8			As to marriage of Nos 1-2, see			
9			testimony of husband and Loren			
10			S. Folsom			
11			No3 on 1896 Roll as Wᵐ G Morris			
12			No4 " 1896 " " Robt A "			
13						
14						
15						
16				Date of Application for Enrollment.	June 5/99	
17						

178

Choctaw By Blood Enrollment Cards 1898-1914

RESIDENCE: Sugar Loaf   COUNTY. **Choctaw Nation**   **Choctaw Roll**   CARD No.
POST OFFICE: Howe, I.T.   *(Not Including Freedmen)*   FIELD No.   2279

Dawes' Roll No.	NAME	Relationship to Person	AGE	SEX	BLOOD	TRIBAL ENROLLMENT		
						Year	County	No.
✓ ✗	1 Lemmons, Ozilla	First Named	23	F	1/32			
DEAD.	2 " Walter F	Son	5	M	1/64			
	3							
	4							
	5							
	6							
	7							
	8	No. 2 HEREON DISMISSED UNDER ORDER OF THE COMMISSION TO THE FIVE						
	9	CIVILIZED TRIBES OF MARCH 31, 1905.						
	10							
	11							
	12	Nos 1&2 denied by Dawes Com in 1896 Choctaw Case #598						
	13							
	14							
	15							
	16							
	17							

TRIBAL ENROLLMENT OF PARENTS

	Name of Father	Year	County	Name of Mother	Year	County
1	A. U. Deaton	1896	Non Citz	Elizabeth Deaton	1896	Choctaw
2	J. G. Lemmons	1896	"	No 1		
3						
4						
5						
6	Admitted by U.S. Court, Central District, Aug 24/97					
7	Case No 94					
8						
9	As to residence see testimony of J.G. Lemmons					
10	N°2 Died Aug 30, 1899, Proof of death filed Oct 31, 1902					
11						
12						
13						
14						
15						
16					Date of Application for Enrollment.	6/5/99
17						

DENIED CITIZENSHIP BY THE CHOCTAW AND CHICKASAW CITIZENSHIP COURT

Choctaw By Blood Enrollment Cards 1898-1914

RESIDENCE: Sugar Loaf   COUNTY. **Choctaw Nation**   **Choctaw Roll**   CARD No.
POST OFFICE: Couser, I.T.   *(Not Including Freedmen)*   FIELD No. **2280**

Dawes' Roll No.	NAME		Relationship to Person	AGE	SEX	BLOOD	TRIBAL ENROLLMENT		
							Year	County	No.
6603	1 Couser, Peter	49	First Named	46	M	1/2	1896	Sugar Loaf	2202
6604	2 " Mary A Dead	32	Wife	29	F	Full	1896	" "	2203
6605	3 " Susie	30	Dau	27	"	3/4	1896	" "	2204
6606	4 " Lue	19	"	16	"	1/4	1896	" "	2205
6607	5 " Julius	17	Son	14	M	1/4	1896	" "	2207
6608	6 " Alice	15	Dau	12	F	1/4	1896	" "	2208
6609	7 " Ada	13	"	10	"	1/4	1896	" "	2209
6610	8 " Simeon	12	Son	9	M	1/4	1896	" "	2210
	9								
	10								
	11								
	12								
	13								
	14								
	15	ENROLLMENT OF NOS. 1,2,3,4,5,6,7,8 HEREON							
	16	APPROVED BY THE SECRETARY							
	17	OF INTERIOR Jan 17 1903							

TRIBAL ENROLLMENT OF PARENTS

	Name of Father	Year	County	Name of Mother	Year	County
1	Couser	Dead	Non Citz	Adaline Couser	Dead	Sugar Loaf
2	William Holson	"	Sugar Loaf	E-ma-te-a	"	" " "
3	No 1			Amy Couser	"	" " "
4	No 1			Jane Couser	"	" " "
5	No 1			" "	"	" " "
6	No 1			" "	"	" " "
7	No 1			" "	"	" " "
8	No 1			" "	"	" " "
9						
10	For child of No6 see NB (Apr 26-06) Card #775					
11	No5 on 1896 roll as Jules Couser					
12	No.4 is wife of Benjamin F. Spring, Choctaw Card No.2192.					
	As to marriage of No1 and Jane Couser, see					
13	testimony of No1					
14						
15	For child of No4 see NB (Mar 3-1905) Card #131				Date of Application for Enrollment	
16	" " " No3 " " " " " " #1104				6/5/99	
17	No4 P.O. Kinta IT 3/17/05					

180

Choctaw By Blood Enrollment Cards 1898-1914

RESIDENCE: Sugar Loaf
POST OFFICE: Cavanal I.T.

COUNTY. **Choctaw Nation**

Choctaw Roll
(Not Including Freedmen)

CARD NO.

FIELD NO. 2281

Dawes' Roll No.	NAME	Relationship to Person	AGE	SEX	BLOOD	TRIBAL ENROLLMENT		
						Year	County	No.
14729	1 Franklin Austin DIED PRIOR TO SEPTEMBER 25, 1902	First Named	21	M	Full	P.R. 1893	Sugar Loaf	213
14730	2 " Green 21	1/2 Bro	18	M	"	1896	Sugar Loaf	3956
	3							
	4	ENROLLMENT						
	5	OF NOS. 1 and 2 HEREON APPROVED BY THE SECRETARY						
	6	OF INTERIOR MAY 20 1903						
	7							
	8							
	9							
	10							
	11							
	12							
	13							
	14							
	15							
	16							
	17							

TRIBAL ENROLLMENT OF PARENTS

	Name of Father	Year	County	Name of Mother	Year	County
1	James Franklin	Dead	Sugar Loaf	Lucy Franklin	Dead	Sugar Loaf
2	" "	"	" " "	" "	"	" " "
3						
4						
5						
6	No 1 On 1893 Pay Roll, Page 21 No 213 Sugar Loaf Co:					
7	See copy of letter from W.A. Welch Jany 26, 1903 as to death of Nº1 and					
8	degree of Choctaw blood possessed by Nºs 1 and 2 filed herein Feby 9, 1903					
9						
10						
11						
12						
13						
14						
15						
16				Date of Application for Enrollment.		6/5/99
17						

| RESIDENCE: Skullyville | COUNTY. | Choctaw Roll | CARD NO. |
| POST OFFICE: Cameron, I.T. | **Choctaw Nation** | (Not Including Freedmen) | FIELD NO. **2282** |

Dawes' Roll No.	NAME		Relationship to Person	AGE	SEX	BLOOD	TRIBAL ENROLLMENT		
							Year	County	No.
6611	1 Wall Thomas J	54	First Named	51	M	1/2	1896	Skullyville	12762
6612	2 " Elizabeth R	54	Wife	51	F	1/4	1896	"	12763
6613	3 McClure Ida	25	Dau	22	"	3/8	1896	"	12764
6614	4 Wall Thomas B	21	Son	18	M	3/8	1896	"	12766
6615	5 " Eva B	19	Dau	16	F	3/8	1896	"	12767
6616	6 " Ella M	18	"	16	"	3/8	1896	"	12768
I.W. 716	7 McClure, Poker J	26	Hus of No3	26	M	I.W.			
	8								
	9	ENROLLMENT OF NOS. ~~ 7 ~~ HEREON APPROVED BY THE SECRETARY							
	10	OF INTERIOR May 7 1904							
	11								
	12	No2 on 1896 roll as Bettie Walls							
	13	No4 " 1896 " " Tom "							
		No5 " 1896 " " Eva "							
	14	No6 " 1896 " " Ella "							
	15	Surname of all appear on				ENROLLMENT OF NOS. 1,2,3,4,5,6 HEREON				
	16	1896 roll as "Walls"				APPROVED BY THE SECRETARY			
	17	No4 P.O. Brooken I.T. 10/6/02				OF INTERIOR Jan 17 1903			

TRIBAL ENROLLMENT OF PARENTS						
Name of Father	Year	County	Name of Mother	Year	County	
1 Thos. Wall	Dead	Skullyville	Catherine Wall	Dead	Skullyville	
2 Joseph Riddle	"	Sans Bois	Phoebe Riddle	"	Non Citz	
3	No 1		No 2			
4	No 1		No 2			
5	No 1		No 2			
6	No 1		No 2			
7 John H McClure		non citizen	Catherine McClure	Dead	non citizen	
8						
9	No3 is now the wife of Poker J McClure on Choctaw Card #D659 Aug 29, 1901					
10	No.7 transferred from Choctaw card #D659. See decision of Feby 27, 1904.					
11	The parents of No2 were married more than sixty years ago. There seems to be no					
12	doubt but that they were lawfully married					
13	but proof cannot be produced					
14	For child of No4 see NB (Mar 3rd 1905) #142					
15	" " " Nos3&7 " " " " #440				Date of Application for Enrollment.	
16	" " " No2 " " " " #564				6/5/99	
17	No3 P.O. Calvin I.T. 3/25/05					

Choctaw By Blood Enrollment Cards 1898-1914

RESIDENCE: Sugar Loaf   COUNTY.

POST OFFICE: Richard, I.T (Reichert) **Choctaw Nation**

Choctaw Roll *(Not Including Freedmen)*

CARD NO.

FIELD NO. 2283

Dawes' Roll No.	NAME		Relationship to Person First Named	AGE	SEX	BLOOD	TRIBAL ENROLLMENT		
							Year	County	No.
6617	1 Curtis, Luvicey	28	First Named	25	F	1/4	1896	Sugar Loaf	2231
6618	2 Robbins, David	13	Son	10	M	1/8	1893	" "	120
6619	3 Curtis, Larabelle	9	Dau	6	F	1/8	1896	" "	2232
6620	4 " Johnnie	7	Son	4	M	1/8	1896	" "	2233
6621	5 " Homer	3	"	3mo	M	1/8			
	6								
	7								
	8								
	9								
	10								
	11								
	12								
	13								
	14								
	15	ENROLLMENT OF NOS. 1,2,3,4,5 HEREON APPROVED BY THE SECRETARY OF INTERIOR JAN 17 1903							
	16								
	17								

TRIBAL ENROLLMENT OF PARENTS

	Name of Father	Year	County	Name of Mother	Year	County
1	Ward	Dead	Non Citz	Tobitha Heavener	1896	Sugar Loaf
2	Bill Robbins	1896	" "	No 1		
3	M. C. Curtis	1896	" "	No 1		
4	" " "	1896	" "	No 1		
5	" " "	1896	" "	No 1		
6						
7						
8						
9	No2 on 1893 Pay Roll, Page 12, No 120, Sugar Loaf County					
10	For child of No.1 see NB (March 3, 1905) #755					
11						
12						
13						
14						
15				#1 to 4		
16			Date of Application for Enrollment.	6/5/99		
17			No5 enrolled Nov 1/99			

183

Choctaw By Blood Enrollment Cards 1898-1914

	RESIDENCE: Sugar Loaf COUNTY.								
	POST OFFICE: Heavener, I.T		**Choctaw Nation**				Choctaw Roll *(Not Including Freedmen)*	CARD NO. / FIELD NO. 2284	

Dawes' Roll No.	NAME	Relationship to Person	AGE	SEX	BLOOD	TRIBAL ENROLLMENT		
						Year	County	No.
6622	1 Camp, Cordelia ⁹	First Named	6	F	1/4	1896	Sugar Loaf	2217
I.W. 1106	2 Goforth, Hanora ²⁸	Mother	28	F	I.W.	1896	Sugar Loaf	14384
	3							
	4							
	5							
	6							
	7							
	8							
	9							
	10							
	11							
	12							
	13							
	14							
	15							
	16							
	17							

ENROLLMENT
OF NOS. 1 HEREON
APPROVED BY THE SECRETARY
OF INTERIOR JAN 17 1903

ENROLLMENT
OF NOS. 2 HEREON
APPROVED BY THE SECRETARY
OF INTERIOR NOV 16 1904

TRIBAL ENROLLMENT OF PARENTS

	Name of Father	Year	County	Name of Mother	Year	County
1	Thomas Camp	Dead	Sugar Loaf	Hanora Goforth	1896	white woman
2	Philip Hennesy	1896	non-citz	Rebecca Hennesy	dead	non-citz
3						
4						
5						
6			Mother Hanora Goforth, on Card No D201			
7						
8						
9						
10			No.2 transferred from Choctaw card #D-201, Oct 31, 1904: See decision of Oct 15, 1904			
11			For child of No2 see NB (Apr 26 '06) #1104			
12						
13						
14						#1
15						Date of Application for Enrollment.
16						6/6/99
17						

Choctaw By Blood Enrollment Cards 1898-1914

RESIDENCE: Sugar Loaf	COUNTY.	CARD No.
POST OFFICE: Poteau, I.T	**Choctaw Nation**	**Choctaw Roll** (Not Including Freedmen)

FIELD No. **2285**

Dawes' Roll No.	NAME Stigler, I.T. 7/26 02	Relationship to Person	AGE	SEX	BLOOD	TRIBAL ENROLLMENT		
						Year	County	No.
✓ *	1 Jones, Nancy E	First Named	24	F	1/32			
✓ *	2 " James E	Son	5	M	1/64			
✓	3 " Hettie M	Dau	7mo	F	1/64			
6623	4 " William P 18	S.Son	15	M	3/16			
6624	5 " Myrtle L 14	S.Dau	11	F	3/16			
✓	6 " Vora Bell	Dau	1	F	1/64			
	7							
	8 Judgement of US Court CD admitting Nos 1&2 vacated and set							
	9 aside by Decree f Choctaw Chickasaw Citizenship Court Dec 7-02							
	10 Nos 1&2 denied by Choctaw Chickasaw Citizenship Court							
	Feb 11 '04 Case #13							
	11							
	12 Nos 1 and 2 DENIED CITIZENSHIP BY THE CHOCTAW AND							
	13 CHICKASAW CITIZENSHIP COURT Feb 11 '04							
	14 * Nos 1 and 2 denied by Dawes Com in 96 Choc Cit Case #598							
	15 ENROLLMENT							
	16 OF NOS. 4, 5 HEREON APPROVED BY THE SECRETARY							
	17 OF INTERIOR JAN 17 1903							

TRIBAL ENROLLMENT OF PARENTS

	Name of Father	Year	County	Name of Mother	Year	County
1	James Biddie	1896	Choctaw	Adaline Biddie	Dead	Non Citz
2	J.S Jones	1896	Non Citz	No 1		
3	" " "	1896	" "	No 1		
4	" " "	1896	" "	Nancy Jones	Dead	Skullyville
5	" " "	1896	" "	" "	"	"
6	" " "	1896	" "	Nº 1		
7						
8	*Nos 1-2 were admitted by the U.S. Court Central district					
9	January 19, 1898. Case No 94					
10	No5 on 1896 roll as Wm P. Jones					
11	No5 " 1896 " " Myrtle M "					
12	Nº6 Born May 11, 1901: enrolled July 26, 1902					
13						
14	Nos DISMISSED MAY 23 1904					
15						
16			Date of Application for Enrollment.	6/6/99		
17						

RESIDENCE: Sugar Loaf	COUNTY.					Choctaw Roll		CARD NO.	
POST OFFICE: Page, I.T.		Choctaw Nation				(Not Including Freedmen)		FIELD NO. 2286	

Dawes' Roll No.	NAME		Relationship to Person	AGE	SEX	BLOOD	TRIBAL ENROLLMENT		
							Year	County	No.
I.W. 244	1 McClure, John H	61	First Named	57	M	I.W.	1896	Sugar Loaf	1459
6625	2 " Biza	29	Wife	26	F	3/8	1896	" "	9121
6626	3 " Nellie C	9	Dau	6	"	3/16	1896	" "	9122
6627	4 " Jesse W	7	Son	4	M	3/16	1896	" "	9123
6628	5 " Rufus R	5	"	2	"	3/16			
6629	6 " Thomas M	2	Son	2mo	M	3/16			
6630	7 " Bertha	1	Dau	6wks	F	3/16			
	8								
	9	ENROLLMENT OF NOS. 1 HEREON APPROVED BY THE SECRETARY OF INTERIOR SEP 12 1903							
	10								
	11								
	12								
	13								
	14								
	15	ENROLLMENT OF NOS 2,3,4,5,6,7 HEREON APPROVED BY THE SECRETARY OF INTERIOR JAN 17 1903							
	16								
	17								

TRIBAL ENROLLMENT OF PARENTS

	Name of Father	Year	County	Name of Mother	Year	County
1	John McClure	Dead	Non Citz	Susan McClure	Dead	Non Citz
2	Thomas Wall	1896	Skullyville	Bettie Wall	1896	Skullyville
3	No 1			No 2		
4	No 1			No 2		
5	No 1			No 2		
6	No.1			No.2		
7	No.1			No.2		
8						
9						
10						
11	No1 on 1896 roll as Jno H McClure. Was admitted					
12	by Dawes Commission as an Intermarried Citizen,					
13	as John H McClure Case No 353					
	No3 admitted in same Case					
14	No4 " " " " as Jessie W McClure			#1 to 5		
15	No.6 Enrolled Aug 31st 1900			Date of Application for Enrollment.		
16	No.7 Born Jany 26, 1902; enrolled March 5, 1902			6/6/99		
17						

Choctaw By Blood Enrollment Cards 1898-1914

	RESIDENCE: Sugar Loaf COUNTY.					

Choctaw Nation   **Choctaw Roll** *(Not Including Freedmen)*

RESIDENCE: Sugar Loaf COUNTY.
POST OFFICE: Heavener, I.T.

CARD NO. FIELD NO. 2287

Dawes' Roll No.	NAME		Relationship to Person First Named	AGE	SEX	BLOOD	TRIBAL ENROLLMENT		
							Year	County	No.
I.W. 1247	1 Wilson, Alice	25		21	F	I.W.			
14731	2 Ward, Jimmie	4	Dau	1	F	1/8			
DP	3 Wilson, Earl		Son	3mo	M	white			
1/29/07	4								
	5								
	6	ENROLLMENT							
	7	OF NOS. 2 HEREON							
	8	APPROVED BY THE SECRETARY OF INTERIOR MAY 20 1903							
	9								
	10	ENROLLMENT							
	11	OF NOS. ~ 1 ~ HEREON							
	12	APPROVED BY THE SECRETARY OF INTERIOR DEC 30 1904							
	13								
	14								
	15								
	16								
	17								

TRIBAL ENROLLMENT OF PARENTS

	Name of Father	Year	County	Name of Mother	Year	County
1	W.I. Robinson	1896	Non Citz	Frances Robinson	1896	Non Citz
2	James Ward	Dead	Sugar Loaf	No 1		
3	Samuel R Wilson	1896	" "	No 1		

No.1 originally listed on this card as Alice Ward
Nº2 See affidavit of Tabitha Heavener as to birth, filed Oct 31, 1902
Sex of Nº2 is female.
No.1 is wife of Samuel R Wilson on Choc Card No 2377
Nº3 Born Sept. 14, 1902. Enrolled Dec 24, 1902
Father of Nº2 James Ward, on 1893 Sugar Loaf Co Choc payroll Nº266
No1 formerly wife of James Ward, 1893 Sugar Loaf No 266,
and who died January 18, 1898.

No.3 REFUSED FEB 7 1907

Date of Application for Enrollment. 6/6/99

187

Choctaw By Blood Enrollment Cards 1898-1914

RESIDENCE: Skullyville COUNTY.
POST OFFICE: Shady Point, I.T.

Choctaw Nation

Choctaw Roll
(Not Including Freedmen)

CARD NO.
FIELD NO. 2288

Dawes' Roll No.	NAME	Relationship to Person	AGE	SEX	BLOOD	TRIBAL ENROLLMENT		
						Year	County	No.
I.W. 104	1 Monks, Francis M 73	First Named	70	M	I.W	1896	Skullyville	14802
	2							
	3							
	4							
	5							
	6							
	7							
	8							
	9							
	10							
	11							
	12							
	13							
	14							
	15	ENROLLMENT OF NOS. 1 ------- HEREON APPROVED BY THE SECRETARY OF INTERIOR JUN 13 1903						
	16							
	17							

TRIBAL ENROLLMENT OF PARENTS

	Name of Father	Year	County	Name of Mother	Year	County
1	James Monks	Dead	Non Citz	Nancy Monks	Dead	Non Citz
2						
3						
4						
5	Further action in connection with allotment to No.1 suspended under protest of					
6	Attorneys for Choctaw and Chickasaw Nation June 23 1904					
7	Protest over ruled by Dept March 31, 1904					
8	Admitted as an Intermarried Citizen by Dawes Commission as F. M. Monks, Case No 367					
9	No 1 is the husband of No2 and father of Nos 3 to 10 inclusive					
10	on Choctaw rejected card #R195					
11						
12						
13						
14						
15						
16				Date of Application for Enrollment.	6/6/99	
17	P.O. Sutter I.T. 4/13/03					

188

Choctaw By Blood Enrollment Cards 1898-1914

Dawes' Roll No.	NAME	Relationship to Person First Named	AGE	SEX	BLOOD	TRIBAL ENROLLMENT Year	County	No.
✓ ✳	1 Deaton, Elizabeth	Named	55	F	1/4			
✓ ✳	2 " Abel	Son	16	M	1/8			
	3							
	4							
	5							
	6							
	7							
	8							
	9							
	10							
	11							
	12							
	13							
	14							
	15							
	16							
	17							

(Watermark: DENIED CITIZENSHIP BY THE CHOCTAW AND CHICKASAW CITIZENSHIP COURT, Feb 1 '04)

TRIBAL ENROLLMENT OF PARENTS

Name of Father	Year	County	Name of Mother	Year	County
1 J. J. Biddie	Dead	Choctaw	Mary J. Biddie	Dead	Non Citz
2 Abel Deaton	1896	Non Citz	No 1		
3					
4					
5					
6					
7 Nos1&2 denied by Dawes Com in 96 Choc Cit Case #598					
8 Admitted by US Court, Central District,					
9 January 18, 1898, Case No 94					
10 As to residence, see testimony of No1					
11					
12					
13					
14					
15					
16			Date of Application for Enrollment.	6/6/99	
17					

189

Choctaw By Blood Enrollment Cards 1898-1914

RESIDENCE:	Sugar Loaf
POST OFFICE:	Heavener, I.T.

Choctaw Nation COUNTY.

Choctaw Roll (Not Including Freedmen)

CARD NO.

FIELD NO. 2290

Dawes' Roll No.	NAME		Relationship to Person First Named	AGE	SEX	BLOOD	TRIBAL ENROLLMENT		
							Year	County	No.
DEAD.	1 Jefferson, Joe			29	M	Full	1896	Sugar Loaf	6490
6631	2 " Jonie	9	Dau	6	F	"	1896	" "	6492
6632	3 " Edna	6	"	3	"	"	1896	" "	6493
I.W. 1298	4 " Annie	18	Wife	18	F	I.W.			
	5								
	6								
	7								
	8	NO. 1 HEREON DISMISSED UNDER							
	9	ORDER OF THE COMMISSION TO THE FIVE							
	10	CIVILIZED TRIBES OF MARCH 31, 1905.							
	11	ENROLLMENT							
	12	OF NOS. 4 HEREON							
	13	APPROVED BY THE SECRETARY OF INTERIOR MAR 14 1905							
	14								
	15	ENROLLMENT							
	16	OF NOS. 2, 3, HEREON APPROVED BY THE SECRETARY							
	17	OF INTERIOR JAN 17 1903							

TRIBAL ENROLLMENT OF PARENTS

	Name of Father	Year	County	Name of Mother	Year	County
1	Henry Jefferson	Dead	Sugar Loaf	Sarah Jefferson	1896	Sugar Loaf
2	No 1			Sis Jefferson	Dead	" "
3	No 1			" "	"	" "
4	Marion Kennedy	dead	non citz	Lou Kennedy		non citz
5						
6						
7	For child of No4 see Chick NB (Apr 26-06) Card #292					
8	Not on 1896 roll as Josiah Jefferson					
9	No2 " 1896 " " Joni "					
10	No1 Died Feby 22, 1902; Proof of death filed Oct 9, 1902					
11	Nos 1 and 4 were married in Jan. 1901. No.4 has not remarried					
12	No.4 originally listed for enrollment on Choctaw card D-934 Dec. 17, 1902; transferred to this card Jan 29,1905. See decision of Jan 13, 1905					
13						
14						
15						
16				Date of Application for Enrollment	6/6/99	
17	No.4 P.O. South McAlester 1/12/05					

Choctaw By Blood Enrollment Cards 1898-1914

RESIDENCE: Sugar Loaf	COUNTY. **Choctaw Nation**	**Choctaw Roll** *(Not Including Freedmen)*	CARD No.
POST OFFICE: Wister, I.T.			FIELD NO. 2291

Dawes' Roll No.	NAME	Relationship to Person First Named	AGE	SEX	BLOOD	TRIBAL ENROLLMENT		
						Year	County	No.
✓	1 Blassingame, Arabella	Named	19	F	1/8			
✓	2 " Bonnie May	Dau	2mo	"	1/16			
✓	3 " Robert Dixie	Son	1mo	M	1/16			
	4							
	5							
N⁰ˢ 2and3 6	DISMISSED							
	7							
	8							
	9							
	10							
	11							
	12							
	13							
	14							
	15							
	16							
	17							

TRIBAL ENROLLMENT OF PARENTS

	Name of Father	Year	County	Name of Mother	Year	County
1	Abel Deaton	1896	Non Citz	Elizabeth Deaton	1896	Choctaw
2	Robt. Blassingame	1896	" "	No 1		
3	" " "	"	" "	No.1		
4						
5	DENIED CITIZENSHIP BY THE CHOCTAW AND					
6	CHICKASAW CITIZENSHIP COURT					
7	No1 denied by Dawes Com in '96 Choc Cit Case #598					
8	Admitted by U.S. Court, Central District, January					
9	19, 1898; Case No 94, as Arabella Deaton					
	As to residence see testimony of No1					
10						
11						
12	No.3 Enrolled July 7th, 1902					
13						
14						
15						
16			Date of Application for Enrollment.	6/6/99		
17						

Choctaw By Blood Enrollment Cards 1898-1914

RESIDENCE:		COUNTY. **Choctaw Nation**				**Choctaw Roll**		CARD NO.
POST OFFICE:						*(Not Including Freedmen)*		FIELD NO. **2292**

Dawes' Roll No.	NAME	Relationship to Person First Named	AGE	SEX	BLOOD	TRIBAL ENROLLMENT		
						Year	County	No.
✓ ✗ 1	Powell, John D	First Named	26	M	1/8			
✓ 2	" Willie	Wife	19	F	I.W.			
✓ 3	" Topsy Belle	Dau	7mo	"	1/16			
✓ 4	" Walcy May	Dau	2mo	F	1/16			
5								
No.1 6	DENIED CITIZENSHIP BY THE CHOCTAW AND							
7	CHICKASAW CITIZENSHIP COURT							
8								
No.? 9	DISMISSED MAY 7 1904							
10								
11								
12								
Nos 13	DISMISSED							
3and4 14	MAY 23 1904							
15								
16								
17								

TRIBAL ENROLLMENT OF PARENTS

	Name of Father	Year	County	Name of Mother	Year	County
1	John Powell	Dead	Non Citz	Elizabeth Deaton	1896	Choctaw
2	Freeland Haley	"	" "	Nancy Haley	Dead	Non Citz
3	No 1			No 2		
4	No 1			No 2		
5						
6	✗No1 Denied by Dawes Com in 96 Choc Cit Case #598					
7	✗No1 Admitted by U.S. Court Central District, January					
8	18, 1898, Case No 94. Married February 18, 1898.					
9	As to residence see his testimony					
	No.4 Enrolled June 13, 1901					
10						
11						
12						
13						
14						
15						
16			Date of Application for Enrollment.	6/6/99		
17						

192

Choctaw By Blood Enrollment Cards 1898-1914

RESIDENCE: Sugar Loaf	COUNTY.							
POST OFFICE: Cavanah, I.T.	**Choctaw Nation**				**Choctaw Roll** (Not Including Freedmen)	CARD NO. FIELD NO. 2293		

Dawes' Roll No.	NAME	Relationship to Person First Named	AGE	SEX	BLOOD	TRIBAL ENROLLMENT		
						Year	County	No.
✓ ✗ 1	Deaton, Lockey		21	M	1/8			
2								
3								
4								
5								
6								
7								
8								
9								
10								
11								
12								
13								
14								
15								
16								
17								

TRIBAL ENROLLMENT OF PARENTS

	Name of Father	Year	County	Name of Mother	Year	County
1	Abel Deaton	1896	Non Citz	Elizabeth Deaton	1896	Choctaw
2						
3						
4						
5						
6						
7	Not denied by Dawes Com in '96 Choc Cit Case #598					
8	Admitted by U.S. Court, Central District, January 19, 1898, Case No 94.					
9	As to residence, see his testimony.					
10	Judgement by U.S. Court affirming was vacated and set aside by Decree of Choctaw Chickasaw Citizenship Court Dec 17/02					
10	Not denied by Choctaw-Chickasaw Citizenship Court Feb 17d					
11						
12						
13						
14						
15						
16	P.O. Wister			Date of Application for Enrollment.	6/6/99	
17	10/11/02					

193

Choctaw By Blood Enrollment Cards 1898-1914

Dawes' Roll No.	NAME		Relationship to Person First Named	AGE	SEX	BLOOD	TRIBAL ENROLLMENT		
							Year	County	No.
6633	1 Hill, Easter	40	First Named	37	F	Full	1896	Sugar Loaf	5234
6634	2 " Sissie	23	Dau	20	"	"	1896	" "	5236
6635	3 " Winnie	18	"	15	"	"	1896	" "	5237
6636	4 " Emma	13	"	10	"	"	1896	" "	5238
	5								
	6								
	7								
	8								
	9								
	10								
	11								
	12								
	13								
	14								
	15								
	16								
	17								

ENROLLMENT
OF NOS. 1, 2, 3, 4,
APPROVED BY THE SECRETARY HEREON
OF INTERIOR JAN 17 1903

TRIBAL ENROLLMENT OF PARENTS

	Name of Father	Year	County	Name of Mother	Year	County
1	George Dwight	1896	Sugar Loaf	Selina Dwight	Dead	Sugar Loaf
2	Coleman Hill	Dead	" "	No 1		
3	" "	"	" "	No 1		
4	" "	"	" "	No 1		
5						
6						
7						
8			No1 on 1896 roll as Esther Hill			
9			No4 " 1896 " " Anna "			
10						
11						
12						
13						
14					Date of Application for Enrollment.	
15						
16					6/6/99	
17						

Choctaw By Blood Enrollment Cards 1898-1914

RESIDENCE: Sugar Loaf	COUNTY. **Choctaw Nation**	**Choctaw Roll** *(Not Including Freedmen)*	CARD NO.
POST OFFICE: Poteau, I.T			FIELD NO. 2295

Dawes' Roll No.	NAME		Relationship to Person	AGE	SEX	BLOOD	TRIBAL ENROLLMENT		
							Year	County	No.
6637	1 Beard, Sillen	47	First Named	44	F	1/2	1896	Sugar Loaf	808
6638	2 " Eric C	13	Son	10	M	1/4	1896	" "	809
	3								
	4								
	5								
	6								
	7								
	8								
	9								
	10								
	11								
	12								
	13								
	14	ENROLLMENT							
	15	OF NOS. 1, 2 HEREON APPROVED BY THE SECRETARY							
	16	OF INTERIOR JAN 17 1903							
	17								

TRIBAL ENROLLMENT OF PARENTS

Name of Father	Year	County	Name of Mother	Year	County
1 Davis James	Dead	Chick Roll	Ta-ma-le-luma	Dead	Skullyville
2 Walter Beard	1896	Non Citz	No 1		
3					
4					
5					
6	No2 on 1896 roll as E.C. Beard				
7					
8					
9					
10					
11					
12					
13					
14					
15					
16			Date of Application for Enrollment.	6/6/99	
17					

195

RESIDENCE: Sugar Loaf		COUNTY.							
POST OFFICE: Wister, I.T			Choctaw Nation				Choctaw Roll (Not Including Freedmen)	CARD No. FIELD No.	2296

Dawes' Roll No.	NAME		Relationship to Person	AGE	SEX	BLOOD	TRIBAL ENROLLMENT		
							Year	County	No.
6639	1 Taylor, Emiline	34	First Named	31	F	Full	1896	Sugar Loaf	11951
6640	2 " Phoebe	9	Dau	6	"	"	1896	" "	11952
6641	3 " Alice	6	"	3	"	"	1896	" "	11953
6642	4 " Charles	3	Son	9mo	M	"			
	5								
	6								
	7								
	8								
	9								
	10								
	11								
	12								
	13								
	14								
	15	ENROLLMENT OF NOS. 1, 2, 3, 4 HEREON APPROVED BY THE SECRETARY OF INTERIOR JAN 17 1903							
	16								
	17								

TRIBAL ENROLLMENT OF PARENTS

	Name of Father	Year	County	Name of Mother	Year	County
1	Tecumseh Perry	Dead	Sugar Loaf	Lizzie Perry	Dead	Sugar Loaf
2	Solomon Taylor	"	" " "	No 1		
3	" "	"	" " "	No 1		
4	" "	"	" " "	No 1		
5						
6						
7						
8	No.4 Enrolled Aug. 28, 1900					
9						
10	No.1 is now Wife of Abel King on Choctaw card #2895. Evidence					
11	of marriage to be supplied, Dec. 18, 1902. For child of No1 see NB (March 3, 1905) #816					
12						
13						
14					#1 to 3	
15						
16				Date of Application for Enrollment:	6/6/99	
17						

196

RESIDENCE: Skullyville   COUNTY.
POST OFFICE: Cameron, I.T.

Choctaw Nation

Choctaw Roll
(Not Including Freedmen)

CARD NO.
FIELD NO. 2297

Dawes' Roll No.	NAME	Relationship to Person First Named	AGE	SEX	BLOOD	TRIBAL ENROLLMENT		
						Year	County	No.
I.W. 903	1 McClure, Mary F (48)	First Named	44	F	I.W.	1896	Skullyville	14857
6643	2 " Garret T (19)	Son	16	M	3/8	1896	"	9067
6644	3 " Albert J (17)	"	14	"	3/8	1896	"	9068
6645	4 " Alfred W (17)	"	14	"	3/8	1896	"	9069
6646	5 " Artemissa (13)	Dau	10	F	3/8	1896	"	9070
6647	6 " Josephine (10)	"	7	"	3/8	1896	"	9071
	7							
	8							
	9							
	10							
	11	ENROLLMENT OF NOS. 1 HEREON APPROVED BY THE SECRETARY OF INTERIOR AUG 3 1904						
	12							
	13							
	14							
	15	ENROLLMENT OF NOS. 2,3,4,5,6 HEREON APPROVED BY THE SECRETARY OF INTERIOR JAN 17 1903						
	16							
	17							

TRIBAL ENROLLMENT OF PARENTS

	Name of Father	Year	County	Name of Mother	Year	County
1	W. S. Hutchison	1896	Non Citz	Rebecca Hutchison	Dead	Non Citz
2	W. W. McClure	Dead	Skullyville	No 1		
3	" " "	"	"	No 1		
4	" " "	"	"	No 1		
5	" " "	"	"	No 1		
6	" " "	"	"	No 1		
7						
8	No5 on 1896 roll as Arty M McClure					
9						
10	As to marriage see her testimony and that of Margaret Wade					
11						
12	For child of No.2 see N.B. (Apr. 26, 1906) Card No 185					
13						
14						
15						
16			Date of Application for Enrollment.	6/6/99		
17	No2 P.O. Cameron IT 4/21/06					

Choctaw By Blood Enrollment Cards 1898-1914

RESIDENCE: Sugar Loaf   COUNTY. **Choctaw Nation**   **Choctaw Roll** CARD No.
POST OFFICE: Poteau, I.T.   (Not Including Freedmen) FIELD No. **2298**

Dawes' Roll No.		NAME		Relationship to Person	AGE	SEX	BLOOD	TRIBAL ENROLLMENT		
								Year	County	No.
6648	1	Sage, Sidney	37	First Named	34	M	1/64	1896	Sugar Loaf	11163
I.W. 1527	2	" Carrie	33	Wife	32	F	I.W.			
6649	3	" Woody	16	Son	13	M	1/128	1896	Sugar Loaf	11164
6650	4	" Cora E	14	Dau	11	F	1/128	1896	" "	11165
6651	5	" John	7	Son	4	M	1/128	1896	" "	11166
6652	6	" Myrtle	5	Son	2	M	1/128			
6653	7	" Maude	3	Dau	5mo	F	1/128			
6654	8	" Eugene	1	Son	1mo	M	1/128			
	9									
	10									
	11	ENROLLMENT								
	12	OF NOS. ~~~ 2 ~~~ HEREON APPROVED BY THE SECRETARY								
	13	OF INTERIOR Mar 14 1906								
	14									
	15	ENROLLMENT OF NOS. 1,3,4,5,6,7,8 HEREON								
	16	APPROVED BY THE SECRETARY								
	17	OF INTERIOR Jan 17 1903								

TRIBAL ENROLLMENT OF PARENTS

	Name of Father	Year	County	Name of Mother	Year	County
1	Jim Sage	1896	Non Citz	Jane F. Sage	1896	Sugar Loaf
2	George French	Dead	" "	Esther French	1896	" "
3	No 1			No 2		
4	No 1			No 2		
5	No 1			No 2		
6	No 1			No 2		
7	No 1			No 2		
8	No 1			No 2		
9						
10	No4 on 1896 roll as Astor Sage					
11	No6 Affidavit of birth to be supplied: Recd June 8/99					
12	As to marriage see testimony of No1 and that of Chas M. Bagwell					
13	No6 is male. Sex changed under Department authority					
14	of March 20, 1906 (I.T. 4562-1906) D.C. 10930-1906		No2 Granted			
15	No7 Enrolled May 24, 1900		Nov 6 – 1905		#1 to 6 inc	
16	No8 Born March 7, 1902: enrolled Aril 25, 1902					
17	For child of Nos 1&2 see NB (March 3, 1905) #790		Date of Application for Enrollment			
	P.O. Talihina I.T				6/6/99	

198

Choctaw By Blood Enrollment Cards 1898-1914

RESIDENCE: Sugar Loaf   COUNTY. **Choctaw Nation**   Choctaw Roll   CARD NO.
POST OFFICE: Poteau, I.T.   *(Not Including Freedmen)*   FIELD NO. 2299

Dawes' Roll No.	NAME		Relationship to Person Named	AGE	SEX	BLOOD	TRIBAL ENROLLMENT		
							Year	County	No.
6655	1 Page, William C	39	First Named	36	M	3/4	1896	Sugar Loaf	10143
6656	2 " Ella L	15	Dau	12	F	3/8	1896	" "	10144
6657	3 " Nellie F	11	"	8	"	3/8	1896	" "	10146
6658	4 " Allen W	8	Son	5	M	3/8	1896	" "	10147
6659	5 " William B	6	"	3	"	3/8	1896	" "	10148
6660	6 " Joseph M	4	"	7mo	"	3/8			
6661	7 " Edmund Monroe	1	Son	3wks	M	3/8			
I.W. 30	8 Page, Jane		Wife of No1	42	F	I.W.			
	9								
	10								
	11								
	12								
	13								
	14								
	15								
	16								
	17								

ENROLLMENT
OF NOS. ~~~ 8 ~~~ HEREON
APPROVED BY THE SECRETARY
OF INTERIOR JUN 13 1903

ENROLLMENT
OF NOS. 1,2,3,4,5,6,7, HEREON
APPROVED BY THE SECRETARY
OF INTERIOR JAN 17 1903

	TRIBAL ENROLLMENT OF PARENTS					
	Name of Father	Year	County	Name of Mother	Year	County
1	John Page	Dead	Skullyville	Jane Page	1896	Skullyville
2	No 1			Jane Page	1896	white woman
3	No 1			" "	1896	" "
4	No 1			" "	1896	" "
5	No 1			" "	1896	" "
6	No 1			" "	1896	" "
7	No 1			" "	1896	" "
8	James Duncan	Dead	Non Citz	Jane Duncan	1896	Non citz
9						
10	No1 on 1896 roll as W^m C Page					
11	No5 " 1896 " " W^m B "					
12						
13	Wife of No1, Jane Page, on Card No D205					
14	No7 Enrolled Sept 24, 1904					
15	No8 transferred from Choctaw card #D205 March 29, 1903			#1 to 6		
16	See decision of March 13, 1903			Date of Application for Enrollment.		
17				6/6/99		

Choctaw By Blood Enrollment Cards 1898-1914

RESIDENCE:	Gaines	COUNTY.								
POST OFFICE:	Wilburton, I.T.		**Choctaw Nation**				**Choctaw Roll** (Not Including Freedmen)	CARD NO. FIELD NO. 2300		

Dawes' Roll No.	NAME	Relationship to Person First Named	AGE	SEX	BLOOD	TRIBAL ENROLLMENT		
						Year	County	No.
✓ *	1 Broome, Alhanan	Named	43	M	1/4			
✓ *	2 " Mary	Wife	31	F	I.W.			
✓ *	3 " Alhanan Jr	Son	6	M	1/8			
✓ *	4 " Eunice	Dau	4	F	1/8			
✓	5 " Mary	Dau	5mo	F	1/8			
✓	6 " Eleanor	Dau	3wks	F	1/8			
	Nos 1,2,3,4 DENIED CITIZENSHIP BY THE CHOCTAW AND							
	8 CHICKASAW CITIZENSHIP COURT							
	9							
	10 Nos 1 to 6 incl denied by Com id 96 Case # 258							
	11 Judgement[sic] of U.S.C.C. admitting Nos 1 to 6 incl vacated and set							
	12 aside by Decree of Choctaw Chickasaw Cit Court Dec 17 '02							
	12 Nos 1,2,3 &4 in C.C.C.C. Case #55 3/12/02							
	13 * Nos 1 to 4 incl denied by C.C.C.C. Case #55 March 14th 04							
	14							
	15							
	16 Nos 5 & 6 DISMISSED							
	17 MAY 23 1904							

TRIBAL ENROLLMENT OF PARENTS

Name of Father	Year	County	Name of Mother	Year	County
1 J. C. Broome	Dead	Non Citz	Mary E Broome	Dead	Choctaw
2 J. H. Lake	"	" "	Rachel Lake	1896	Non Citz
3	No 1		No 2		
4	No 1		No 2		
5	No 1		No 2		
6	No 1		No 2		
7	All admitted by U.S. Court Central District, September				
8	1, 1897, Case No 241				
9	No 1 was admitted as Alhannan Broome				
	No 3 " " " Alhannan "				
10	No 2 " " " an Intermarried Citz				
11					
12	As to residence, see testimony of No 1				
13	No 5 Enrolled May 24, 1900.				
14	No 6 born Nov 17, 1901: Enrolled Dec. 7, 1901.				
15				Date of Application for Enrollment.	
16				6/6/99	
17					

Choctaw By Blood Enrollment Cards 1898-1914

RESIDENCE: Gaines   COUNTY. **Choctaw Nation**   **Choctaw Roll** *(Not Including Freedmen)*   CARD No.

POST OFFICE: Wilburton, I.T.   FIELD No. 2301

Dawes' Roll No.	NAME	Relationship to Person First Named	AGE	SEX	BLOOD	TRIBAL ENROLLMENT		
						Year	County	No.
✓	1 Broome, Frank P	Named	45	M	1/4			
✓	2 " Elizabeth	Wife	36	F	I.W.			
	3							
	4							
	5							
	6							
	7							
	8							
	v9							
	10							
	11							
	12							
	13							
	14							
	15							
	16							
	17							

TRIBAL ENROLLMENT OF PARENTS

	Name of Father	Year	County	Name of Mother	Year	County
1	J. C. Broome	Dead	Non Citz	Mary E Broome	Dead	Choctaw
2	George Back	"	" "	America Back	"	Non Citz
3						
4						
5						
6						
7	Nos 1and2 denied by Com in '96 Case #1258					
8	Nos 1&2 Admitted by U.S. Court, Central District,					
9	Sept 1, 1897, Case No 241					
	As to residence, see testimony of No 1					
10	Judgment by U.S. Court finding Nos 1and2 ~~~					
11						
12						
13						
14						
15						
16				Date of Application for Enrollment.	6/6/99	
17						

DENIED CITIZENSHIP BY THE CHOCTAW AND CHICKASAW CITIZENSHIP COURT

201

Choctaw By Blood Enrollment Cards 1898-1914

RESIDENCE: Sugar Loaf   COUNTY, **Choctaw Nation**   **Choctaw Roll**   CARD No.
POST OFFICE: Howe I.T.   (Not Including Freedmen)   FIELD No. 2302

Dawes' Roll No.	NAME		Relationship to Person	AGE	SEX	BLOOD	TRIBAL ENROLLMENT		
							Year	County	No.
6662	1 Benton Edward	34	First Named	31	M	Full	1896	Sugar Loaf	794
I.W. 105	2 " " Evline[sic]	28	Wife	25	F	I.W.			
	3								
	4								
	5								
	6								
	7								
	8								
	9								
	10								
	11								
	12								
	13								
	14								
	15								
	16								
	17								

ENROLLMENT OF NOS. 1 HEREON APPROVED BY THE SECRETARY OF INTERIOR JAN 17 1903

ENROLLMENT OF NOS. 2 ~~~~ HEREON APPROVED BY THE SECRETARY OF INTERIOR JUN 13 1903

TRIBAL ENROLLMENT OF PARENTS

	Name of Father	Year	County	Name of Mother	Year	County
1	Mia-shan-ta	Dead			Dead	
2	Hugh McVey	Dead	Non-citizen	Mary McVey		Non-citizen
3						
4						
5						
6		No. 2	Enrolled June 14,	1900.		
7						
8						
9						
10						
11						
12						
13						
14						#1
15					Date of Application for Enrollment	
16					For No 1 - 6/6/99	
17						

Choctaw By Blood Enrollment Cards 1898-1914

RESIDENCE: Sans Bois
POST OFFICE: Stigler I.T.

COUNTY. **Choctaw Nation**

Choctaw Roll
(Not Including Freedmen)

CARD NO.
FIELD NO. **2303**

Dawes' Roll No.	NAME	Relationship to Person First Named	AGE	SEX	BLOOD	TRIBAL ENROLLMENT Year	County	No.
I.W. 1628	1 Allen Andrew J 63	First Named	60	M	I.W.			
16193	2 " Elizabeth 65	Wife	62	F	1/8			
15551A	3							
	4 DP No. L&2 2/15/06							
	5 No-1 Dismissed							
	6 Sept 20 1904							
	7 No.2 Dismissed							
	8 Nov 4-1905							
	9 Granted Dec 19 1906							
	10							
	11		March 1, 1909 Department requests report as to No.2					
	12		March 25, 1909 Full report to Department					
	13				1&2 Granted			
	14	ENROLLMENT OF NOS. ~~~ 1 ~~~ HEREON APPROVED BY THE SECRETARY OF INTERIOR Feb 19 1907						
	15			ENROLLMENT OF NOS. ~~ 2 ~~ HEREON APPROVED BY THE SECRETARY OF INTERIOR Mar 4 1907				
	16							
	17							

TRIBAL ENROLLMENT OF PARENTS

	Name of Father	Year	County	Name of Mother	Year	County
1	Nathan A Allen	Dead	Non Citz	Nancy Allen	Dead	Non Citz
2	Thomas Samuel	"	Mississippi	Nancy Reed	"	Mississippi
3	No.1 restored to roll by Departmental authority of January 19, 1909) File 5-51					
4	Enrollment of No.1 cancelled by order of Department March 4, 1907					
5	Nos 1and 2 admitted by Dawes Com 96 cet Case #488 No1 also admitted in 96 case 49-0					
6	No1 Andrew J Allen admitted by U.S. Courts at S. McAlester					
7	Aug 25-97 Case #T32 as intermarried citizen in name					
8	of A.J. Allen. Elizabeth Allen admitted at the same time as a citizen by blood					
9	As to residence see testimony of Andrew J Allen above					
10	Judgement[sic] of U.S.Court admitting Nos 1and 2 vacated and set aside by Decree of Choctaw Chickasaw Citizenship					
11	No appeal to C.C.C.C.					Ct Decd 17'02
12						
13	[On back]					
14	By authority of Departmental letter of September 18,1909 (File 551) words and lines					Date of Application for Enrollment.
15	purporting cancellation to be regarded as eased and without effect in so far as					
16	they relate to name opposite number 15551; said number for identification to be distinguished by the addition of the letter "A"					6/6/99
17						

(over)
203

Choctaw By Blood Enrollment Cards 1898-1914

RESIDENCE: San Bois		COUNTY.							
POST OFFICE: San Bois I.T.									

Choctaw Nation

Choctaw Roll (*Not Including Freedmen*)

CARD NO.

FIELD NO. 2304

Dawes' Roll No.	NAME		Relationship to Person	AGE	SEX	BLOOD	TRIBAL ENROLLMENT		
							Year	County	No.
6663	1 Cobb, Lewis W	54	First Named	51	M	Full	1896	Jacks Fork	3001
6664	2 Loman William	19	Neph	16	M	"	1896	" "	8369
	3								
	4								
	5								
	6								
	7								
	8								
	9								
	10								
	11								
	12								
	13								
	14								
	15								
	16								
	17								

ENROLLMENT
OF NOS. 1, 2 HEREON
APPROVED BY THE SECRETARY
OF INTERIOR JAN 17 1903

TRIBAL ENROLLMENT OF PARENTS

	Name of Father	Year	County	Name of Mother	Year	County
1	William Cobb	Dead	Towson	Sophia Cobb	Dead	Towson
2	John Loman	"	Jacks Fork	Mary Loman	"	Atoka
3						
4						
5						
6	On 1896 roll as L.W. Cobb					
7						
8						
9						
10						
11						
12						
13						
14						
15						
16					Date of Application for Enrollment.	6/6/99
17						

204

Choctaw By Blood Enrollment Cards 1898-1914

RESIDENCE: Sugar Loaf
POST OFFICE: Monroe I.T.

COUNTY. **Choctaw Nation**

Choctaw Roll (Not Including Freedmen)

CARD NO.
FIELD NO. 2305

Dawes' Roll No.	NAME	Relationship to Person Named	AGE	SEX	BLOOD	TRIBAL ENROLLMENT		
						Year	County	No.
I.W. 31	1 Tucker Edward T 36	First Named	33	M	I.W.	1896	Sugar Loaf	15093
6665	2 " Lona 29	Wife	26	F	1/4	1896	" "	11959
6666	3 " Ethel 9	Dau	6	F	1/8	1896	" "	11960
6667	4 " Simual[sic] C 8	Son	5	M	1/8	1896	" "	11961
6668	5 " Edith 7	Dau	4	F	1/8	1896	" "	11962
6669	6 Griffith Ida L 19	Sister in Law	16	F	1/4	1896	" "	4676
6670	7 Tucker, Hilda 2	Dau	6mo	F	1/8			
	8							
	9							
	10							
	11	ENROLLMENT OF NOS. ~~~ 1 ~~~ HEREON APPROVED BY THE SECRETARY OF INTERIOR JUN 13 1903				No		
	12							
	13							
	14	ENROLLMENT OF NOS. 2,3,4,5,6,7 HEREON APPROVED BY THE SECRETARY OF INTERIOR JAN 17 1903						
	15							
	16							
	17							

TRIBAL ENROLLMENT OF PARENTS

	Name of Father	Year	County	Name of Mother	Year	County
1	J.B. Tucker	1896	Non Citz	Elizabeth Tucker	1896	Non Citz
2	Monroe Griffith	Dead	Non Citz	Martha Griffith	Dead	Sugar Loaf
3	No 1			No 2		
4	No 1			No 2		
5	No 1			No 2		
6	Monroe Griffith	Dead	Non Citz	Martha Griffith	Dead	Sugar Loaf
7	No.1			No.2		
8						
9	No1 On 1896 roll as Edward Tucker					
10	No4 " " " " Samuel C Tucker					
11	No6 Sister of Lona Tucker above on 1896 roll as Ida Lee Griffith					
12	No1 admitted as an intermarried citizen, and Nos 2,3and4 (Error should be 3,4,&5)					
13	as citizens by blood by Dawes Commission Choctaw case #294: No appeal.					
14	No.7 Enrolled June 25, 1901					#1 to 6
15	N°6 Evidence of marriage to Thomas B Wall filed Jany 2, 1903					Date of Application for Enrollment.
16	For child of No6 see NB (Mar 3rd 1905) Card #142 " children " No1&2 " " " " " " #295					6/6/99
17	P.O. Cameron, I.T. 12/7/02					

Choctaw By Blood Enrollment Cards 1898-1914

RESIDENCE: Sugar Loaf   COUNTY. **Choctaw Nation**   **Choctaw Roll** CARD NO.
POST OFFICE: Gilmon I.T.   *(Not Including Freedmen)*   FIELD NO. 2306

Dawes' Roll No.	NAME	Relationship to Person	AGE	SEX	BLOOD	TRIBAL ENROLLMENT		
						Year	County	No.
I.W. 1107	1 Williams John R 61	First Named	64	M	IW	1896	Sugar Loaf	15153
	2							
	3							
	4							
	5							
	6							
	7							
	8							
	9							
	10							
	11							
	12							
	13							
	14							
	15							
	16							
	17							

ENROLLMENT
OF NOS. ~~ 1 ~~ HEREON
APPROVED BY THE SECRETARY
OF INTERIOR NOV 16 1904

TRIBAL ENROLLMENT OF PARENTS

Name of Father	Year	County	Name of Mother	Year	County
1 Israel Williams	Dead	Non Citz	Elizabeth Williams	Dead	Non Citz
2					
3					
4					
5					
6					
7	On 1896 Roll as Jno. R. Williams and admitted by Dawes				
8	Com as intermarried citizen as J.R. Williams				
9					
10					
11					
12					
13					
14					
15					
16			Date of Application for Enrollment.	6/6/99	
17 P.O. Page IT 2/3/03 Gilmon I.T.					

Choctaw By Blood Enrollment Cards 1898-1914

RESIDENCE: Skullyville   COUNTY.
POST OFFICE: Oak Lodge I.T.

Choctaw Nation

Choctaw Roll
(Not Including Freedmen)

CARD NO.
FIELD NO. 2307

Dawes' Roll No.		NAME		Relationship to Person Named	AGE	SEX	BLOOD	TRIBAL ENROLLMENT		
								Year	County	No.
6671	1	Folsom Frank D	26	First Named	23	M	3/8	1896	Skullyville	3945
6672	2	" Augusta Victoria	2	Dau	9mo	F	3/16			
I.W. 184	3	" Mary G		Wife	36	F	I.W.			
	4									
	5									
	6									
	7									
	8									
	9									
	10									
	11									
	12									
	13									
	14									
	15									
	16									
	17									

ENROLLMENT
OF NOS. 1, 2 HEREON
APPROVED BY THE SECRETARY
OF INTERIOR JAN 17 1903

ENROLLMENT
OF NOS. ~~~ 3 ~~~ HEREON
APPROVED BY THE SECRETARY
OF INTERIOR JUN 13 1903

TRIBAL ENROLLMENT OF PARENTS

	Name of Father	Year	County	Name of Mother	Year	County
1	William Folsom	1896	Tobucksy	Rosa Folsom	1896	Skullyville
2	No 1			Mary G Folsom		Non Citz
3	James Funk		non-citz	Elizabeth Funk		" "
4						
5						
6			Nº3 transferred from Choctaw card #D516			
7			See decision of May 1, 1903			
8						
9						
10						
11						
12			Wife on Card D516			
13			No.2 Born February 8, 1901: Enrolled Nov 6, 1901			
14			For children of Nos 1&3 see NB (Mar 3,1905) #619			
15					Date of Application for Enrollment.	
16					#1&2	6/6/99
17					#3 Dec. 17, 1902	

207

| RESIDENCE: Sugar Loaf COUNTY.
POST OFFICE: Monroe I.T. | | | | | **Choctaw Nation** | | | **Choctaw Roll**
(Not Including Freedmen) | CARD NO.
FIELD NO. **2308** | |

Dawes' Roll No.	NAME		Relationship to Person	AGE	SEX	BLOOD	TRIBAL ENROLLMENT		
							Year	County	No.
I.W. 1470	1 Tucker William N	30	First Named	27	M	I.W	1896	Sugar Loaf	15094
6673	2 " Anna N	25	Wife	22	F	1/4	1896	" "	11963
6674	3 " Ida M	9	Dau	6	F	1/8	1896	" "	11964
6675	4 " Ulysses G	7	Son	4	M	1/8	1896	" "	11965
6676	5 " Sestos	5	Dau	2	F	1/8			
6677	6 " Chester	2	Son	1mo	M	1/8			
6678	7 " McCurtain	1	Son	2mo	M	1/8			
	8 No1 Dismissed								
	9 Sep 23 1904								
	10 Such action rescinded and No.1- Granted May 23 1905						ENROLLMENT		
	11						OF NOS. One HEREON		
	12 No.1 No appeal to C.C.C.C.						APPROVED BY THE SECRETARY OF INTERIOR Aug 22 1905		
	13								
	14		ENROLLMENT						
	15		OF NOS. 2,3,4,5,6,7 HEREON						
	16		APPROVED BY THE SECRETARY OF INTERIOR Jan 17 1903						
	17								

	TRIBAL ENROLLMENT OF PARENTS						
	Name of Father	Year	County	Name of Mother	Year	County	
1	J.B. Tucker	1896	non citz	Elizabeth Tucker	1896	non citz	
2	Monroe Griffith	Dead	non citz	Martha Griffith	Dead	Sug. Loaf	
3	No 1			No 2			
4	No 1			No 2			
5	No 1			No 2			
6	No.1			No.2			
7	No.1			No.2			
8	Jan 23 1904 Intermarried status of No1 taken						
9	No1 On Roll 1896 as William Tucker						
10	No5 Affidavit of birth to be supplied. Recd June 8/99 No.6 Enrolled November 14th, 1900.						
11	No.1 admitted by U.S. Court Central District, Ind. Terrty, July 1st, 1897						
12	Court case #155: Wm N. Tucker vs Choctaw Nation						
13	Nos 3 and 4 admitted by Dawes Commission in 1896 as citizens by blood: Choctaw case #288: No appeal. Enrollment of No.1 Cancelled by order						
14	No.7 Born May 29th 1902: Enrolled July 15th 1902: Department March 4,1907						
15	No.1 Admitted by Dawes Com in 96 case #288. Appealed				# 1 to 5		
16	Poteau I.T. Jan 23 '04			Date of Application for Enrollment.	6/6/99		
17	Judgement[s] of US Ct admitting No1 vacated and set aside by Decree of Choctaw Chickasaw Citizenship Court Decr 17 '02						

Not restored to roll by Departmental authority of January 18, 1909 (File 5-51)

RESIDENCE: Sugar Loaf
POST OFFICE: Howe I.T.

COUNTY. **Choctaw Nation**

Choctaw Roll
(Not Including Freedmen)

CARD NO.
FIELD NO. 2309

Dawes' Roll No.	NAME	Relationship to Person	AGE	SEX	BLOOD	TRIBAL ENROLLMENT		
						Year	County	No.
6679	1 MᶜCurtain Mack ²³	First Named	20	M	Full	1896	Sugar Loaf	9090
	2							
	3							
	4							
	5							
	6							
	7							
	8							
	9							
	10							
	11							
	12							
	13							
	14							
	15							
	16							
	17							

ENROLLMENT
OF NOS. 1 HEREON
APPROVED BY THE SECRETARY
OF INTERIOR JAN 17 1903

TRIBAL ENROLLMENT OF PARENTS

	Name of Father	Year	County	Name of Mother	Year	County
1	Frank MᶜCurtain	Dead	Sugar Loaf	Sophia MᶜCurtain	Dead	Sug. Loaf
2						
3						
4						
5						
6						
7	On 1896 roll as MᶜAlester MᶜCurtain					
8	For child of No. 1 see N.B. (Apr 26, 1906) Card No. 260					
9						
10						
11						
12						
13						
14						
15						
16				Date of Application for Enrollment		6/6/99
17						

RESIDENCE: Sugar Loaf	COUNTY.							CARD NO.
POST OFFICE: Summerfield I.T.	**Choctaw Nation**					Choctaw Roll *(Not Including Freedmen)*		FIELD NO. 2310

Dawes' Roll No.	NAME		Relationship to Person	AGE	SEX	BLOOD	TRIBAL ENROLLMENT		
							Year	County	No.
6680	₁ Jackson, Mila	45	First Named	42	F	Full	1896	Sugar Loaf	8501
6681	₂ Moore Thompson	14	Son	11	M	"	1896	" "	8502
6682	₃ Jackson, William B	1	Son	2mo	M	"			
	4								
	5								
	6								
	7								
	8								
	9								
	10								
	11								
	12								
	13								
	14								
	15	ENROLLMENT OF NOS 1, 2, 3, HEREON APPROVED BY THE SECRETARY OF INTERIOR JAN 17 1903							
	16								
	17								

TRIBAL ENROLLMENT OF PARENTS

	Name of Father	Year	County	Name of Mother	Year	County
₁	Simon Peter	1896	Sugar Loaf	Na-mia-ho-na	Dead	Nashoba
₂	Robert Moore	Dead	Sugar Loaf	No 1		
₃	Henry Jackson on Choctaw		Card #2380	No 1		
4						
5						
6						
7						
8						
9	No1 On 1896 roll as Mary Moore					
10	No3 Born May 6ᵗʰ 1902: Enrolled July 16" 1902					
11	No1 Now the wife of Henry Jackson on Choctaw Card #2380 Evidence requested July 16" 1902 Filed Oct 13 1902					
12						
13						
14						
15					#1&2	
16				Date of Application for Enrollment.	6/6/99	
17						

RESIDENCE: Sugar Loaf   COUNTY. **Choctaw Nation**   **Choctaw Roll**   CARD No.

POST OFFICE: Heavener I.T.   *(Not Including Freedmen)*   FIELD No. 2311

Dawes' Roll No.	NAME		Relationship to Person	AGE	SEX	BLOOD	TRIBAL ENROLLMENT		
							Year	County	No.
6683	1 Jefferson Israel	34	First Named	31	M	Full	1896	Sugar Loaf	6488
I.W. 32	2 " Sarah	30	Wife	27	F	I.W.	1896	" "	14685
6684	3 ~~Lucy Ann~~ DIED PRIOR TO SEPTEMBER 25,1902		Dau	11	F	1/2	1896	" "	6489
	4								
	5								
	6								
	7								
	8								
	9								
	10								
	11								
	12								
	13								
	14								
	15	ENROLLMENT OF NOS. 1, 3, HEREON APPROVED BY THE SECRETARY OF INTERIOR JAN 17 1903		ENROLLMENT OF NOS. 2 HEREON APPROVED BY THE SECRETARY OF INTERIOR JUN 13 1903						
	16								
	17								

TRIBAL ENROLLMENT OF PARENTS

	Name of Father	Year	County	Name of Mother	Year	County
1	Henry Jefferson	Dead	Sugar Loaf	Sarah Ann Jefferson	1896	Sugar Loaf
2	Beal Wilds	"	Non Citz	Mina Wilds	Dead	Non Citz
3	No 1			No 2		
4						
5						
6						
7	No3 On 1896 roll as Rosa Ann					
8	Nos1-2: Evidence of marriage filed December 20, 1902					
9	No.3 Died Sept 10" 1902: Proof of death filed Decr 20" 1902					
10	No.3 died Sept 10, 1902. Enrollment cancelled by Department [illegible]					
11						
12						
13						
14						
15						
16				Date of Application for Enrollment.	6/6/99	
17						

211

Choctaw By Blood Enrollment Cards 1898-1914

RESIDENCE: Sugar Loaf COUNTY.
POST OFFICE: Heavener I.T.

Choctaw Nation

Choctaw Roll
(Not Including Freedmen)

CARD NO.
FIELD NO. 2312

Dawes' Roll No.	NAME	Relationship to Person	AGE	SEX	BLOOD	TRIBAL ENROLLMENT		
						Year	County	No.
~~6685~~	1 ~~Jefferson Charley~~ DIED PRIOR TO SEPTEMBER 25 1902	First Named	23	M	Full	1896	Sugar Loaf	6494
DEAD.	2 " ~~Bettie~~							
DEAD.	3 " ~~Tilda M~~							
	4							
	5							
	No.2 and 3 HEREON DISMISSED UNDER ORDER OF THE COMMISSION TO THE FIVE CIVILIZED TRIBES OF MARCH 31, 1905.							
	8							
	9							
	10							
	11							
	12							
	13							
	14							
	15 ENROLLMENT OF NOS. 1 HEREON							
	16 APPROVED BY THE SECRETARY OF INTERIOR JAN 17 1903							
	17							

TRIBAL ENROLLMENT OF PARENTS

	Name of Father	Year	County	Name of Mother	Year	County
1	Henry Jefferson	Dead	Sugar Loaf	Sarah Ann Jefferson	1896	Sugar Loaf
2	John Simmal	Dead	Non Citz	Nancy Simmal	1896	Non Citz
3	No 1			No 2		
4						
5						
6						
7	No.1 Died in 1900: Proof of Death filed December 20" 1902;					
8	No.2 Died in 1901: Proof of Death filed December 20" 1902;					
9	No.3 Died in 1899: Proof of Death filed December 20" 1902;					
10	[Entry completely illegible]					
11						
12						
13						
14						
15						
16				Date of Application for Enrollment.	6/6/99	
17						

Choctaw By Blood Enrollment Cards 1898-1914

| RESIDENCE: Sugar Loaf | COUNTY. | Choctaw Nation | Choctaw Roll | CARD No. |
| POST OFFICE: Heavener I.T. | | | *(Not Including Freedmen)* | FIELD No. 2313 |

Dawes' Roll No.	NAME	Relationship to Person Named	AGE	SEX	BLOOD	TRIBAL ENROLLMENT		
						Year	County	No.
6686	DIED PRIOR TO SEPTEMBER 25, 1902 1 Jefferson Sarah	First Named	58	F	Full	1896	Sugar Loaf	6486
6687	DIED PRIOR TO SEPTEMBER 25, 1902 2 Sissy	Dau	20	F	Full	1896	" "	6487
	3							
	4							
	5							
	6							
	7							
	8							
	9							
	10							
	11							
	12							
	13							
	14							
	15	ENROLLMENT						
	16	OF NOS. 1, 2 HEREON APPROVED BY THE SECRETARY						
	17	OF INTERIOR JAN 17 1903						

TRIBAL ENROLLMENT OF PARENTS

	Name of Father	Year	County	Name of Mother	Year	County
1	M. Jack	Dead	Sugar Loaf		Dead	Sugar Loaf
2	Charley Griffith	"	" "	No 1		
3						
4						
5						
6		No.1 Died in 1900: Proof of Death filed December 20" 1902				
7		No.1 Died in 1900: Proof of Death filed December 20" 1902				
8						
9						
10						
11						
12						
13						
14						
15						
16				Date of Application for Enrollment.	6/6/99	
17						

Choctaw By Blood Enrollment Cards 1898-1914

RESIDENCE: Sugar Loaf	COUNTY.	Choctaw Nation	Choctaw Roll (Not Including Freedmen)	CARD NO.
POST OFFICE: LeFlore I.T.				FIELD NO. 2314

Dawes' Roll No.	NAME	Relationship to Person First Named	AGE	SEX	BLOOD	TRIBAL ENROLLMENT		
						Year	County	No.
✓ ✗ 1	Walters Benjamin A		22	M	1/16			
2								
3								
4								
5								
6								
7								
8								
9								
10								
11								
12								
13								
14								
15								
16								
17								

TRIBAL ENROLLMENT OF PARENTS

	Name of Father	Year	County	Name of Mother	Year	County
1	Thomas Walters	1896	Non Citz	Sarah McFarland	1896	Sugar Loaf
2						
3						
4						
5		Admitted by U.S. Court South McAlester Jan 19th 1898 Case No 94				
6		as Benjamin Walters. As to residence see his testimony.				
7	Judgement by U.S. Court admitting No 1 vacated and set aside by Decree of Choctaw Chickasaw Citizenship Court Dec' 17'02					
8	No. 1 denied by Choctaw-Chickasaw Citizenship Court Feb 2 '04					
9						
10						
11						
12						
13						
14						
15						
16				Date of Application for Enrollment.	6/6/99	
17						

214

RESIDENCE: Sugar Loaf COUNTY. **Choctaw Nation** Choctaw Roll CARD No.
POST OFFICE: Houston I.T. *(Not Including Freedmen)* FIELD No. 2315

Dawes' Roll No.	NAME	Relationship to Person First Named	AGE	SEX	BLOOD	TRIBAL ENROLLMENT		
	Rau, I.T. 12/30 --					Year	County	No.
6688	1 McCurtain Houston 41	First Named	38	M	3/4	1896	Sugar Loaf	9080
I.W. 33	2 " Rosie 32	Wife	29	F	I.W.	1896	" "	14858
6689	3 " Mary V.J. 13	Dau	10	F	3/8	1896	" "	9881
	4							
	5							
	6							
	7							
	8							
	9							
	10							
	11							
	12							
	13							
	14							
	15	ENROLLMENT OF NOS. 1, 3 HEREON APPROVED BY THE SECRETARY OF INTERIOR JAN 17 1903		ENROLLMENT OF NOS. ~~ 2 ~~ HEREON APPROVED BY THE SECRETARY OF INTERIOR JUN 13 1903				
	16							
	17							

TRIBAL ENROLLMENT OF PARENTS

	Name of Father	Year	County	Name of Mother	Year	County
1	John McCurtain	Dead	Sugar Loaf	Rhoda McCurtain	Dead	Sugar Loaf
2	Sam Clayton	"	Non Citz	Eliza Clayton	"	Non Citz
3	No 1			No 2		
4						
5						
6	No3 On 1896 roll as Viola J. McCurtain					
7	Nos 1-2 Evidence of marriage filed Dec 20, 1902					
8						
9						
10						
11						
12						
13						
14						
15						
16			Date of Application for Enrollment:	6/6/99		
17						

215

Choctaw By Blood Enrollment Cards 1898-1914

RESIDENCE:	Sugar Loaf	COUNTY.						
POST OFFICE:	Fanshaw I.T.	**Choctaw Nation**			Choctaw Roll *(Not Including Freedmen)*	CARD NO. FIELD NO. 2316		

Dawes' Roll No.	NAME	Relationship to Person First Named	AGE	SEX	BLOOD	TRIBAL ENROLLMENT		
						Year	County	No.
6690	₁ Harris Gilbert *DIED PRIOR TO SEPTEMBER 25 1902*		30	M	3/4	1896	Sugar Loaf	5248
6691	₂ " Lena ³³	Wife	30	F	Full	1896	" "	2219
6692	₃ " Mattie ⁷	Dau	4	F	7/8	1896	" "	5265
15045	₄ Harris Buddy ⁵	Son	18mo	M	7/8			
6693	₅ " Mitchell ¹¹	Neph	8	M	7/8	1896	Sugar Loaf	5251
6694	₆ Harris Josie ²	Son	4mo	M	7/8			
	₇							
	₈							
	₉							
	₁₀							
	₁₁							
	₁₂							
	₁₃							
	₁₄							
	₁₅							
	₁₆							
	₁₇							

ENROLLMENT OF NOS. 1,2,3,5,6 HEREON APPROVED BY THE SECRETARY OF INTERIOR JAN 17 1903

ENROLLMENT OF NOS. 4 HEREON APPROVED BY THE SECRETARY OF INTERIOR FEB 16 1904

TRIBAL ENROLLMENT OF PARENTS

	Name of Father	Year	County	Name of Mother	Year	County
₁	Joseph Harris	Dead	Sugar Loaf	Nellie Harris	Dead	Sugar Loaf
₂	Sam Allen	"	" "	A-tok-o-ntema	"	" "
₃	No 1			No 2		
₄	No 1			No 2		
₅	Watson Harris	Dead	Sugar Loaf	Louisa Harris	Dead	Sugar Loaf
₆	No.1			No.2		
₇						
₈			No3 On 1896 roll as Mandy Harris			
₉			No2 " 1896 " " Lena Colbert			
₁₀			No.6 Enrolled Feby 20, 1901			
₁₁			Evidence of birth of No.4 filed Feby 20, 1901			
₁₂			No.1 Died Jan 12ᵗ 1901: Proof of death filed Dec 20", 1902			
			No.2 is now wife of Frazier Jefferson Choctaw Card #2389			
₁₃			Nº4 Born Jany 28 1898 and is a male. See letter of Nº1 in Gen Off files Nº 34171-1903			
₁₄			No.1 died Jan 12, 1901: Enrollment cancelled by Department July 8, 1904			
₁₅						#1 to 5
₁₆					Date of Application for Enrollment.	6/6/99
₁₇	P.O. Wister I.T. 3/7/07					

216

Choctaw By Blood Enrollment Cards 1898-1914

RESIDENCE: Sugar Loaf   COUNTY. **Choctaw Nation**   **Choctaw Roll** *(Not Including Freedmen)*   CARD NO.

POST OFFICE: Poteau, I.T.   FIELD NO. 2317

NAME		Relationship to Person	AGE	SEX	BLOOD	TRIBAL ENROLLMENT		
						Year	County	No.
James, Wesley W	31	First Named	28	M	1/64	1896	Sugar Loaf	6495
" Clara	25	Wife	22	F	I.W.			
" Clarice	2	Dau	2wk	F	1/128			
4								
5								
6								
7								
8								
9								
10								
11								
12								
13								
14								
15								
16								
17								

ENROLLMENT
OF NOS. 1, 3, HEREON
APPROVED BY THE SECRETARY
OF INTERIOR JAN 17 1903

ENROLLMENT
OF NOS ~~ 2 ~~ HEREON
APPROVED BY THE SECRETARY
OF INTERIOR JUN 13 1903

TRIBAL ENROLLMENT OF PARENTS

	Name of Father	Year	County	Name of Mother	Year	County
1	Morton V. James	Dead	Chickasaw	Julia A Beard		Sugar Loaf
2	L. E. Watson		Non Citz	Mattie Watson		Non Citz
3	No.1			No.2		
4						
5						
6						
7			No1 on 1896 Roll as Wesley James			
8			No.3 Enrolled Oct 16th, 1900			
9						
10						
11						
12						
13						
14						
15				#1&2		
16				Date of Application for Enrollment.	June 6/99	
17						

217

Choctaw By Blood Enrollment Cards 1898-1914

RESIDENCE: Gaines   COUNTY. **Choctaw Nation**   **Choctaw Roll** *(Not Including Freedmen)*   CARD NO.
POST OFFICE: Vireton I.T.   FIELD NO. 2318

Dawes' Roll No.	NAME		Relationship to Person	AGE	SEX	BLOOD	TRIBAL ENROLLMENT		
							Year	County	No.
6697	1 White Osborne	36	First Named	33	M	Full	1896	Sans Bois	12695
6698	2 " Malsey	41	Wife	38	F	"	1896	" "	12696
6699	3 " Alzira J.	14	Dau	11	F	"	1896	" "	12697
6700	4 Beams Jesse	18	Step Son	15	M	"	1896	" "	595
	5								
	6								
	7								
	8								
	9								
	10								
	11								
	12								
	13								
	14								
	15								
	16								
	17								

ENROLLMENT
OF NOS. 1, 2, 3, 4, HEREON
APPROVED BY THE SECRETARY
OF INTERIOR JAN 17 1903

TRIBAL ENROLLMENT OF PARENTS

	Name of Father	Year	County	Name of Mother	Year	County
1	Reuben White	Dead	Gaines	Malsey Norman	Dead	Sugar Loaf
2	"	"	Sans Bois	Rhoda Woolridge	"	Sans Bois
3	No 1			No 2		
4	Joseph Beams	Dead	Sans Bois	No 2		
5						
6						
7						
8			No3 on roll as A. J. White			
9						
10						
11						
12						
13						
14						
15						
16				Date of Application for Enrollment.	6/6/99	
17						

Choctaw By Blood Enrollment Cards 1898-1914

RESIDENCE: Sugar Loaf   COUNTY. **Choctaw Nation**   **Choctaw Roll**   CARD NO.
POST OFFICE: Poteau I.T.   (Not Including Freedmen)   FIELD NO. **2319**

Dawes' Roll No.		NAME		Relationship to Person First Named	AGE	SEX	BLOOD	TRIBAL ENROLLMENT Year	County	No.
6701	1	Wilburn Martha	47	First Named	44	F	3/4	1896	Sugar Loaf	12914
6702	2	" Lizzie N	25	Dau	22	F	3/8	1896	" "	12915
Dead	3	DEAD Alice S DEAD		Dau	17	F	3/8	1896	" "	12916
6703	4	" Charles S	18	Son	15	M	3/8	1896	" "	12917
6704	5	" Blanche	16	Dau	13	F	3/8	1896	" "	12918
6705	6	" John C	14	Son	11	M	3/8	1896	" "	12919
6706	7	" Sarah	12	Dau	9	F	3/8	1896	" "	12920
6707	8	" Annie	10	Dau	7	F	3/8	1896	" "	129212
6708	9	" Estella	8	Dau	5	F	3/8	1896	" "	12922
6709	10	" Jesse H	6	Son	3	M	3/8	1896	" "	12923
6710	11	" Frederick	4	Son	1	M	3/8			
	12									
	13									
	14									
	15									
	16									
	17									

No. three hereon dismissed under order of the Commission to the Five Civilized Tribes of March 31, 1905.

ENROLLMENT
OF NOS. 1,2,4,5,6,7,8,9,10,11 HEREON
APPROVED BY THE SECRETARY
OF INTERIOR Jan 17 1903

TRIBAL ENROLLMENT OF PARENTS

	Name of Father	Year	County	Name of Mother	Year	County
1	Greenwood LeFlore	Dead	Skullyville	Effie Fisher	Dead	Towson
2	Charles Wilburn	1896	Non Citz	No 1		
3	" "	"	" "	No 1		
4	" "	"	" "	No 1		
5	" "	"	" "	No 1		
6	" "	"	" "	No 1		
7	" "	"	" "	No 1		
8	" "	"	" "	No 1		
9	" "	"	" "	No 1		
10	" "	"	" "	No 1		
11	" "	"	" "	No 1		
12	No2 On 1896 roll as Lizzie K Wilburn					
13	No4 " " " " Charley Wilburn					
	No6 " " " " J. Curtis Wilburn					
14	No10 " " " " Jessie Wilburn					
15	No.3 died Aug 24, 1899 Proof of death filed Aug 20 1901					
16	For child of No5 see NB (Apr 26-06) Card #518			Date of Application for Enrollment.	6/6/99	
17	" " " No2 " " " " #897 " " " " (Mar 3-05) " #1476					

Choctaw By Blood Enrollment Cards 1898-1914

RESIDENCE:	Sugar Loaf		COUNTY.						CARD NO.	
POST OFFICE:	Monroe I.T.		**Choctaw Nation**				**Choctaw Roll** *(Not Including Freedmen)*		FIELD NO.	**2320**

Dawes' Roll No.	NAME		Relationship to Person	AGE	SEX	BLOOD	TRIBAL ENROLLMENT		
							Year	County	No.
6711	1 Pickens Edmond	35	First Named	32	M	1/2	1896	Sugar Loaf	10149
I.W. 35	2 " Jane	37	Wife	34	F	I.W.			
6712	3 " William	12	Son	9	M	1/4	1896	Sugar Loaf	10150
6713	4 " Nellie	9	Dau	6	F	1/4	1896	" "	10151
6714	5 " DeWitt	7	Son	4	M	1/4	1896	" "	10152
6715	6 " Coleman	4	Son	9mo	M	1/4			
	7								
	8								
	9								
	10								
	11								
	12								
	13								
	14								
	15	ENROLLMENT OF NOS. 1,3,4,5,6 HEREON APPROVED BY THE SECRETARY OF INTERIOR Jan 17 1903		ENROLLMENT OF NOS ~~ 2 ~~ HEREON APPROVED BY THE SECRETARY OF INTERIOR Jun 13 1903						
	16								
	17								

TRIBAL ENROLLMENT OF PARENTS

	Name of Father	Year	County	Name of Mother	Year	County
1	Dave Pickens	Dead	Chickasaw	Mary Pickens	Dead	Sugar Loaf
2	Marion Choate	1896	Non Citz	Mollie Choate	Dead	Non Citz
3	No 1			No 2		
4	No 1			No 2		
5	No 1			No 2		
6	No 1			No 2		
7						
8			No1 on 1896 roll as Edward Picken			
9			No3 " " " " Wm Picken			
10						
11			Evidence of marriage to be supplied. Received June 7 – 99			
12			No6 Affidavit of birth to be supplied " " " "			
13						
14						
15					Date of Application for Enrollment.	
16					6/6/99	
17						

Choctaw By Blood Enrollment Cards 1898-1914

RESIDENCE: Sugar Loaf

POST OFFICE: Monroe, I.T.

COUNTY. **Choctaw Nation**

Choctaw Roll *(Not Including Freedmen)*

CARD NO.

FIELD NO. 2321

Dawes' Roll No.	NAME	Relationship to Person	AGE	SEX	BLOOD	TRIBAL ENROLLMENT		
						Year	County	No.
6716	1 Wilson, Archey 19	First Named	16	M	1/4	1896	Sugar Loaf	12877
	2							
	3							
	4							
	5							
	6							
	7							
	8							
	9							
	10							
	11							
	12							
	13							
	14							
	15							
	16							
	17							

ENROLLMENT
OF NOS. 1 HEREON
APPROVED BY THE SECRETARY
OF INTERIOR JAN 17 1903

TRIBAL ENROLLMENT OF PARENTS

	Name of Father	Year	County	Name of Mother	Year	County
1	Chas Wilson	Dead	Sugar Loaf	Lizzie Wilson	Dead	Non Citz
2						
3						
4						
5						
6						
7			On 1896 roll as Archy Wilson. As to marriage of parents			
8			see testimony of Edmond Pickens			
9						
10						
11						
12						
13						
14						
15						
16				Date of Application for Enrollment.	6/6/99	
17						

Choctaw By Blood Enrollment Cards 1898-1914

RESIDENCE:	Sugar Loaf	COUNTY.						CARD NO.	
POST OFFICE:	Wister, I.T.	**Choctaw Nation**				Choctaw Roll *(Not Including Freedmen)*		FIELD NO.	2322

Dawes' Roll No.	NAME		Relationship to Person	AGE	SEX	BLOOD	TRIBAL ENROLLMENT		
							Year	County	No.
6717	1 Quinn, Eastman	45	First Named	42	M	Full	1896	Sugar Loaf	10654
6718	2 " Thomas	22	Son	19	"	"	1896	" "	10655
~~6719~~	3 DIED PRIOR TO SEPTEMBER 25 1902 ~~Austin~~		"	~~15~~	"	"	~~1896~~	" "	~~10656~~
6720	4 " James	9	"	16	"	"	1896	" "	10657
	5								
	6								
	7								
	8								
	9								
	10								
	11								
	12								
	13								
	14								
	15	ENROLLMENT OF NOS. 1, 2, 3, 4, HEREON APPROVED BY THE SECRETARY OF INTERIOR JAN 17 1903							
	16								
	17								

TRIBAL ENROLLMENT OF PARENTS

	Name of Father	Year	County	Name of Mother	Year	County
1	E-ma-han-tubby	Dead	Sugar Loaf	Wisey	Dead	Sugar Loaf
2	No 1			Wasey Quinn	"	" "
3	No 1			" "	"	" "
4	No 1			Martha Quinn	"	" "
5						
6						
7						
8	No3 Died April 22nd 1901; Proof of death filed Decr 23 1902					
9	No.2 is now husband of Nancy Jefferson on Choctaw Card #2389 Dec. 18, 02					
10	No.3 died April 22, 1901; Enrollment cancelled by Department July 8, 1904					
11						
12						
13						
14						
15				Date of Application for Enrollment		
16				6/6/99		
17						

Choctaw By Blood Enrollment Cards 1898-1914

RESIDENCE: Sugar Loaf COUNTY. **Choctaw Nation** **Choctaw Roll** CARD NO.
POST OFFICE: Wister, I.T. 12-18-02-Victor, I.T. (Not Including Freedmen) FIELD NO. 2323

Dawes' Roll No.	NAME	Relationship to Person	AGE	SEX	BLOOD	TRIBAL ENROLLMENT		
						Year	County	No.
6721	1 Lofton, Charles W 29	First Named	26	M	1/4	1896	Sugar Loaf	7817
I.W. 36	2 " Sarah E 32	Wife	29	F	I.W.			
	3							
	4							
	5							
	6							
	7							
	8							
	9							
	10							
	11							
	12							
	13							
	14							
	15							
	16							
	17							

ENROLLMENT OF NOS. 1 HEREON APPROVED BY THE SECRETARY OF INTERIOR JAN 17 1903

ENROLLMENT OF NOS. 2 HEREON APPROVED BY THE SECRETARY OF INTERIOR JUN 13 1903

TRIBAL ENROLLMENT OF PARENTS

	Name of Father	Year	County	Name of Mother	Year	County
1	John Lofton	Dead	Non Citz	Sarah J Lofton	Dead	Sugar Loaf
2	Andrew Going	1896	" "	Linda Going	"	Non Citz
3						
4						
5						
6						
7						
8	No 1 on 1896 roll as Chas W Lofton					
9						
10						
11						
12						
13						
14						
15						
16				Date of Application for Enrollment.	6/6/99	
17						

223

Choctaw By Blood Enrollment Cards 1898-1914

RESIDENCE: Sugar Loaf
POST OFFICE: LeFlore, I.T.

COUNTY. **Choctaw Nation**

Choctaw Roll (Not Including Freedmen)

CARD NO.
FIELD NO. 2324

Dawes' Roll No.	NAME		Relationship to Person	AGE	SEX	BLOOD	TRIBAL ENROLLMENT		
							Year	County	No.
6722	1 Culberson, James	32	First Named	29	M	1/2	1896	Sugar Loaf	2220
I.W. 37	2 " Martha [?]	30	Wife	27	F	I.W.			
6723	3 " Sophia	23	Sister	20	"	1/2	1896	Sugar Loaf	2222
6724	4 DIED PRIOR TO SEPTEMBER 25, 1902 Jacob		Bro	17	M	1/2	1896	" "	2221
6725	5 " Johnanna	18	Sister	15	F	1/2	1896	" "	2223
6726	6 " James Matthew[1]		Son	5mo	M	1/4			
I.W. 1108	7 Evans, Lucy	56	Mother	56	F	I.W.			
	8								
	9								
	10								
	11								
	12	No. 1 to [?] 6 & 8 [?] enrollmen[?]							
	13	cancelled by Department July 8, 1904							
	14								

15 ENROLLMENT OF NOS. 1,3,4,5,6 HEREON APPROVED BY THE SECRETARY OF INTERIOR JAN 17 1903	ENROLLMENT OF NOS. ~~2~~ HEREON APPROVED BY THE SECRETARY OF INTERIOR JUN 13 1903	ENROLLMENT OF NOS. ~~7~~ HEREON APPROVED BY THE SECRETARY OF INTERIOR NOV 16 1904

TRIBAL ENROLLMENT OF PARENTS

	Name of Father	Year	County	Name of Mother	Year	County
1	John Culberson	Dead	Skullyville	Lucy Culberson	1896	Non Citz
2	M. H. Harris	1898	Non Citz	Elizabeth Harris	1896	" "
3	John Culberson	Dead	Skullyville	Lucy Culberson	1896	" "
4	" "	" "	" "	" "	1896	" "
5	" "	" "	" "	" "	1896	" "
6	No 1			No 2		
7	Alex McDonald	dead	non-citizen	Catherine McDonald	dead	Non-Citz
8						
9	No5 on 1896 roll as Johana Culberson					
10	For child of Nos 1&2 see NB (March 3 1905) #752					
11	As to marriage of parents of Nos 1-3-4-5, see his testimony and that of Simon Peter					
12	No 6 born July 18, 1901: Enrolled Dec 7, 1901					
13	No.4 Died October 8" 1901: Proof of death filed December 20" 1902					
14						
15			#1 to 5			
16			Date of Application for Enrollment. 6/6/99			
17	No.7 transferred from Choctaw card #D-515, Oct 31, 1904; See decision of Oct. 15, 1904					

Choctaw By Blood Enrollment Cards 1898-1914

RESIDENCE: Sugar Loaf   COUNTY. **Choctaw Nation**   **Choctaw Roll**   CARD NO.
POST OFFICE: Howe, I.T.   *(Not Including Freedmen)*   FIELD NO.   2325

Dawes' Roll No.	NAME			Relationship to Person First Named	AGE	SEX	BLOOD	TRIBAL ENROLLMENT		
								Year	County	No.
6727	1	Mᶜ Noel, Joel	53		50	M	Full	1896	Sugar Loaf	9083
6728	2	" Sap	23	Son	20	"	"	1896	" "	9084
	3									
	4									
	5									
	6									
	7									
	8									
	9									
	10									
	11									
	12									
	13									
	14									
	15	ENROLLMENT OF NOS. 1, 2, HEREON APPROVED BY THE SECRETARY OF INTERIOR JAN 17 1903								
	16									
	17									

TRIBAL ENROLLMENT OF PARENTS

	Name of Father	Year	County	Name of Mother	Year	County
1	Bobbie	Dead	Sugar Loaf		Dead	Sugar Loaf
2	No 1			Nancy Mᶜ Noel	"	" "
3						
4						
5						
6						
7						
8						
9						
10						
11						
12						
13						
14						
15					Date of Application for Enrollment.	
16					6/6/99	
17						

225

Choctaw By Blood Enrollment Cards 1898-1914

RESIDENCE: Sugar Loaf   COUNTY. **Choctaw Nation**   **Choctaw Roll** CARD NO.
POST OFFICE: Gilmore, I.T.   *(Not Including Freedmen)*   FIELD NO. **2326**

Dawes' Roll No.	NAME	Relationship to Person First Named	AGE	SEX	BLOOD	TRIBAL ENROLLMENT Year	County	No.
DEAD.	1 Harrison, Walter DEAD.		22	M	I.W.	1896	Sugar Loaf	14606
6729	2 " Delia 22	Wife	19	F	1/4	1896	Sugar Loaf	5247
6730	3 " William C.E.6	Son	2	M				
6731	4 " Clarence 4	"	3mo	"				
6732	5 " Walter Hamlet 1	"	9mo	M				
	6							
	7							
	8							
	9							
	10							
	11							
	12							
	13							
	14							
	15							
	16							
	17							

No. 1 HEREON DISMISSED UNDER ORDER OF THE COMMISSION TO THE FIVE CIVILIZED TRIBES OF MARCH 31, 1905.

ENROLLMENT OF NOS. 2,3,4,5 HEREON APPROVED BY THE SECRETARY OF INTERIOR JAN 17 1903

TRIBAL ENROLLMENT OF PARENTS

	Name of Father	Year	County	Name of Mother	Year	County
1	Jack Harrison	1896	Non Citz	Mary A Harrison	1896	Non Citz
2	Chas Wilson	Dead	Sugar Loaf	Lizzie Wilson	Dead	" "
3	No 1			No 2		
4	No 1			No 2		
5	No.1			No 2		
6						
7						
8						
9	No1 was admitted by Dawes Com as an Intermarried Citz					
10	Case No 1368					
11	As to marriage of parents of No2 see evidence in case of her					
12	brother Archey Wilson					
13						
14	No3-4 Affidavits of birth to be supplied. Recd June 8/99					
15	No.5 born Nov. 9, 1901; Enrolled July 7, 1902					
16	No.1 Died Aug 15, 1901: Proof of death filed Dec 24, 1902 #1 to 4 inc					
17	For child of No.1 see NB (Mar 3,1905) #615 Date of Application for Enrollment. 6/6/99					

Choctaw By Blood Enrollment Cards 1898-1914

RESIDENCE: Sugar Loaf   COUNTY. **Choctaw Nation**   **Choctaw Roll** *(Not Including Freedmen)*   CARD NO.
POST OFFICE: Couser, I.T.   FIELD NO. 2327

Dawes' Roll No.	NAME	Relationship to Person	AGE	SEX	BLOOD	TRIBAL ENROLLMENT		
						Year	County	No.
6733	1 McCurtain, Mollie ³²	First Named	29	F	Full	1896	Sugar Loaf	9089
	2							
	3							
	4							
	5							
	6							
	7							
	8							
	9							
	10							
	11							
	12							
	13							
	14							
	15							
	16							
	17							

ENROLLMENT
OF NOS. 1 HEREON
APPROVED BY THE SECRETARY
OF INTERIOR JAN 17 1903

TRIBAL ENROLLMENT OF PARENTS

	Name of Father	Year	County	Name of Mother	Year	County
1	Thomas James	Dead	Sugar Loaf	Nicey Fisher	Dead	Sugar Loaf
2						
3						
4						
5						
6						
7						
8						
9						
10						
11						
12						
13						
14						
15						
16			Date of Application for Enrollment.	6/6/99		
17	P.O. Sutter, I.T. 1/11/07					

Choctaw By Blood Enrollment Cards 1898-1914

RESIDENCE: Sugar Loaf COUNTY. **Choctaw Nation** **Choctaw Roll** *(Not Including Freedmen)* CARD No.
POST OFFICE: Kennedy, I.T. FIELD No. 2328

Dawes' Roll No.	NAME		Relationship to Person	AGE	SEX	BLOOD	TRIBAL ENROLLMENT		
							Year	County	No.
6734	1 Peter, Davis	49	First Named	46	M	Full	1896	Sugar Loaf	10135
6735	2 " Mary Ann	33	Wife	30	F	"	1896	" "	10136
6736	3 " Larly	16	Dau	13	"	"	1896	" "	10137
6737	4 " Wynie	14	"	11	"	"	1896	" "	10138
6738	5 " Callis	10	Son	7	M	"	1896	" "	10139

ENROLLMENT
OF NOS. 1,2,3,4,5 HEREON
APPROVED BY THE SECRETARY
OF INTERIOR JAN 17 1903

TRIBAL ENROLLMENT OF PARENTS

	Name of Father	Year	County	Name of Mother	Year	County
1	Simon Peter	1896	Sugar Loaf	Na-me-a-ho-na	Dead	Skullyville
2	A-tok-lan-tubby	Dead	Skullyville	Ba-la-le-hu-na	"	"
3	No1			No2		
4	No1			No2		
5	No1			No2		

No1 on 1896 roll as Davis Petter
No2 " 1896 " " Mary Ann "
No3 " 1896 " " Larly "
No4 " 1896 " " Wynie "
No5 " 1896 " " Callis "

Date of Application for Enrollment. 6/6/99

228

Choctaw By Blood Enrollment Cards 1898-1914

RESIDENCE: Sugar Loaf COUNTY. **Choctaw Nation** Choctaw Roll CARD NO.

POST OFFICE: Summerfield, I.T *(Not Including Freedmen)* FIELD NO. 2329

Dawes' Roll No.	NAME	Relationship to Person	AGE	SEX	BLOOD	TRIBAL ENROLLMENT		
						Year	County	No.
DEAD.	Tisho, Tennessee DEAD. First	Named	26	F	Full	1896	Sugar Loaf	11974
6739 2	" Ida 9	Dau	6	"	"	1896	" "	11975
3								
4								
5								
6								
7								
8								
9								
10								
11	No. 1 HEREON DISMISSED UNDER							
12	ORDER OF THE COMMISSION TO THE FIVE							
13	CIVILIZED TRIBES OF MARCH 31, 1905.							
14								
15	ENROLLMENT OF NOS. 2 HEREON							
16	APPROVED BY THE SECRETARY							
17	OF INTERIOR JAN 17 1903							

TRIBAL ENROLLMENT OF PARENTS

	Name of Father	Year	County	Name of Mother	Year	County
1	John Tolbert	Dead	Sugar Loaf	Nellie Tolbert	Dead	Sugar Loaf
2	Charley Tisho	"	" "	No 1		
3						
4						
5						
6	No1 on 1896 roll as Tennessee Tishue					
7	No2 " 1896 " " Ida "					
8	No.1 Died October 6, 1899. Evidence of death filed March 29, 1901					
9	No.2 lives with James McCurley, Summerfield, I.T. – Dec 18, 1902					
	The wife of James McCurley is on Choctaw Card #2362 as Rhoda Curley					
10						
11						
12						
13						
14					Date of Application for Enrollment.	
15						
16					6/6/99	
17						

Choctaw By Blood Enrollment Cards 1898-1914

RESIDENCE: Sugar Loaf	COUNTY.							
POST OFFICE: Poteau I.T.								

Choctaw Nation — **Choctaw Roll** *(Not Including Freedmen)* — CARD NO. FIELD NO. **2330**

Dawes' Roll No.	NAME	Relationship to Person First Named	AGE	SEX	BLOOD	TRIBAL ENROLLMENT Year	County	No.
6740	1 Brown, Permelia 23		20	F	1/2	1893	Kiamitia	303
6741	2 " Judy 6	Dau	3	"	1/4			
6742	3 " Pink 5	"	1	"	1/4			
~~6743~~	~~4 DIED PRIOR TO SEPTEMBER 25, 1902 Hiram~~	~~Son~~	~~2mo~~	~~M~~	~~1/4~~			
I.W. 818	5 " Mat (31)	Hus	31	M	I.W.			
	6							
	7							
	8							
	9							
	10							
	11							
	12							
	13							
	14							
	15							
	16							
	17							

ENROLLMENT OF NOS. 5 HEREON APPROVED BY THE SECRETARY OF INTERIOR May 21 1904

No.4 died April 6, 1901 · Enrollment cancelled by Department July 8, 1904

ENROLLMENT OF NOS. 1,2,3,4 HEREON APPROVED BY THE SECRETARY OF INTERIOR Jan 17 1903

TRIBAL ENROLLMENT OF PARENTS

	Name of Father	Year	County	Name of Mother	Year	County
1	Ismon Hart	1896	Kiamitia	Mattie Hart	1896	Non Citz
2	Mat Brown	1896	Non Citz	No 1		
3	" "	1896	" "	No 1		
4	~~" "~~	~~1896~~	~~" "~~	~~No 1~~		
5	Morris Brown		non citizen	Jane L Brown		non citizen
6						
7						
8	For child of Nos 1&2 see NB (Apr 26 '06) Card #232					
9	" " " " " " " " (March 3,1905) " #1199					
10	No1 on 1893 Pay roll, Kiamitia County, Page 36 No 303 as Pelemary Hart					
11	No.1 on Choctaw 1896 roll as Amelia Brown page 35: #1414					
12	No.2 " " " " " Judith " " " " #1415					
13	No.1 is wife of Mat Brown on Choctaw Card D-949 Evidence of marriage of parents with Choctaw 1512					
14	Mother of No.1 on Choctaw card #D.587					
15	No.4 Enrolled November 7th, 1900			Date of Application for Enrollment.		
16	No.4 Died April 6" 1902: Proof of death filed December 20 1902			6/6/99		
17	No5 transferred from Choctaw card D949 April 15, 1904 See decision of March 15, 1904					

P.O. Wister I T 4/17/05

Choctaw By Blood Enrollment Cards 1898-1914

RESIDENCE: Chickasaw Nation COUNTY. **Choctaw Nation** **Choctaw Roll** CARD NO.
POST OFFICE: Opie, I.T. *(Not Including Freedmen)* FIELD NO. 2331

Dawes' Roll No.	NAME	Relationship to Person	AGE	SEX	BLOOD	TRIBAL ENROLLMENT		
						Year	County	No.
I.W. 786	1 Trout, S. G. ㊺	First Named	52	M	I.W.	1896	Chick. Dist	15122
2								
3	ENROLLMENT							
4	OF NOS. 1 HEREON APPROVED BY THE SECRETARY							
5	OF INTERIOR							
6								
8	Judgement... by U.S. Court C.D. #153 admitting No. 1... and set aside by Decree of Choctaw Chickasaw Citizenship Court Dec. 17-02.							
9	Not admitted by C.C.C.C. Case #46 Jan 27 '04							
10								
11								
12								
13								
14								
15								
16								
17								

TRIBAL ENROLLMENT OF PARENTS

	Name of Father	Year	County	Name of Mother	Year	County
1	G.W. Trout	Dead	Non Citz	Catherine Trout	Dead	Non Citz
2						
3						
4						
5						
6						
7						
8						

9 Admitted by Dawes Commission, as an Intermarried Citz.
10 as S.G. Trout, Case No 297. Judgment sustained.
   Also admitted by U.S. Court Central District
11 July 13, 1897, Case No 153, as S.G. Trout
12
   On 1896 roll as G.S. Trout
13 See additional testimony of no.1 taken Oct 15, 1902.
14 Nº1 is father of Nºs 2-3 and 4 on Choctaw card #2340. He is also now the husband
15 of Annis Snider on Choctaw card #2340, Oct 15, 1902.

Date of Application for Enrollment. 6/6/99

17 P.O. Ryan, I.T.

231

Choctaw By Blood Enrollment Cards 1898-1914

RESIDENCE: Sugar Loaf
POST OFFICE: Monroe I.T.

COUNTY, **Choctaw Nation**

Choctaw Roll
(Not Including Freedmen)

CARD NO.
FIELD NO. **2332**

Dawes' Roll No.	NAME		Relationship to Person	AGE	SEX	BLOOD	TRIBAL ENROLLMENT		
							Year	County	No.
6744	1 Self Ida	24	First Named	21	F	1/4	1896	Sugar Loaf	11216
~~6745~~	2 ~~DIED PRIOR TO SEPTEMBER 25 1902~~ ~~Ola~~		~~Dau~~	~~4~~	~~F~~	~~1/8~~	~~1896~~	~~" "~~	~~11217~~
6746	3 " Eula	5	Dau	18mo	F	1/8			
6747	4 " Estella	3	Dau	5mo	F	1/8			
6748	5 " Earl	1	Son	1mo	M	1/8			
I.W.**38**	6 Self John L		Husband of No 1	33	M	I.W.	1896	Sugar Loaf	15027
	7								
	8	ENROLLMENT							
	9	OF NOS. ~~~ 6 ~~~ HEREON							
	10	APPROVED BY THE SECRETARY OF INTERIOR JUN 13 1903							
	11								
	12	ENROLLMENT							
	13	OF NOS. 1,2,3,4,5, HEREON							
	14	APPROVED BY THE SECRETARY OF INTERIOR JAN 17 1903							
	15								
	16 No.2 died Aug 14, 1900: Enrollment								
	17 cancelled by Department July 8, 1904								

TRIBAL ENROLLMENT OF PARENTS

	Name of Father	Year	County	Name of Mother	Year	County
1	Charley Wilson	Dead	Sugar Loaf	Lizzie Wilson	Dead	Non Citz
2	~~John L Self~~	~~1896~~	~~" "~~	~~No 1~~		
3	" " "	1896	" "	No 1		
4	" " "	"	" "	No 1		
5	" " "	"	" "	No 1		
6	V.G. Self	1896	" "	Mary M Self	1896	Non Citz
7	No 1 For evidence of marriage of father & mother see enrollment					
8	of her brother Archey Wilson					
9	Husband of Ida Self on W.C. No D206					
10	No3 Affidavit of birth to be supplied Received June 8-1899					
11						
12	No4 Enrolled June 5, 1900					
13	Nº5 Born April 25 1902: enrolled June 13, 1902					
	No.2 Died August 14" 1900: Proof of death filed December 20th 1902					
14	No.6 transferred from Choctaw card #D206 March 29 1903					
15	See decision of March 13, 1903				Date of Application for Enrollment.	
16				For Nos 1,2 and 3	6/6/99	
17						

Choctaw By Blood Enrollment Cards 1898-1914

RESIDENCE: Sugar Loaf
POST OFFICE: Wister I.T.

COUNTY. **Choctaw Nation**

Choctaw Roll
(Not Including Freedmen)

CARD No.
FIELD No. 2333

Dawes' Roll No.	NAME		Relationship to Person First Named	AGE	SEX	BLOOD	TRIBAL ENROLLMENT		
							Year	County	No.
6749	1 Whistler Ellis	37	First Named	34	M	Full	1896	Sugar Loaf	12844
6750	2 " Allie	31	Wife	28	F	"	1896	" "	12845
6751	3 " Belle	17	Dau	14	F	"	1896	" "	12846
6752	4 " Lillie M	14	Dau	11	F	"	1896	" "	12847
6753	5 " Ada	8	Dau	5	F	"	1896	" "	12848
6754	6 McClure Walter L	17	Neph	14	M	"	1896	" "	9102
6755	7 Thompson Webster	12	"	9	M	"	1896	" "	11968
6756	8 Whistler Neoma M	2	Dau	6mo	F	"			
	9								
	10								
	11								
	12								
	13								
	14								
	15	ENROLLMENT OF NOS. 1,2,3,4,5,6,7,8 HEREON APPROVED BY THE SECRETARY OF INTERIOR Jan 17 1903							
	16								
	17								

TRIBAL ENROLLMENT OF PARENTS

	Name of Father	Year	County	Name of Mother	Year	County
1	Tom Whistler	Dead	Sugar Loaf	Mary Nakicho	1896	Wade
2	Harris Daney	"	" "	Melvina Potts	Dead	Sugar Loaf
3	No 1			No 2		
4	No 1			No 2		
5	No 1			No 2		
6	Alfred McClure	1896	Tobucksy	Minnie McClure	Dead	Sugar Loaf
7	Gilbert Thompson	1896	Wade	Minnie Thompson	"	" " "
8	No 1			No 2		
9						
10		No4 On 1896 roll as Lillie Whistler				
11		No6 " " " " Lee McClure				
12		No7 " " " " G.W. Thompson Jr				
		No.8 Enrolled May 6, 1901				
13						
14						#1 to 7
15					Date of Application for Enrollment	
16						6/6/99
17						

233

Choctaw By Blood Enrollment Cards 1898-1914

RESIDENCE: Sugar Loaf   COUNTY. **Choctaw Nation**   **Choctaw Roll** *(Not Including Freedmen)*   CARD No.

POST OFFICE: Wister, I.T.   FIELD No. 2334

Dawes' Roll No.	NAME		Relationship to Person First Named	AGE	SEX	BLOOD	TRIBAL ENROLLMENT		
							Year	County	No.
6757	1 Curtis, Ella	24	First Named	21	F	1/2	1896	Sugar Loaf	3965
6758	2 Free, Rosetta	21	Sister	18	F	1/2	1896	" "	3966
6759	3 " Lonnie	17	Bro	14	M	1/2	1896	" "	3967
6760	4 " Maudie	14	Sist.	11	F	1/2	1896	" "	3968
6761	5 " William	12	Bro	9	M	1/2	1896	" "	3969
6762	6 " Lona	10	Sist.	7	F	1/2	1896	" "	3970
6763	7 " Nettie	8	Sist.	5	F	1/2	1896	" "	3971
6764	8 Curtis Willie C	2	Son	2mo	M	1/4			
	9								
	10								
	11								
	12								
	13								
	14								
	15								
	16								
	17								

ENROLLMENT
OF NOS. 1,2,3,4,5,6,7,8 HEREON
APPROVED BY THE SECRETARY
OF INTERIOR JAN 17 1903

TRIBAL ENROLLMENT OF PARENTS

	Name of Father	Year	County	Name of Mother	Year	County
1	Walker Free	Dead	Non Citz	Elizabeth Free	Dead	Sugar Loaf
2	" "	"	" " "	Elizabeth Free	"	" " "
3	" "	"	" " "	" "	"	" " "
4	" "	"	" " "	" "	"	" " "
5	" "	"	" " "	" "	"	" " "
6	" "	"	" " "	" "	"	" " "
7	" "	"	" " "	" "	"	" " "
8	Thomas A Curtis		" "	No.1		
9						
10		No2 On 1896 roll as Rosie L Free				
11		No3 " " " " Alonzo Free				
12		No.1 is now the wife of Thomas Curtis Oct 2d 1900				
13		No8 Enrolled Oct 2nd 1900				
		For child of No.1 see NB (March 3,1905) #760				
14						
15					#1 to 7	
16				Date of Application for Enrollment.	6/6/99	
17	P.O. Richart[sic] I.T. 3/3/05					

Choctaw By Blood Enrollment Cards 1898-1914

RESIDENCE: Sugar Loaf   COUNTY. **Choctaw Nation**   **Choctaw Roll**   CARD NO.
POST OFFICE: Wister I.T.   *(Not Including Freedmen)*   FIELD NO.   2335

Dawes' Roll No.	NAME	Relationship to Person First Named	AGE	SEX	BLOOD	TRIBAL ENROLLMENT Year	County	No.
DEAD.	1 Johnson George W	Named	58	M	I.W.			
6765	2 McClure, Mary A 23	Dau	20	F	1/4	1896	Skullyville	6476
14732	3 Tucker, Martha Belle 21	Dau	18	F	1/4	1896	"	6477
6766	4 McClure, Isaac W 1	Gr.Son	4mo	M	3/16			
14733	5 Tucker Oscar McK 1	Gr.Son	4½ mo	M	1/8			
	6							
	7							
	8 Father of Nº5 is Oscar Tucker non-citz							
	9 Mother of Nº5 is Nº3							
	10							
	11 No. 1 HEREON DISMISSED UNDER							
	12 ORDER OF THE COMMISSIONER TO THE FIVE CIVILIZED TRIBES OF JULY 18, 1905.							
	13							
	14							
	15 ENROLLMENT OF NOS. 2, 4, HEREON							
	16 APPROVED BY THE SECRETARY							
	17 OF INTERIOR JAN 17 1903							

ENROLLMENT OF NOS. 3 and 5 HEREON APPROVED BY THE SECRETARY OF INTERIOR MAY 20 1903

TRIBAL ENROLLMENT OF PARENTS

	Name of Father	Year	County	Name of Mother	Year	County
1	John Johnson	Dead	Non Citz	Eliza Johnson	Dead	Non Citz
2	No 1			Sahar Jane Johnson	"	Sugar Loaf
3	No 1			" " "	"	" "
4	Newton McClure	1896	Blue	Nº2		
5	No1 Admitted by Dawes Com as intermarried citizen case #1046 as G.W.					
6	Johnson. Judgment sustained					
7	No2 On 1896 roll as Mary Johnson					
8	No.1 died in fall of 1900: Proof of death filed August 11, 1906					
9	See letter enclosed as to marriage of No.1 to white woman.					
10	Nº1 married out, see original 1896 papers and letter referred to above					
11	Nº3 is now the wife of Oscar Tucker-non-citizen, evidence of marriage requested Oct. 15, 1902. Recd and filed Oct 24, 1902					
12	Nº5 Born May 28, 1902; enrolled Oct. 15, 1902					
13	For child of No2 see NB (Apr 26-06) Card #576					
14	Nº2 is now the wife of Newton McClure on Choctaw card #3345. Evidence of marriage filed Sept 10, 1902					
15	Nº4 Born May 15, 1902; enrolled Sept 10, 1902					
16	For child of No.3 see NB (Mar 3 '05) #546					
17	No3 Cameron 8/4/05			Date of Application for Enrollment.	6/6/99	

Choctaw By Blood Enrollment Cards 1898-1914

Dawes' Roll No.	NAME		Relationship to Person First Named	AGE	SEX	BLOOD	TRIBAL ENROLLMENT		
							Year	County	No.
6767	1 Jones Joseph	52	First Named	49	M	Full	1896	Sugar Loaf	6509
6768	2 " Sallie	53	Wife	50	F	"	1896	" "	11214
~~6769~~	~~3 DIED PRIOR TO SEPTEMBER 25 1902 Isabelle~~		~~Dau~~	~~24~~	~~F~~	~~"~~	~~1896~~	~~" "~~	~~6511~~
6770	4 " Ida	20	Dau	17	F	"	1896	" "	6512
6771	5 Sam Elizabeth	12	Step Dau	9	F	"	1896	" "	11215
	6								
	7								
	8								
	9								
	10								
	11								
	12								
	13								
	14								
	15	ENROLLMENT OF NOS. 1, 2, 3, 4, 5 HEREON APPROVED BY THE SECRETARY OF INTERIOR Jan 17 1903								
	16								
	17								

TRIBAL ENROLLMENT OF PARENTS

	Name of Father	Year	County	Name of Mother	Year	County
1	Joel Jones	Dead	Sugar Loaf	Ish-tqa-ho-ke	Dead	Skullyville
2	Hom-be	"	Skullyville	Em-ma	"	" "
3	~~No 1~~			~~Betsy Ushta~~	"	" "
4	John Jones	Dead	Skullyville	Nicey Jones	"	" "
5	Charley Sam	"	Sugar Loaf	No 2		
6						
7						
8	No2 On 1896 roll as Sallie Sam					
9	No.3 Died January 12" 1901: Proof of death filed December 20" 1902					
10	No.3 died Jan 12, 1901: Enrollment cancelled by Department July 8, 1904					
11	No.4 is duplicate of Lottie Jones No.1 on Choctaw roll card #927 roll #2566. Enrollment					
12	thereon cancelled under Departmental instructions of N9ovember 27, 1905 (I.T.D.					
13	15574-1905) D.C. 53806-1905					
14						
15					Date of Application for Enrollment.	
16					6/6/99	
17						

Choctaw By Blood Enrollment Cards 1898-1914

Dawes' Roll No.	NAME		Relationship to Person First Named	AGE	SEX	BLOOD	TRIBAL ENROLLMENT		
							Year	County	No.
6772	1 Watson William	72	First Named	69	M		1896	Sugar Loaf	12857
6773	2 " Betsy	83	Wife	80	F		1896	" "	12858
	3								
	4								
	5								
	6								
	7								
	12								
	13								
	14								
	15								
	16								
	17								

ENROLLMENT
OF NOS. 1, 2,   HEREON
APPROVED BY THE SECRETARY
OF INTERIOR JAN 17 1903

TRIBAL ENROLLMENT OF PARENTS

	Name of Father	Year	County	Name of Mother	Year	County
1	Rama-se-lo-bi	Dead	Mississippi	Ka-hla-ho-na	Dead	Sugar Loaf
2				Tsa-ha-ho-ke	"	" " "
3						
4						
5		No1 On 1896 roll as William Wartson				
6		No2 " " " " Betsy Wartson				
7						
8						
9						
10						
11						
12						
13						
14						
15						
16					Date of Application for Enrollment.	6/6/99
17						

Choctaw By Blood Enrollment Cards 1898-1914

RESIDENCE: Sugar Loaf POST OFFICE: Monroe I.T.	COUNTY.	Choctaw Nation				Choctaw Roll (Not Including Freedmen)		CARD NO. FIELD NO. 2338	

Dawes' Roll No.	NAME	Relationship to Person First Named	AGE	SEX	BLOOD	TRIBAL ENROLLMENT		
						Year	County	No.
6771	1 Anderson Annie ⁴⁰	First Named	37	F	Full	1896	Sugar Loaf	59
DEAD.	2 " William DEAD.	Son	4	M	"	1896	" "	60
DEAD.	3 Harmby Sibbie DEAD.	Dau	18	F	"	" "		5230
	4							
	5							
	6							
	7 No. 2&3 HEREON DISMISSED UNDER							
	8 ORDER OF THE COMMISSION TO THE FIVE CIVILIZED TRIBES OF MARCH 31, 1905.							
	9							
	10							
	11							
	12							
	13							
	14							
	15 ENROLLMENT OF NOS. 1 HEREON							
	16 APPROVED BY THE SECRETARY OF INTERIOR JAN 17 1903							
	17							

TRIBAL ENROLLMENT OF PARENTS

	Name of Father	Year	County	Name of Mother	Year	County
1	William Watson	1896	Sugar Loaf	Ki-a-ho-na	Dead	Sugar Loaf
2	Hickman Anderson	1896	Wade	No 1		
3	Willis Harmby	Dead	Sugar Loaf	No 1		
4						
5						
6						
7		No3 On 1896 Roll as Sibbie Humby				
8		No3 died November 5 1900: Proof of death filed Aug 6 1901				
9		\Nº2 Died Aug 2 1902: Proof of death filed Aug 27, 1902				
10						
11						
12						
13						
14						
15						
16				Date of Application for Enrollment.	6/6/99	
17						

RESIDENCE: Sugar Loaf

POST OFFICE: Howe, I.T.

COUNTY. **Choctaw Nation**

Choctaw Roll *(Not Including Freedmen)*

CARD No.

FIELD No. 2339

Dawes' Roll No.	NAME		Relationship to Person First Named	AGE	SEX	BLOOD	TRIBAL ENROLLMENT		
							Year	County	No.
6775	1 Jack, Loman	55	First Named	52	M	Full	1896	Sugar Loaf	6505
6776	2 " Hama	58	Wife	55	F	"	1896	" "	6506
	3								
	4								
	5								
	6								
	7								
	8								
	9								
	10								
	11								
	12								
	13								
	14								
	15								
	16								
	17								

ENROLLMENT
OF NOS. 1, 2, HEREON
APPROVED BY THE SECRETARY
OF INTERIOR JAN 17 1903

TRIBAL ENROLLMENT OF PARENTS

	Name of Father	Year	County	Name of Mother	Year	County
1	E-ya-ka-yo	Dead	Sugar Loaf	Ho-na	Dead	Sugar Loaf
2	Hok-le-chubbee	"	" " "	Okla-me-a	"	" " "
3						
4						
5						
6		No2 on 1896 roll as Hamma Jack				
7						
8						
9						
10						
11						
12						
13						
14						
15						
16				Date of Application for Enrollment.	6/6/99	
17						

239

Choctaw By Blood Enrollment Cards 1898-1914

RESIDENCE:	Chickasaw Natn	COUNTY.						
POST OFFICE:	Opie, I.T.							

Choctaw Nation

Choctaw Roll (Not Including Freedmen)

CARD NO.

FIELD NO. 2340

Dawes' Roll No.	NAME		Relationship to Person	AGE	SEX	BLOOD	TRIBAL ENROLLMENT		
							Year	County	No.
6777	1 Snider, Annis	33	First Named	30	F	1/16	1896	Tobucksy	11281
6778	2 Trout, John R	17	Son	14	M	1/32	1896	"	12020
6779	3 " Lillie V	14	Dau	11	F	1/32	1896	"	12021
6780	4 " Katie M	12	"	9	"	1/32	1896	"	12022
6781	5 Key, Ambrose	9	Son	6	M	1/32	1896	"	7493
6782	6 Snider, Beatrice	7	Dau	4	F	1/32	1896	"	11282
	7								
	8								
	9								
	10								
	11								
	12								
	13								
	14								
	15	ENROLLMENT OF NOS. 1,2,3,4,5,6 HEREON							
	16	APPROVED BY THE SECRETARY OF INTERIOR JAN 17 1903							
	17								

TRIBAL ENROLLMENT OF PARENTS

	Name of Father	Year	County	Name of Mother	Year	County
1	Andrew Stanton	Dead	Skullyville	Eliz Stanton	1896	Non Citz
2	S. G. Trout	1896	white man	No 1		
3	" " "	1896	" "	No 1		
4	" " "	1896	" "	No 1		
5	Charley Key	Dead	Non Citz	No 1		
6	Tom Snider	1896	" "	No 1		
7						
8	No1 on 1896 roll as Annie Snider					
9	No2 " 1896 " " John Trout					
10	No3 " 1896 " " Viola "					
11	No4 " 1896 " " Maud "					
12	No5 " 1896 " " Ambrose Keys					
	Evidence of marriage of parents of No1 to be supplied					
13	For Evidence of marriage see enrollment of Elizabeth G. Folsom					
14	N°1 is now the wife of Seth G Trout on Choctaw card #2331. See testimony					
	of Seth G Trout filed with Choctaw #2331, Oct 15, 1902.					

Date of Application for Enrollment.

15		6/6/99
16		
17	P.O. Ran, I.T.	

Choctaw By Blood Enrollment Cards 1898-1914

RESIDENCE: Sugar Loaf   COUNTY. **Choctaw Nation**   Choctaw Roll   CARD NO.
POST OFFICE: Howe, I.T.   *(Not Including Freedmen)*   FIELD NO. 2341

Dawes' Roll No.	NAME		Relationship to Person First Named	AGE	SEX	BLOOD	TRIBAL ENROLLMENT		
							Year	County	No.
6783	1 Billy, Tyles	33	First Named	30	M	Full	1896	Sugar Loaf	798
6784	2 " Marlin	12	Son	9	"	"	1896	" "	799
6785	3 " Jackson	10	"	7	"	"	1896	" "	800
	4								
	5								
	6								
	7								
	8								
	9								
	10								
	11								
	12								
	13								
	14								
	15	ENROLLMENT OF NOS. 1, 2, 3, HEREON							
	16	APPROVED BY THE SECRETARY							
	17	OF INTERIOR JAN 17 1903							

TRIBAL ENROLLMENT OF PARENTS

	Name of Father	Year	County	Name of Mother	Year	County		
1	Jackson Billy	Dead	Sugar Loaf	Me-ha-le	Dead	Sugar Loaf		
2	No 1			Rabie Billy	"	" "		
3	No 1			" "	"	" "		
4								
5								
6			No2 on 1896 roll as Martin Billy					
7								
8								
9								
10								
11								
12								
13								
14						Date of Application for Enrollment		
15								
16						6/6/99		
17								

241

Choctaw By Blood Enrollment Cards 1898-1914

RESIDENCE: Skullyville   COUNTY. **Choctaw Nation**   **Choctaw Roll** *(Not Including Freedmen)*   CARD NO.

POST OFFICE: Pocola, I.T.   FIELD NO. 2342

Dawes' Roll No.	NAME	Relationship to Person	AGE	SEX	BLOOD	TRIBAL ENROLLMENT		
						Year	County	No.
I.W. 904	1 Folsom, Mary Elizabeth	First Named	50	F	I.W.	1896	Skullyville	14514
	2							
	3							
	4							
	5							
	6							
	7							
	8							
	9							
	10							
	11							
	12							
	13							
	14							
	15							
	16							
	17							

ENROLLMENT
OF NOS.   1   HEREON
APPROVED BY THE SECRETARY
OF INTERIOR   AUG 3 1904

TRIBAL ENROLLMENT OF PARENTS

Name of Father	Year	County	Name of Mother	Year	County
1 James Jones	Dead	Non Citz	Susan Jones	1896	Non Citz
2					
3					
4					
5	wife of Willis Frances Folsom 1893 Skullyville #181 & 1896 Skullyville #3921 Died Oct 22 '98				
6	License exhibited and found satisfactory but				
7	not in a condition to be filed Certified copy of marriage certificate				
8	filed December 20, 1902				
9					
10					
11					
12					
13					
14					
15	No1 Evidence requested 4/2/04				
16			Date of Application for Enrollment.	6/6/99	
17	P.O. Wilburton I.T. 5/8/04				

Choctaw By Blood Enrollment Cards 1898-1914

RESIDENCE: Sugar Loaf   COUNTY. **Choctaw Nation**   **Choctaw Roll** *(Not Including Freedmen)*   CARD No.

POST OFFICE: Howe, I.T.   FIELD No. 2343

Dawes' Roll No.	NAME		Relationship to Person First Named	AGE	SEX	BLOOD	TRIBAL ENROLLMENT		
							Year	County	No.
6786	₁ Billy, Watson	27	First Named	24	M	3/4	1896	Sugar Loaf	822
I.W. 1299	₂ " Minnie	21	Wife	18	F	I.W.			
	₃								
	₄								
	₅								
	₆								
	₇								
	₈								
	₉								
	10								
	11	ENROLLMENT							
	12	OF NOS. 2 HEREON							
	13	APPROVED BY THE SECRETARY OF INTERIOR MAR 14 1905							
	14								
	15	ENROLLMENT							
	16	OF NOS. 1 HEREON APPROVED BY THE SECRETARY OF INTERIOR JAN 17 1903							
	17								

TRIBAL ENROLLMENT OF PARENTS

	Name of Father	Year	County	Name of Mother	Year	County
₁	Simon Billy	1896	Sugar Loaf	Lettie Billy	Dead	Sugar Loaf
₂	John Anderson	1896	Non Citz	Nancy B Anderson	"	Non Citz
₃						
₄						
₅						
₆						
₇		As to evidence of marriage, see testimony of No1				
₈		and that of William Watson				
₉						
10		Nos 1 and 2 have separated For child of No1 see NB (Apr 26, 1906) Card #234			Minor	
11						
12						
13						
14						
15						
16				Date of Application for Enrollment.	6/6/99	
17						

243

Choctaw By Blood Enrollment Cards 1898-1914

RESIDENCE: Sugar Loaf   COUNTY.   **Choctaw Nation**   Choctaw Roll   CARD NO.
POST OFFICE: Wister, I.T.   (Not Including Freedmen)   FIELD NO. 2344

Dawes' Roll No.	NAME		Relationship to Person First Named	AGE	SEX	BLOOD	TRIBAL ENROLLMENT		
							Year	County	No.
6787	1 Freeman, George	39		36	M	Full	1896	Sugar Loaf	3958
6788	2 " Memiss	59	Wife	56	F	"	1896	" "	3959
	3								
	4								
	5								
	6								
	7								
	8								
	9								
	10								
	11								
	12								
	13								
	14								
	15	ENROLLMENT OF NOS. 1, 2, HEREON							
	16	APPROVED BY THE SECRETARY OF INTERIOR JAN 17 1903							
	17								

TRIBAL ENROLLMENT OF PARENTS

	Name of Father	Year	County	Name of Mother	Year	County	
1	A-te-ka-tubbee	Dead	Nashoba	Ha-te-ma	Dead	Sugar Loaf	
2	O-ola-lin-tubbee	"	Sugar Loaf	She-ne-pa	"	"	"
3							
4							
5							
6							
7							
8			No's 1 and 2 have separated.				
9							
10							
11							
12							
13							
14							
15							
16				Date of Application for Enrollment.	6/6/99		
17							

244

Choctaw By Blood Enrollment Cards 1898-1914

RESIDENCE: Sugar Loaf

POST OFFICE: Wister, I.T.

COUNTY

Choctaw Nation

Choctaw Roll
(Not Including Freedmen)

CARD NO.

FIELD NO. 2345

Dawes' Roll No.	NAME		Relationship to Person First Named	AGE	SEX	BLOOD	TRIBAL ENROLLMENT		
							Year	County	No.
6789	1 Dwight, George	66	First Named	63	M	Full	1896	Sugar Loaf	3246
6790	2 " Sallie	57	Wife	54	F	"	1896	" "	3247
6791	3 Colbert, Sam	10	Ward	7	M	"	1896	" "	2244
	4								
	5								
	6								
	7								
	8								
	9								
	10								
	11								
	12								
	13								
	14								
	15	ENROLLMENT OF NOS. 1, 2, 3, HEREON APPROVED BY THE SECRETARY OF INTERIOR JAN 17 1903							
	16								
	17								

TRIBAL ENROLLMENT OF PARENTS

	Name of Father	Year	County	Name of Mother	Year	County
1	Fa-la-me	Dead	Skullyville	Te-fah-ke	Dead	Sugar Loaf
2	E-ma-ko-tubbee	"	Sugar Loaf		"	" "
3	Silas Colbert	"	" "	Sisa Colbert	"	" "
4						
5						
6						
7		No2 on 1896 roll as Sally Ann Dwight				
8		Nos 1&3 Died prior to Sept 25, 1902; Not entitled to land or money				
9		See I.O.L.G.F. 907-1911				
10						
11						
12						
13						
14						
15					Date of Application for Enrollment.	
16					6/6/99	
17						

Choctaw By Blood Enrollment Cards 1898-1914

RESIDENCE: Sugar Loaf	COUNTY.							CARD NO.
POST OFFICE: Wister, I.T.	Choctaw Nation			Choctaw Roll (Not Including Freedmen)			FIELD NO.	2346

Dawes' Roll No.	NAME	Relationship to Person First Named	AGE	SEX	BLOOD	TRIBAL ENROLLMENT		
						Year	County	No.
6792	1 Dwight, Jackson DIED PRIOR TO SEPTEMBER 25, 1902		51	M	Full	1896	Sugar Loaf	3268
6793	2 " Susan 20	Wife	17	F	"	1896	" "	8506
	3							
	4							
	5							
	6							
	7							
	8							
	9							
	10							
	11							
	12							
	13							
	14							
	15 ENROLLMENT OF NOS. 1, 2, HEREON							
	16 APPROVED BY THE SECRETARY OF INTERIOR JAN 17 1903							
	17							

TRIBAL ENROLLMENT OF PARENTS

Name of Father	Year	County	Name of Mother	Year	County
1 Fa-la-me	Dead	Skullyville	Te-fah-ke	Dead	Sugar Loaf
2 John Martin	"	Sugar Loaf	Maley Martin	"	" " "
3					
4					
5					
6		No2 on 1896 roll as Susan Martin			
7		No.1 Died February 15" 1901: Proof of death filed December 20" 1902			
8		No.1 died Feb 15 1901: Enrollment cancelled by Department July 8, 1904			
9					
10					
11					
12					
13					
14					
15					
16			Date of Application for Enrollment.	6/6/99	
17					

246

RESIDENCE: Sugar Loaf	COUNTY.			CARD NO.			
POST OFFICE: Howe, I.T.	Choctaw Nation			Choctaw Roll (Not Including Freedmen)		FIELD NO. 2347	

Dawes' Roll No.	NAME	Relationship to Person	AGE	SEX	BLOOD	TRIBAL ENROLLMENT		
						Year	County	No.
6794	1 Powell, Ernest 23	First Named	20	M	3/8	1896	Sugar Loaf	10116
6795	2 McCartney, Elsie 20	Sister	17	F	3/8	1896	" "	10134
6796	3 McCartney, Argie 3	Son of No2	1mo	M	3/16			
6797	4 " Elvia 1	Dau of No2	1mo	F	3/16			
	5							
	6							
	7							
	8							
	9							
	10							
	11							
	12							
	13							
	14							
	15	ENROLLMENT OF NOS. 1, 2, 3, 4, HEREON						
	16	APPROVED BY THE SECRETARY						
	17	OF INTERIOR JAN 17 1903						

TRIBAL ENROLLMENT OF PARENTS

	Name of Father	Year	County	Name of Mother	Year	County
1		Dead	Non Citz	Melvina	Dead	Sugar Loaf
2		"	" "	"	"	" "
3	Charley McCartney		" "	No.2		
4	C. E. McCartney		" "	No2		
5						
6						
7		Claim never to have known father's name				
8		No.2 is now the wife of Chas E McCartney				
9		Evidence of marriage filed February 14, 1901				
10		No.3 Enrolled February 15, 1901				
11		No4 Born July 19, 1902; enrolled Oct. 9, 1902				
12		For child of No.2 see NB (Mar 3-1905) card #569				
13						
14						
15				#1&2		
16				Date of Application for Enrollment.	6/6/99	
17						

247

Choctaw By Blood Enrollment Cards 1898-1914

RESIDENCE: Sugar Loaf   COUNTY. **Choctaw Nation** **Choctaw Roll**   CARD NO.

POST OFFICE: Howe, I.T.   (Not Including Freedmen)   FIELD NO. 2348

Dawes' Roll No.	NAME		Relationship to Person	AGE	SEX	BLOOD	TRIBAL ENROLLMENT		
							Year	County	No.
6798	1 Billy, Simon	51	First Named	48	M	Full	1896	Sugar Loaf	802
I.W. 39	2 " Ida	32	Wife	29	F	I.W.			
6799	3 " Albert	14	Son	11	M	1/2	1896	Sugar Loaf	803
6800	4 " Dennis	10	"	7	"	1/2	1896	" "	804
6801	5 " Gilbert	1	Son	3mo	M	1/2			
	6								
	7								
	8								
	9								
	10								
	11								
	12								
	13								
	14								
	15	ENROLLMENT OF NOS. 1, 2, 3, 4, 5 HEREON APPROVED BY THE SECRETARY OF INTERIOR		ENROLLMENT OF NOS. ~~ 2 ~~ HEREON APPROVED BY THE SECRETARY OF INTERIOR JUN 13 1903					
	16								
	17								

TRIBAL ENROLLMENT OF PARENTS

	Name of Father	Year	County	Name of Mother	Year	County
1	Jackson Billy	Dead	Sugar Loaf	Me-ha-le	Dead	Sugar Loaf
2	Hatfield	"	Non Citz	Cyntha[sic] Hatfield	1896	Non Citz
3	No1			No2		
4	No1			No2		
5	No.1			No.2		
6						
7						
8						
9			No⁵ Born Nov 15, 1901; enrolled Feby 20, 1902			
10						
11						
12						
13						
14					#1 to 4	
15						
16				Date of Application for Enrollment.	6/6/99	
17						

Choctaw By Blood Enrollment Cards 1898-1914

RESIDENCE: Sugar Loaf   COUNTY. **Choctaw Nation**   **Choctaw Roll**   CARD No.
POST OFFICE: Wister, I.T   (Not Including Freedmen)   FIELD No. 2349

Dawes' Roll No.	NAME		Relationship to Person	AGE	SEX	BLOOD	TRIBAL ENROLLMENT		
							Year	County	No.
6802	1 James, Elissie	33	First Named	30	F	Full	1896	Sugar Loaf	6498
	2								
	3								
	4								
	5								
	6								
	7								
	8								
	9								
	10								
	11								
	12								
	13								
	14								
	15								
	16								
	17								

ENROLLMENT
OF NOS. 1 HEREON
APPROVED BY THE SECRETARY
OF INTERIOR JAN 17 1903

TRIBAL ENROLLMENT OF PARENTS

	Name of Father	Year	County	Name of Mother	Year	County
1	To-spa-tubbee	Dead	Sugar Loaf	She-ne-pa	Dead	Sugar Loaf
2						
3						
4						
5						
6						
7						
8		No 1 on 1896 roll as Elisie James				
9						
10		"Died prior to September 25, 1902: not entitled to land or money"				
11		See Indian Office letter May 13, 1910, D.C.				
12						
13						
14						
15						
16				Date of Application for Enrollment.	6/6/99	
17						

249

Choctaw By Blood Enrollment Cards 1898-1914

RESIDENCE: Sugar Loaf COUNTY.		Choctaw Nation				Choctaw Roll (Not Including Freedmen)		CARD NO.	
POST OFFICE: Summerfield, I.T.								FIELD NO. 2350	

Dawes' Roll No.	NAME	Relationship to Person	AGE	SEX	BLOOD	TRIBAL ENROLLMENT		
						Year	County	No.
6803	1 Sexton, Henry 30	First Named	27	M	1/2	1896	Sugar Loaf	11175
15574	2 " Minnie 20	Wife	17	F	1/8	1896	" "	11227
	3							
	4							
	5							
	6							
	7							
	8							
	9							
	10							
	11	ENROLLMENT						
	12	OF NOS. ~~ 2 ~~ HEREON APPROVED BY THE SECRETARY						
	13	OF INTERIOR SEP 22 1904						
	14							
	15	ENROLLMENT OF NOS. 1 HEREON						
	16	APPROVED BY THE SECRETARY						
	17	OF INTERIOR JAN 17 1903						

TRIBAL ENROLLMENT OF PARENTS

	Name of Father	Year	County	Name of Mother	Year	County
1	Alfred Sexton	Dead	Wade	Julie Sexton	Dead	Sugar Loaf
2	Robt Satterfield	1896	non citizen	Drusilla Satterfield	1896	" "
3						
4						
5						
6						
7	No 1 is now husband of Minnie Satterfield on Choctaw card D230					
8	Evidence of marriage filed Dec. 26, 1902.					
9	N*2 transferred from Choctaw card #D230					
10	For children of Nos 1&2 see NB (March 3, 1905) #997					
11						
12						
13						
14						
15						
16			DATE OF APPLICATION FOR ENROLLMENT.	6/6/99		
17						

250

Choctaw By Blood Enrollment Cards 1898-1914

RESIDENCE: Sugar Loaf COUNTY.
POST OFFICE: Howe, I.T.

Choctaw Nation

Choctaw Roll (Not Including Freedmen)

CARD No. FIELD No. 2351

Dawes' Roll No.	NAME		Relationship to Person First Named	AGE	SEX	BLOOD	TRIBAL ENROLLMENT		
							Year	County	No.
6804	1 Runton, Carnolie	30	First Named	27	M	1/4	1896	Sugar Loaf	10713
I.W. 40	2 " Tabitha	28	Wife	25	F	I.W.			
6805	3 " Wilson E	6	Son	3	M	1/8	1896	Sugar Loaf	10714
6806	4 " Burton	3	"	3mo	M	1/8			
6807	5 " Bertha	3	Dau	3mo	F	1/8			
6808	6 " Bessie May	1	Dau	2mo	F	1/8			
	7								
	8								
	9								
	10								
	11	ENROLLMENT							
	12	OF NOS. ~~~ 2 ~~~ HEREON APPROVED BY THE SECRETARY							
	13	OF INTERIOR JUN 13 1903							
	14								
	15	ENROLLMENT							
	16	OF NOS. 1,3,4,5,6 HEREON APPROVED BY THE SECRETARY							
	17	OF INTERIOR JAN 17 1903							

TRIBAL ENROLLMENT OF PARENTS

	Name of Father	Year	County	Name of Mother	Year	County
1	James Runton	Dead	Sugar Loaf	Nancy Runton	Dead	Non Citz
2	John M Doyle	"	Non Citz	Lutetia Doyle	"	" "
3	No 1			No 2		
4	No 1			No 2		
5	No 1			No 2		
6	No 1			No 2		
7						
8	As to marriage of parents of No1, see testimony of					
9	William Watson also as to marriage of No1 and No2					
10						
11	No3 on 1896 roll as Wilson Runton					
12	No.6 Born August 26, 1901 and enrolled October 28, 1901					
13	For children of Nos 1&2 see NB (Mar 3 1905) card #603					
14					#1 to 5	
15					Date of Application for Enrollment.	
16					6/6/99	
17	P.O. Heavener, I.T. 4/1/05				Nos 4-5 enrolled Oct 6/99	

251

Choctaw By Blood Enrollment Cards 1898-1914

RESIDENCE: Sugar Loaf COUNTY. **Choctaw Nation** **Choctaw Roll** CARD No.
POST OFFICE: Summerfield, I.T. *(Not Including Freedmen)* FIELD No. 2352

Dawes' Roll No.	NAME	Relationship to Person Named	AGE	SEX	BLOOD	TRIBAL ENROLLMENT Year	County	No.
6809 ₁	Bell, Davis DIED PRIOR TO SEPTEMBER 25 1902	First Named	49	M	Full	1896	Sugar Loaf	764
6810 ₂	" Allie DIED PRIOR TO SEPTEMBER 25 1902	Wife	20	F	"	1896	" "	765
6811 ₃	" Davis Jr 20	Son	17	M	1/2	1896	" "	766
₄								
₅								
₆								
₇								
₈								
₉								
₁₀								
₁₁								
₁₂								
₁₃								
₁₄								
₁₅	ENROLLMENT OF NOS. 1, 2 and 3 HEREON							
₁₆	APPROVED BY THE SECRETARY OF INTERIOR JAN 17 1903							
₁₇								

TRIBAL ENROLLMENT OF PARENTS

	Name of Father	Year	County	Name of Mother	Year	County
₁	Wesley Bell	Dead	Skullyville		Dead	Sugar Loaf
₂	John Tolbert	"	Sugar Loaf	Nellie Tolbert	"	" " "
₃	No 1			Ellen Bell	"	Non Citz
₄						
₅	No.1 Died Oct 16" 1901: Proof of death filed Decr 23 1902					
₆	No.2 Died in 1900: Proof of death filed Decr 23 1902					
₇						
₈	As to marriage of parents of No3, see testimony of No1					
₉	and that of S.E. Lewis					
₁₀	No 1 died Oct 16 1901; No 2 died -- 1900; Enrollment cancelled by Department July 8 1904					
₁₁						
₁₂						
₁₃						
₁₄						
₁₅						
₁₆				Date of Application for Enrollment.	6/6/99	
₁₇						

Choctaw By Blood Enrollment Cards 1898-1914

RESIDENCE: Sugar Loaf	COUNTY.					CARD NO.	
POST OFFICE: Reichert, I.T.	**Choctaw Nation**			Choctaw Roll *(Not Including Freedmen)*		FIELD NO. 2353	

Dawes' Roll No.	NAME	Relationship to Person	AGE	SEX	BLOOD	TRIBAL ENROLLMENT		
						Year	County	No.
6812	1 Reichert, Josephine 32	First Named	29	F	3/8	1896	Sugar Loaf	781
6813	2 " William W 5	Son	2	M	3/16			
6814	3 " Johanna Marie 2	dau	2wks	F	3/16			
6815	4 " Owilie Josephine 1	Dau	2wks	F	3/16			
I.W 1491	5 " William	Husband	45	M	I.W.	1896	Sugar Loaf	14962
	6							
	7							
	8							
	9							
	10							
	11							
	12							
	13							
	14							
	15							
	16							
	17							

ENROLLMENT OF NOS. Five HEREON APPROVED BY THE SECRETARY OF INTERIOR AUG 22 1905

ENROLLMENT OF NOS. 1, 2, 3 and 4 HEREON APPROVED BY THE SECRETARY OF INTERIOR HAN 17 1903

TRIBAL ENROLLMENT OF PARENTS

	Name of Father	Year	County	Name of Mother	Year	County
1	W. A. Lewis	Dead	Non Citz	Lucinda Lewis	Dead	Tobucksy
2	William Reichert	1896	white man	No 1		
3	" "			No 1		
4	" "		on Choctaw Card #D212	No 1		
5	F.C. Reichert	dead	non citz	Louisa Reichert	dead	non citz
6						
7	On 1896 roll as Josephine Beicherd					
8						
9	Husband on Card No D212					
	No4 Born June 20" 1902; Enrolled July 3rd 1902					
10	No.5 was rejected by Commission in 1896 under name of William Richard, see 1896 Docket					
11	"C" page 386; Case #1117. No record of any appeal					
	No.5 on 1896 roll as William Ritchie					
12	No.5 1885 Sugar Loaf No 284 as William Richard. Former wife of No.5 on 1885 Sugar Loaf,					
13	No 285 as Martha Richard					
14	No.5 originally listed for enrollment on Choctaw card #D-212 6/6/99; transferred to this card					
15	July 12, 1905 See decision of May 6, 1905 No.3 enrolled 6/5/1900					
16	Martha Reichert former wife of No.5 died in 1889.					
17	P.O. Wynnewood I.T.			Date of Application for Enrollment.	#1&2 6/6/99	

253

Choctaw By Blood Enrollment Cards 1898-1914

RESIDENCE: Sugar Loaf COUNTY.			**Choctaw Nation**			**Choctaw Roll** (Not Including Freedmen)	CARD No.	
POST OFFICE: Summerfield, I.T.							FIELD No. **2354**	

Dawes' Roll No.	NAME	Relationship to Person	AGE	SEX	BLOOD	TRIBAL ENROLLMENT		
						Year	County	No.
6816	1 Bell, Malinda 33	First Named	30	F	Full	1896	Sugar Loaf	824
	2							
	3							
	4							
	5							
	6							
	7							
	8							
	9							
	10							
	11							
	12							
	13							
	14							
	15	ENROLLMENT OF NOS. 1 HEREON APPROVED BY THE SECRETARY OF INTERIOR Jan 17 1903						
	16							
	17							

TRIBAL ENROLLMENT OF PARENTS

	Name of Father	Year	County	Name of Mother	Year	County
1	Tecumseh Perry	Dead	Skullyville	Lizzie Perry	Dead	Sugar Loaf
2						
3						
4						
5	On 1896 roll as Melinda Bell					
6	Nº1 is wife of Stephen Collin Choctaw Card #2229. Certificate					
7	of marriage filed Jany 21, 1903.					
8						
9						
10						
11						
12						
13						
14						
15						
16				Date of Application for Enrollment	6/6/99	
17						

Choctaw By Blood Enrollment Cards 1898-1914

RESIDENCE: Sugar Loaf   COUNTY. **Choctaw Nation**   **Choctaw Roll**   CARD NO.
POST OFFICE: Reichert I.T.   *(Not Including Freedmen)*   FIELD NO. **2355**

Dawes' Roll No.	NAME		Relationship to Person	AGE	SEX	BLOOD	TRIBAL ENROLLMENT		
							Year	County	No.
6817	1 Sims Lula	22	First Named	19	F	3/4	1896	Skullyville	714
6818	2 " Elam A	4	Son	6mo	M	3/8			
6819	3 " Mary Ann	2	Dau	1mo	F	3/8			
	4								
	5								
	6								
	7								
	8								
	9								
	10								
	11								
	12								
	13								
	14								
	15	ENROLLMENT OF NOS. 1,2 and 3 HEREON APPROVED BY THE SECRETARY OF INTERIOR Jan 17 1903							
	16								
	17								

TRIBAL ENROLLMENT OF PARENTS

	Name of Father	Year	County	Name of Mother	Year	County
1	Lyman Bohanan	Dead	Skullyville	Celia Bohanan	Dead	Skullyville
2	T.J. Sims	1896	Non Citz	No 1		
3	Tom Sims			No 1		
4						
5						
6			No1 on 1896 roll as Lula Bohanan			
7			No.3 Enrolled April 25, 1901			
8			For child of No.1 see N.B. (Apr 26, 1906) Card No. 268			
9			" " " " " " (Mar 3, 1905) " " 155			
10						
11						
12						
13						
14						
15				#1 & 2		
16				Date of Application for Enrollment	6/6/99	
17	P.O. Wister I.T. 9/3/03					

255

Choctaw By Blood Enrollment Cards 1898-1914

RESIDENCE:	Sugar Loaf	COUNTY.					
POST OFFICE:	Summerfield, I.T.						

Choctaw Nation

Choctaw Roll (Not Including Freedmen)

CARD No.

FIELD No. 2356

Dawes' Roll No.	NAME	Relationship to Person First Named	AGE	SEX	BLOOD	TRIBAL ENROLLMENT		
						Year	County	No.
6820	1 Pain, Elsie DIED PRIOR TO SEPTEMBER 25, 1902	First Named	47	F	Full	1896	Skullyville	10105
	2							
	3							
	4							
	5							
	6							
	7							
	8							
	9							
	10							
	11							
	12							
	13							
	14							
	15							
	16							
	17							

ENROLLMENT
OF NOS. 1 HEREON
APPROVED BY THE SECRETARY
OF INTERIOR JAN 17 1903

TRIBAL ENROLLMENT OF PARENTS

	Name of Father	Year	County	Name of Mother	Year	County
1	Hampton Bell	Dead	Skullyville		Dead	Sans Bois
2						
3						
4						
5						
6						
7	No1 Died June 17" 1900: Proof of death filed Dec'r 23" 1902					
8	No.1 died June 17, 1900: Enrollment cancelled by Department July 8, 1904					
9						
10	On 1896 roll as Eliza Paine					
11						
12						
13						
14						
15						
16			Date of Application for Enrollment.	6/6/99		
17						

Choctaw By Blood Enrollment Cards 1898-1914

RESIDENCE: Sugar Loaf   COUNTY. **Choctaw Nation**   **Choctaw Roll** CARD NO.
POST OFFICE: Howe, I.T.   *(Not Including Freedmen)* FIELD NO. **2357**

Dawes' Roll No.	NAME	Relationship to Person First Named	AGE	SEX	BLOOD	TRIBAL ENROLLMENT Year	County	No.
6821	1 Jackson Joseph ³⁸	First Named	35	M	Full	1896	Sugar Loaf	6507
6822	2 " Rosie ³⁹	Wife	36	F	"	1896	" "	6508
6823	3 " Robert ⁶	Son	2	M	"			
6824	4 Hickman, Sandy ¹⁶	S.Son	13	"	3/4	1896	Sugar Loaf	5232
6825	5 Fisher, Alice ~~DIED PRIOR TO SEPTEMBER 25, 1902~~	Sister in Law	4 14	F	Full	1896	" "	3957
6826	6 Jackson, Emiline ¹	Dau	2mo	F	"			
	7							
	8							
	9							
	10							
	11							
	12							
	13							
	14							
	15	ENROLLMENT OF NOS. 1,2,3,4,5 and 6 HEREON APPROVED BY THE SECRETARY OF INTERIOR Jan 17 1903						
	16							
	17							

TRIBAL ENROLLMENT OF PARENTS

	Name of Father	Year	County	Name of Mother	Year	County
1	Reuben Jackson	Dead	Cedar	Liza Jackson	Dead	Sugar Loaf
2	Charley Fisher	"	Sugar Loaf	Winnie Fisher	"	" "
3	No 1			No 2		
4	Tom Hickman	Dead	Sugar Loaf	No 2		
5	Charley Fisher	"	" "	Natsie Fisher	Dead	Sugar Loaf
6	No.1			No.2		
7						
8						
9	No.3 Affidavit of birth to be supplied. Recd June 8/99					
10	No.6 born Nov 22d, 1901: Enrolled Jany 20th, 1902					
11	No.5 Died in October 1901: Proof of death filed Decr 23 1902 = Is No.5 duplicate of No.1 on C.C. #976? = No 976 Cancelled					
12	~~No.5 died Oct - 1901: Enrollment cancelled by Department July 8, 1904~~					
13	For child of Nos 1 and 2 see NB (March 3, 1905) #1222.					
14						
15				Date of Application for Enrollment. #1 to 5		
16				6/6/99		
17	P.O. Couser, I.T. 12/16 '02					

P.O. Heavener I.T. 4/22/05

257

Choctaw By Blood Enrollment Cards 1898-1914

RESIDENCE:	Sugar Loaf	COUNTY.	Choctaw Nation	Choctaw Roll	CARD NO.
POST OFFICE:	Howe, I.T.			(Not Including Freedmen)	FIELD NO. 2358

Dawes' Roll No.	NAME	Relationship to Person First Named	AGE	SEX	BLOOD	TRIBAL ENROLLMENT Year	County	No.
Dead	1 Washington, Benson DEAD.	Named	26	M	Full	1896	Sugar Loaf	12925
6827	2 " Losan 39	Wife	36	F	"	1896	" "	12896
6828	3 Allen, Sam 15	S.Son	12	M	"	1893	" "	9
	4							
	5							
	6 No. 1 HEREON DISMISSED UNDER							
	7 ORDER OF THE COMMISSION TO THE FIVE CIVILIZED TRIBES OF MARCH 31, 1905							
	8							
	9							
	10							
	11							
	12							
	13							
	14							
	15 ENROLLMENT OF NOS. 2 and 3 HEREON							
	16 APPROVED BY THE SECRETARY OF INTERIOR JAN 17 1903							
	17							

TRIBAL ENROLLMENT OF PARENTS

Name of Father	Year	County	Name of Mother	Year	County
1 Amos Washington	Dead	Sugar Loaf	Kon-to-na	Dead	Sugar Loaf
2 Jackson Billy	"	" " "	Me-ha-le	"	" " "
3 John Allen	"	Sans Bois	No 2		
4					
5					
6					
7 No3 on 1893 Pay roll, Sugar Loaf Co, Page 1, No 9					
8 as Samson Allen					
9 No.1 Died Oct 30, 1898, Proof of death filed March 27, 1902					
10 No.1 Date of death was Oct. 30, 1899[sic]. See letter of No2 filed Nov 4, 1902					
11					
12					
13					
14					
15				Date of Application for Enrollment.	
16				6/6/99	
17					

258

RESIDENCE:	Sugar Loaf	COUNTY.	**Choctaw Nation**	**Choctaw Roll**	CARD NO.	
POST OFFICE:	Wister, I.T.			*(Not Including Freedmen)*	FIELD NO.	2359

Dawes' Roll No.	NAME		Relationship to Person	AGE	SEX	BLOOD	TRIBAL ENROLLMENT		
							Year	County	No.
6829	1 Monroe, Milton	29	First Named	26	M	Full	1896	Sugar Loaf	8498
6830	2 " Annie	23	Wife	20	F	"	1896	" "	8499
6831	3 " Millie	6	Dau	2	"	"			
6832	4 " Bennett	3	Son	14mo	M	"			
6833	5 " Carrie	1	Dau	1mo	F	"			
	6								
	7								
	8								
	9								
	10								
	11								
	12								
	13								
	14								
	15	ENROLLMENT OF NOS. 1,2,3,4 and 5 HEREON							
	16	APPROVED BY THE SECRETARY OF INTERIOR JAN 17 1903							
	17								

TRIBAL ENROLLMENT OF PARENTS

	Name of Father	Year	County	Name of Mother	Year	County
1	William Monroe	Dead	Sugar Loaf	Phoebe Monroe	Dead	Sugar Loaf
2	Davis Peter	1896	" "	Sophia Peter	1896	Skullyville
3	No1			No2		
4	No.1			No.2		
5	Nº1			Nº2		
6						
7						
8			No1 on 1896 roll as Walton Moore			
9			No2 " 1896 " " Annie "			
10			No3 Affidavit of birth to be supplied; Recd Oct 6/99			
11			No.4 Enrolled March 4, 1901			
12			Nº5 Born March 4, 1902; enrolled April 25, 1902			
13						
14						#1 to 5
15						
16					6/6/99	
17						

Choctaw By Blood Enrollment Cards 1898-1914

RESIDENCE: Sugar Loaf COUNTY. **Choctaw Nation** **Choctaw Roll** CARD NO.
POST OFFICE: Red Oak I.T. *(Not Including Freedmen)* FIELD NO. 2360

Dawes' Roll No.	NAME	Relationship to Person	AGE	SEX	BLOOD	TRIBAL ENROLLMENT		
						Year	County	No.
6834	1 Thompson Miston ⁴⁰	First Named	37	M	Full	1896	Gaines	11997
	2							
	3							
	4							
	5							
	6							
	7							
	8							
	9							
	10							
	11							
	12							
	13							
	14							
	15	ENROLLMENT OF NOS. 1 HEREON APPROVED BY THE SECRETARY OF INTERIOR JAN 17 1903						
	16							
	17							

TRIBAL ENROLLMENT OF PARENTS

	Name of Father	Year	County	Name of Mother	Year	County
1	Ka-nia-cha-be	Dead	Sugar Loaf	La-poy-me	Dead	Sugar Loaf
2						
3						
4						
5	No1 Died prior to September 25, 1902; not entitled to land or money					
6	(See Indian Office letter September 20, 1910 D.C. #1291-1910)					
7						
8						
9						
10						
11						
12						
13						
14						
15						
16				Date of Application for Enrollment	6/6/99	
17						

Choctaw By Blood Enrollment Cards 1898-1914

RESIDENCE: Sugar Loaf
POST OFFICE: Wister, I.T.

COUNTY. **Choctaw Nation**

Choctaw Roll (Not Including Freedmen)

CARD NO.
FIELD NO. **2361**

Dawes' Roll No.	NAME	Relationship to Person First Named	AGE	SEX	BLOOD	TRIBAL ENROLLMENT Year	County	No.
DEAD	₁ Cricklin, Thomas DEAD		24	M	Full	1896	Sugar Loaf	2139
6835	₂ Peter Emiline ²³	Wife	20	F	"	1896	" "	9095
14734	₃ Cricklin Fred ⁸	Son	5	M	"			
6836	₄ McClure, Harry ¹⁷	Bro in Law	14	"	"	1896	Sugar Loaf	9096
6837	₅ Cricklin, Wilson ³	Son	2mo	"	"			
6838	₆ Peter, Minnie ¹	Dau of No2	3mo	F	"			
	₇							
	₈							
	₉ No.1 hereon dismissed under order of							
	₁₀ the Commission to the Five Civilized							
	₁₁ Tribes of March 31, 1905.							
	₁₂							
	₁₃							
	₁₄							
	₁₅ ENROLLMENT OF NOS. 2,4,5,6 HEREON			ENROLLMENT OF NOS. 3 HEREON				
	₁₆ APPROVED BY THE SECRETARY			APPROVED BY THE SECRETARY				
	₁₇ OF INTERIOR Jan 17 1903			OF INTERIOR May 20 1903				

TRIBAL ENROLLMENT OF PARENTS

	Name of Father	Year	County	Name of Mother	Year	County
₁	Jesse Cricklin	1896	Skullyville	Louisa Cricklin	Dead	Skullyville
₂	Wallace McClure	Dead	Sugar Loaf	Elsie McClure	1896	Sugar Loaf
₃	No 1			Louisa Jones	Dead	Sans Bois
₄	Wallace McClure	Dead	Sugar Loaf	Elsie McClure	1896	Sugar Loaf
₅	No 1			No 2		
₆	Barnabas Peter	1896	Sugar Loaf	N°2		
₇						
₈	No1 Dead: Evidence of Death filed June 21ˢᵗ 1902. Died May 8ᵗʰ 1900					
₉	No2 on 1896 roll as Anna McClure					
₁₀	N°2 is now the wife of Barnabas Peter on Choctaw card #2214. Evidence					
₁₁	of marriage filed Aug. 29, 1902					
₁₂	N°6 Born May 13, 1902> enrolled Aug 29, 1902					
₁₃	Mother of No3 on 1893 San Bois Co Choctaw pay roll No 531					
₁₄	For child of No.2 see NB (Mar 3-1905) Card #143					
₁₅						
₁₆				Date of Application for Enrollment	6/6/99	
₁₇				No5 Enrolled Nov 24/99		

Choctaw By Blood Enrollment Cards 1898-1914

RESIDENCE:	Sugar Loaf	COUNTY.	**Choctaw Nation**		**Choctaw Roll**	CARD No.
POST OFFICE:	Summerfield, I.T.				*(Not Including Freedmen)*	FIELD No. **2362**

Dawes' Roll No.	NAME		Relationship to Person First Named	AGE	SEX	BLOOD	TRIBAL ENROLLMENT		
							Year	County	No.
6839	1 Curley, Rhoda	27	First Named	24	F	Full	1896	Sugar Loaf	2253
6840	2 " Annie	9	Dau	6	"	1/2	1896	" "	2254
6841	3 " Arizona	7	"	4	"	1/2	1896	" "	2255
	4								
	5								
	6								
	7								
	8								
	9								
	10								
	11								
	12								
	13								
	14								
	15	ENROLLMENT OF NOS. 1,2 and 3 HEREON APPROVED BY THE SECRETARY OF INTERIOR Jan 17 1903							
	16								
	17								

TRIBAL ENROLLMENT OF PARENTS

	Name of Father	Year	County	Name of Mother	Year	County
1	John Tolbert	Dead	Sugar Loaf	Nellie Tolbert	Dead	Sugar Loaf
2	James Curley	1896	Non Citz	No 1		
3	" "	1896	" "	No 1		
4						
5						
6						
7						
8						
9	No3 on 1896 roll as Zona Curley					
10						
11	For child of No.1 see NB (March 3, 1905) #1380					
12						
13	No.1 also on 1893 Leased District Pay Roll, Sugar Loaf Co, P.52, #493, as Rhoda McCurley					
14	No.2 " " " " " " " " " 52, #494, as Ann McCurley					
15					Date of Application for Enrollment.	
16					6/6/99	
17						

Choctaw By Blood Enrollment Cards 1898-1914

RESIDENCE: Sugar Loaf
POST OFFICE: Howe I.T.

COUNTY. **Choctaw Nation**

Choctaw Roll
(Not Including Freedmen)

CARD No.
FIELD No. **2363**

Dawes' Roll No.	NAME		Relationship to Person First Named	AGE	SEX	BLOOD	TRIBAL ENROLLMENT		
							Year	County	No.
6842	₁ Hoteyabi, Ben	43	First Named	40	M	Full	1896	Sugar Loaf	5259
6843	₂ " Sillis	38	Wife	35	F	"	1896	" "	5260
6844	₃ " Lou	10	Dau	7	"	"	1896	" "	5261
6845	₄ Frances		"	7mo	"	"			
6846	₅ Turnbull, Thomas	16	S.Son	13	M	"	1896	Sugar Loaf	11948

DIED PRIOR TO SEPTEMBER 25, 1902

ENROLLMENT OF NOS. 1,2,3,4 and 5 HEREON APPROVED BY THE SECRETARY OF INTERIOR Jan 17 1903

TRIBAL ENROLLMENT OF PARENTS

	Name of Father	Year	County	Name of Mother	Year	County
1	Ho-tey-a-bi	Dead	Skullyville	Do-na	Dead	Skullyville
2	E-lige-hom-be	"	Sugar Loaf	Mih-yo-ke	"	Sugar Loaf
3	No 1			No 2		
4	No 1			No 2		
5	Geo Turnbull	Dead	Blue	No 2		

No3 on 1896 roll as Leo Hoteyabi

No4 died Sept 8, 1900: Proof of death filed Dec 15, 1902
No.4 died Sept 8, 1902: Enrollment cancelled by Department Sept. 16, 1904.

263

Choctaw By Blood Enrollment Cards 1898-1914

RESIDENCE: Sugar Loaf

POST OFFICE: Howe, I.T.

Choctaw Nation

Choctaw Roll _(Not Including Freedmen)_

CARD NO.

FIELD NO. 2364

Dawes' Roll No.	NAME		Relationship to Person First Named	AGE	SEX	BLOOD	TRIBAL ENROLLMENT		
							Year	County	No.
6847	1 Moore, William	61	First Named	58	M	Full	1896	Sugar Loaf	8492
6848	2 " Ellen	59	Wife	56	F	"	1896	" "	8493
6849	3 " Sopha	20	Dau	17	"	"	1896	" "	8496
6850	4 " Liffie	15	"	12	"	"	1896	" "	8497
6851	5 Folsom, Amanda	4	G.Dau	10mo	"	"			
	6								
	7								
	8								
	9								
	10								
	11								
	12								
	13								
	14	ENROLLMENT OF NOS. 1,2,3,4 and 5 HEREON APPROVED BY THE SECRETARY OF INTERIOR JAN 17 1903							
	15								
	16								
	17								

TRIBAL ENROLLMENT OF PARENTS

	Name of Father	Year	County	Name of Mother	Year	County
1	Pisa-ubbee	Dead	Sugar Loaf	En-la-hu-na	Dead	Sugar Loaf
2	Amos Camp	"	" "		"	" " "
3	No 1			No 2		
4	No 1			No 2		
5	Isael[sic] Folsom	1896	Sugar Loaf	Liley Folsom	Dead	Sugar Loaf
6				No.4	Born	Feb. 29-06
7						
8						
9			For child of #3 see NB (Apr 26 '06) card #234			
10			" " " #4 " "	" " " " #939		
11						
12						
13						
14						
15						
16						6/6/99
17						

264

RESIDENCE: Sugar Loaf	COUNTY.	CARD NO.
POST OFFICE: Houston, I.T.	Choctaw Nation — Choctaw Roll (Not Including Freedmen)	FIELD NO. 2365

Dawes' Roll No.	NAME	Relationship to Person First Named	AGE	SEX	BLOOD	TRIBAL ENROLLMENT Year	County	No.
6852	1 Perry, Nail ⁶⁷	First Named	64	M	1/2	1896	Sugar Loaf	10109
6853	2 " Matilda ²²	Dau	19	F	1/2	1896	" "	10110
6854	3 Covey, Frank DIED PRIOR TO SEPTEMBER 25, 1902	G.Son	8mo	M	1/4			
	4							
	5							
	6							
	7							
	8							
	9							
	10							
	11							
	12							
	13							
	14							
	15	ENROLLMENT OF NOS. 1, 2, and 3, HEREON APPROVED BY THE SECRETARY OF INTERIOR JAN 17 1903						
	16							
	17							

TRIBAL ENROLLMENT OF PARENTS

	Name of Father	Year	County	Name of Mother	Year	County
1	Hardy Perry	Dead	Sugar Loaf	Sophie Perry	Dead	Sugar Loaf
2	No 1			Eliza Perry	"	" "
3	John Covey	1896	Non Citz	No 2		
4						
5						
6						
7	No3 Affidavit of birth to be supplied. Recd June 16/99					
8	No3 Died in November 1899: Proof of death filed December 20" 1902					
9	No.2 is now wife of No.1 on Choc. Card #2393, 12/17 ⁰²					
10	No.3 died Nov – 1899 Enrollment cancelled by Department July 8, 1904					
11						
12						
13						
14						
15				Date of Application for Enrollment. #1 to 3 6/6/99		
16						
17						

Choctaw By Blood Enrollment Cards 1898-1914

RESIDENCE: Sugar Loaf   COUNTY. **Choctaw Nation**   Choctaw Roll   CARD NO.
POST OFFICE: Houston, I.T   *(Not Including Freedmen)*   FIELD NO. 236

Dawes' Roll No.	NAME		Relationship to Person	AGE	SEX	BLOOD	TRIBAL ENROLLMENT		
							Year	County	No.
6855	1 Sexton, George	39	First Named	36	M	Full	1896	Sugar Loaf	11208
6856	2 " Lillie A	39	Wife	36	F	1/2	1896	" "	11209
6857	3 " Henry Jr	12	Son	9	M	3/4	1896	" "	11210
6858	4 " Mary J	9	Dau	6	F	3/4	1896	" "	11211
6859	5 " Etha M	7	"	4	"	3/4	1896	" "	11212
Dead	6 " Roma		"	1	"	3/4			
6860	7 " Theodore Floyd	1	Son	1mo	M	3/4			
	8								
	9								
	10	No. 6 HEREON DISMISSED UNDER ORDER OF THE COMMISSION TO THE FIVE CIVILIZED TRIBES OF MARCH 31, 1905.							
	11								
	12								
	13								
	14								
	15	ENROLLMENT OF NOS. 1,2,3,4,5 and 7 HEREON APPROVED BY THE SECRETARY OF INTERIOR JAN 17 1903							
	16								
	17								

TRIBAL ENROLLMENT OF PARENTS

	Name of Father	Year	County	Name of Mother	Year	County
1	Thompson Sexton	1896	Sugar Loaf	Judie Sexton	Dead	Wade
2	Garrett Thompson	Dead	Wade	Eliza Perry	"	Sugar Loaf
3	No1			No2		
4	No1			No2		
5	No1			No2		
6	No1			No2		
7	Nº1			Nº2		
8						
9	No2 on 1896 roll as Lillie Sexton					
10	No6 Affidavit of birth to be supplied. Recd June 16/99					
11	No5 on 1896 roll as Ether M Sexton					
12	No6 Died October 22, 1899. Evidence of death filed March 21, 1901					
13	Nº7 Born Aug 30, 1901. Enrolled Sept. 30, 1902.					
14						
15						
16				DATE OF APPLICATION FOR ENROLLMENT.	6/6/99	
17						

266

Choctaw By Blood Enrollment Cards 1898-1914

RESIDENCE: Sugar Loaf   COUNTY. **Choctaw Nation**   **Choctaw Roll**   CARD No.
POST OFFICE: Howe, I.T.   *(Not Including Freedmen)*   FIELD No.   2367

Dawes' Roll No.	NAME	Relationship to Person First Named	AGE	SEX	BLOOD	TRIBAL ENROLLMENT Year	County	No.
6861	1 Washington, John ²⁶		23	M	Full	1896	Sugar Loaf	12880
	2							
	3							
	4							
	5							
	6							
	7							
	8							
	9							
	10							
	11							
	12							
	13							
	14							
	15							
	16							
	17							

ENROLLMENT
OF NOS. 1 HEREON
APPROVED BY THE SECRETARY
OF INTERIOR JAN 17 1903

TRIBAL ENROLLMENT OF PARENTS

	Name of Father	Year	County	Name of Mother	Year	County
1	Amos Washington	Dead	Sugar Loaf	Kon-to-na	Dead	Sugar Loaf
2						
3						
4						
5						
6			On 1896 roll as Jno. Washington			
7						
8						
9						
10						
11						
12						
13						
14						
15						
16				Date of Application for Enrollment.	6/6/99	
17						

267

Choctaw By Blood Enrollment Cards 1898-1914

RESIDENCE:	Sugar Loaf	COUNTY.					
POST OFFICE:	Klondike I.T.						

Choctaw Nation Choctaw Roll (Not Including Freedmen)

CARD NO.
FIELD NO. **2368**

Dawes' Roll No.	NAME	Relationship to Person First Named	AGE	SEX	BLOOD	TRIBAL ENROLLMENT Year	County	No.
6862	1 Washington, Levi 37	First Named	34	M	Full	1896	Sugar Loaf	12895
6863	2 " George 9	Son	6	M	"	1896	" "	12929
	3							
	4							
	5							
	6							
	7							
	8							
	9							
	10							
	11							
	12							
	13							
	14							
	15	ENROLLMENT OF NOS. 1 and 2 HEREON						
	16	APPROVED BY THE SECRETARY OF INTERIOR Jan 17 1903						
	17							

TRIBAL ENROLLMENT OF PARENTS

	Name of Father	Year	County	Name of Mother	Year	County
1	Amos Washington	Dead	Sugar Loaf	Kon-to-na	Dead	Sugar Loaf
2	No1			Liley Washington	"	" "
3						
4						
5						
6						
7			No1 On 1896 roll as Levia Washington			
8			For child of No.1 see NB (Mar 3, 05) #481			
9						
10						
11						
12						
13						
14						
15				Date of Application for Enrollment.		
16						6/7/99
17	P.O. Wister I.T.					

Choctaw By Blood Enrollment Cards 1898-1914

RESIDENCE: Skullyville COUNTY. **Choctaw Nation** **Choctaw Roll** CARD NO.
POST OFFICE: Pocola I.T. *(Not Including Freedmen)* FIELD NO. 2369

Dawes' Roll No.	NAME	Relationship to Person First Named	AGE	SEX	BLOOD	TRIBAL ENROLLMENT		
						Year	County	No.
✓ ✓ 1	McLarty Sarah		24	F	1/8			
✓ ✓ 2	" Elton E	Son	5	M	1/16			
✓ ✓ 3	" Bum	Son	3	M	1/16			
✓ DP 4	" Ida Bolin	Dau	3mo	F	1/16			
5								
6								
7								
8								
9								
10								
11								
12								
13								
14								
15								
16								
17								

DISMISSED MAY 27 1904

DENIED CITIZENSHIP BY THE CHOCTAW AND CHICKASAW CITIZENSHIP COURT

ENROLLMENT OF NOS. .... HEREON APPROVED BY THE SECRETARY OF INTERIOR.................

Duplicate record in Choctaw 4575 See C 132

TRIBAL ENROLLMENT OF PARENTS

	Name of Father	Year	County	Name of Mother	Year	County
1	William Vandergriff	1896	Non Citz	Hazey Ann F Vandergriff	1896	Skullyville
2	Harvey E McLarty	1896	" "	No 1		
3	" " "	1896	" "	No 1		
4	" " "	"	" "	No 1		
5						
6	No 1,2 and 3 denied by Com in 96 Case #916					
7	Nos 1-2 and 3 admitted by U.S. Court Central Dist I.T. as citizens of Choc Nation Sept 11-1897 Court Case					
8	No 62 at So M°Alester. All under name of McClarty As to residence see testimony of Harvey E McLarty					
9	No 4 Enrolled Oct 8th 1900					
10	Judgement[s] of U.S. Court admitting Nos 1,2 & 3 vacated and set aside by Decree of Choctaw					
11	Chickasaw Citizenship Court Decr 17 '02					
12	For children of No1 see NB #1010 – (Act Aor 26 '06)					
13						
14						
15						
16				Date of Application for Enrollment.	6/7/99	
17						

Choctaw By Blood Enrollment Cards 1898-1914

RESIDENCE: Sugar Loaf   COUNTY. **Choctaw Nation**   Choctaw Roll   CARD NO.
POST OFFICE: Couser I.T.   *(Not Including Freedmen)*   FIELD NO. **2370**

Dawes' Roll No.	NAME		Relationship to Person	AGE	SEX	BLOOD	TRIBAL ENROLLMENT		
							Year	County	No.
6864	1 Perry Hampton	43	First Named	40	M	Full	1896	Sugar Loaf	10124
6865	2 " Peggy	DIED PRIOR TO SEPTEMBER 25, 1902	Wife	33	F	"	1896	" "	10125
6866	3 " Daniel	18	Son	15	M	"	1896	" "	10126
6867	4 " Jonas	14	Son	11	M	"	1896	" "	10127
6868	5 " Edward	11	Son	8	M	"	1896	" "	10128
6869	6 " Gilbert	9	Son	6	M	"	1896	" "	10129
6870	7 " Harriet	6	Dau	2	F	"			
6871	8 Nolen Thomas Jr	16	Neph	13	M	"	1896	" "	9570
6872	9 " Cephus	14	Neph	11	M	"	1896	" "	9571
15423	10 Perry, Sydney	2	Son	21mo	M	"			
	11								
	12								
	13								
	14								
	15								
	16								
	17								

ENROLLMENT
OF NOS. 1234567889 HEREON
APPROVED BY THE SECRETARY
OF INTERIOR Jan 17 1903

ENROLLMENT
OF NOS. ~10~ HEREON
APPROVED BY THE SECRETARY
OF INTERIOR May 9 1904

TRIBAL ENROLLMENT OF PARENTS

	Name of Father	Year	County	Name of Mother	Year	County
1	Daniel Perry	Dead	Sugar Loaf	Elizabeth Perry	Dead	Sugar Loaf
2	Elijah Hom-by	"	" "	Hannah Hom-by	"	" "
3	No 1			No 2		
4	No 1			No 2		
5	No 1			No 2		
6	No 1			No 2		
7	No 1			No 2		
8	Rason Nolen	Dead	Sugar Loaf	Loney Nolan[sic]	Dead	Sugar Loaf
9	" "	"	" "	" "	"	" "
10	No 1			No 2		
11	N°10 Born Jany 21, 1901. Application made Dec 15,1901, proof of birth filed April 7, 1904					
12	No2 On 1896 roll as Pinkie Perry					
13	No4 " " " " Jones Perry / No9 " " " " Saphus Perry					
14	No2 died February 20, 1902: Proof of death filed Dec 20 1902					
15	No.2 died Feb 20, 1902: Enrollment cancelled by				Date of Application for Enrollment.	
16	Department July 8, 1904 / For child of No.1 see NB (March 3,1905) #816				6/7/99	
17						

Choctaw By Blood Enrollment Cards 1898-1914

RESIDENCE: Sugar Loaf   COUNTY. **Choctaw Nation**   Choctaw Roll   CARD NO.
POST OFFICE: Fan-shaw I.T.   *(Not Including Freedmen)*   FIELD NO. 2371

Dawes' Roll No.	NAME	Relationship to Person	AGE	SEX	BLOOD	TRIBAL ENROLLMENT		
						Year	County	No.
6873	1 Verner Nettie ²²	First Named	19	F	1/8	1896	Sugar Loaf	11954
6874	2 " Richard ⁴	Son	4mo	M	1/16			
6875	3 " Rody Maree ²	Dau	3mo	F	1/16			
6876	4 " Walter Green ¹	Son	1mo	M	1/16			
	5							
	6							
	7							
	8							
	9							
	10							
	11							
	12							
	13							
	14							
	15							
	16							
	17							

ENROLLMENT
OF NOS. 1,2,3 and 4 HEREON
APPROVED BY THE SECRETARY
OF INTERIOR JAN 17 1903

TRIBAL ENROLLMENT OF PARENTS

	Name of Father	Year	County	Name of Mother	Year	County
1	Enoch Tucker	Dead	Non Citz	Rhoda Tucker	Dead	Sug. Loaf
2	Frank Verner	1896	Non Citz	No 1		
3	Frank Verner		Non Citz	No 1		
4	" "		" "	No 1		
5						
6						
7			No1 on 1896 roll as Nettie Tucker			
8			No.3 Enrolled January 15, 1901			
9			Nº4 Born March 34, 1902: enrolled April 2, 1902			
10			For child of No.1 see NB (March 3 1905) #700			
11						
12						
13						
14						
15				Date of Application for Enrollment.	For Nos 1&2	
16					6/7/99	
17	Hughes I.T.					

Choctaw By Blood Enrollment Cards 1898-1914

RESIDENCE: Sugar Loaf   COUNTY. **Choctaw Nation**   **Choctaw Roll**   CARD NO.
POST OFFICE: Fanshaw I.T.   *(Not Including Freedmen)*   FIELD NO.   2372

Dawes' Roll No.	NAME		Relationship to Person	AGE	SEX	BLOOD	TRIBAL ENROLLMENT		
							Year	County	No.
DEAD.	1 Stephens Robert	DEAD.	First Named	40	M	1/4	1896	Sugar Loaf	11194
6877	2 " Martha	31	Wife	28	F	1/8	1896	" "	11195
6878	3 " Charley	23	Son	20	M	1/8	1896	" "	11196
6879	4 " Roscoe	10	Son	7	M	3/16	1896	" "	11197
6880	5 " Catherine	8	Dau	5	F	3/16	1896	" "	11198
6881	6 " Indianola	6	Dau	3	F	3/16	1896	" "	11199
6882	7 " Ida M	4	Dau	9mo	F	3/16			
	8								
	9								
	10								
	11								
	12								
	13								
	14								
	15	ENROLLMENT OF NOS. 2,3,4,5,6 and 7 HEREON							
	16	APPROVED BY THE SECRETARY OF INTERIOR JAN 17 1903							
	17								

TRIBAL ENROLLMENT OF PARENTS

	Name of Father	Year	County	Name of Mother	Year	County
1	Tandy Stephens	1896	Non Citz	Catherine Stephens	Dead	Skullyville
2	Enoch Tucker	Dead	Non Citz	Rhoda Tucker	"	Sugar Loaf
3	No 1			Sally Stephens	1896	Non Citz
4	No 1			No 2		
5	No 1			No 2		
6	No 1			No 2		
7	No 1			No 2		
8						
9				No1 See his testimony and Herman P Lyle's as to marriage of		
10				Robert Stephens and Sally Price		
11				No.1 Proof of death filed March 13, 1901		
12						
13						
14						
15					Date of Application for Enrollment.	
16					6/7/99	
17						

Choctaw By Blood Enrollment Cards 1898-1914

RESIDENCE: Sugar Loaf   COUNTY. **Choctaw Nation**   **Choctaw Roll** *(Not Including Freedmen)*   CARD No.
POST OFFICE: Heavener I.T.   FIELD No. 2373

Dawes' Roll No.	NAME	Relationship to Person First Named	AGE	SEX	BLOOD	TRIBAL ENROLLMENT Year	County	No.
DEAD	1 Crawford Lonie	18	18	F	5/8	1896	Sugar Loaf	2230
6883	2 " Charles ⁶	Son	3	M	5/16	1896	" "	2265
6884	3 " Jessie ⁴	Dau	6mo	F	5/16			
6885	4 " Ben ¹	Son	8mo	M	5/16			
	5							
	6 No. 1 HEREON DISMISSED UNDER							
	7 ORDER OF THE COMMISSION TO THE FIVE							
	8 CIVILIZED TRIBES OF MARCH 31, 1905.							
	9							
	10							
	11							
	12							
	13							
	14							
	15 ENROLLMENT OF NOS. 2, 3 and 4 HEREON							
	16 APPROVED BY THE SECRETARY							
	17 OF INTERIOR JAN 17 1903							

TRIBAL ENROLLMENT OF PARENTS

	Name of Father	Year	County	Name of Mother	Year	County
1	Watson Benton	Dead	Sugar Loaf	Julia Benton	Dead	Sug Loaf
2	Oliver Crawford	1896	Non Citz	No 1		
3	" "		" "	No 1		
4	" "		" "	No 1		
5						
6						
7			No2 On Roll 1896 as Chas C Croford			
8						
9		No4 born April 5, 1901: Enrolled Dec 17th 1901				
10		Nº1 Died April 24, 1901, Proof of death filed Oct 31, 1902				
11						
12						
13						
14						
15						
16					Date of Application for Enrollment.	6/7/99
17	c/o Oliver Crawford – father					

273

RESIDENCE: Sugar Loaf		COUNTY. **Choctaw Nation**				**Choctaw Roll** (*Not Including Freedmen*)		CARD NO. 2374
POST OFFICE: Conser I.T.								FIELD NO.

Dawes' Roll No.	NAME	Relationship to Person	AGE	SEX	BLOOD	TRIBAL ENROLLMENT		
						Year	County	No.
6886	1 McCurtain Elum ⁴⁵	First Named	42	M	3/4	1896	Sugar Loaf	9103
DEAD.	2 " Susie	Wife	26	F	7/8	1896	" "	9104
6887	3 " Nail P ¹⁷	Son	14	M	3/4	1896	" "	9105
6888	4 " Zack T ⁹	Son	6	M	13/16	1896	" "	9106
6889	5 " Green ⁷	Son	4	M	13/16	1896	" "	9107
	6							
	7							
	8 No. 2 HEREON DISMISSED UNDER ORDER OF THE COMMISSION TO THE FIVE							
	9 CIVILIZED TRIBES OF MARCH 31, 1905.							
	10							
	11							
	12							
	13							
	14							
	15 ENROLLMENT OF NOS. 1 and 3, 4, 5 HEREON							
	16 APPROVED BY THE SECRETARY OF INTERIOR JAN 17 1903							
	17							

TRIBAL ENROLLMENT OF PARENTS

	Name of Father	Year	County	Name of Mother	Year	County
1	Johnson McCurtain	Dead	Sugar Loaf	Rhoda McCurtain	Dead	Sugar Loaf
2	John Carshall	"	" "	Betsy Carshall	"	" "
3	No 1			Seanna McCurtain	"	" "
4	No 1			No 2		
5	No 1			No 2		
6						
7	No3 On 1896 roll as N. P. McCurtain					
8	Nº2 Died in June 1900. See letter #16862-1902 Gen Off files Proof of death filed Nov 4 1902					
9	Nº1 is now the husband of Ruthie Harris on Choctaw card #2272 Oc6 6, 1902					
10						
11						
12						
13						
14						
15						
16				Date of Application for Enrollment.	6/7/99	
17						

RESIDENCE: Sugar Loaf   COUNTY. **Choctaw Nation**   **Choctaw Roll**   CARD NO.
POST OFFICE: Houston, I.T.   *(Not Including Freedmen)*   FIELD NO.   2375

Dawes' Roll No.	NAME		Relationship to Person First Named	AGE	SEX	BLOOD	TRIBAL ENROLLMENT		
							Year	County	No.
6890	1 Bird, Billy	22	First Named	19	M	1/2	1893	Kiamitia	66
I.W. 996	2 " Edna	24	Wife	21	F	I.W.			
	3								
	4								
	5								
	6								
	7								
	8								
	9								
	10								
	11	ENROLLMENT OF NOS. 2 HEREON APPROVED BY THE SECRETARY OF INTERIOR OCT 21 1904							
	12								
	13								
	14								
	15	ENROLLMENT OF NOS. 1 HEREON APPROVED BY THE SECRETARY OF INTERIOR JAN 17 1903							
	16								
	17								

TRIBAL ENROLLMENT OF PARENTS

	Name of Father	Year	County	Name of Mother	Year	County
1	Dick Bird	1896	Non Citz	Belle Bird	Dead	Sugar Loaf
2	Jefferson Chriss		non citizen	Ellie Chriss	"	non citizen
3						
4						
5	No2 transferred from Choctaw card D832 August 11, 1904					
6	See decision of July 26, 1904					
7	No1 is now husband of Edna Bird a non citizen on Choctaw card D#832					
8	For child of Nos 1 and 2 see NB (Mar 3, 1905) #485					
9	On 1893 Pay Roll, Page 118, No 66, Kiamitia Co					
10	as Billy Byrd					
11	Also on 1896 Roll, Page 48, No 1985, Jacks Fork Co					
12						
13						
14					#1	
15					Date of Application for Enrollment.	
16					6/7/99	
17	P.O. Owl I.T. (?)					

RESIDENCE:	Tobucksy	COUNTY.						

RESIDENCE: Tobucksy **COUNTY.** **Choctaw Nation** **Choctaw Roll** (Not Including Freedmen) **CARD No. FIELD No.** 2376
POST OFFICE: South McAlester, I.T.

Dawes' Roll No.	NAME	Relationship to Person	AGE	SEX	BLOOD	TRIBAL ENROLLMENT		
						Year	County	No.
6891	1 Lyles, Hermon P 43	First Named	40	M	1/4	1896	Tobucksy	7864
VOID.	2 " Viola	Dau	20	F	1/8	1896	"	7865
	3							
	4							
	5							
	6 Sept 4/99 No2 has been							
	7 placed upon Card No 4484,							
	8 with husband Frank A Karl							
	9							
	10							
	11							
	12							
	13							
	14							
	15 ENROLLMENT OF NOS. 1 HEREON							
	16 APPROVED BY THE SECRETARY OF INTERIOR JAN 17 1903							
	17							

TRIBAL ENROLLMENT OF PARENTS

Name of Father	Year	County	Name of Mother	Year	County
1 John Lyles	Dead	Skullyville	Mary Lyles	1896	Non Citz
2 No 1			Mary Lyles	Dead	" "
3					
4					
5					
6					
7		No 1 on 1896 as Hermon Lyles			
8					
9		As to marriage of parents of No2, see testimony			
10		of No 1 and Robert Stephens			
11		Evidence of marriage of parents of No 1			
12		to be supplied. See testimony of Mary A McCarty			
13					
14					
15					
16			Date of Application for Enrollment.	6/7/99	
17					

Choctaw By Blood Enrollment Cards 1898-1914

RESIDENCE: Sugar Loaf   COUNTY. **Choctaw Nation**   **Choctaw Roll**   CARD NO.
POST OFFICE: Heavener, I.T.   *(Not Including Freedmen)*   FIELD NO. 2377

Dawes' Roll No.	NAME	Relationship to Person	AGE	SEX	BLOOD	TRIBAL ENROLLMENT		
						Year	County	No.
IW 1248	1 Wilson, Samuel R ⁴¹	First Named	38	M	I.W	1896	Sugar Loaf	15152
6892	2 " Josephine ¹⁸	Dau	15	F	1/4	1896	" "	12850
6893	3 " Dora ¹⁴	"	11	"	1/4	1896	" "	12851
6894	4 " Luella ¹¹	"	8	"	1/4	1896	" "	12852
6895	5 " Ed ⁹	Son	6	M	1/4	1896	" "	12853
6896	6 Morris, Lee ²⁰	S.Son	17	"	1/2	1896	" "	8490
	7							
	8							
	9							
	10							
	11							
	12							
	13							
	14							
	15							
	16							
	17							

ENROLLMENT
OF NOS. ~ 1 ~ HEREON
APPROVED BY THE SECRETARY
OF INTERIOR DEC 30 1904

ENROLLMENT
OF NOS. 2,3,4,5 and 6 HEREON
APPROVED BY THE SECRETARY
OF INTERIOR JAN 17 1903

TRIBAL ENROLLMENT OF PARENTS

	Name of Father	Year	County	Name of Mother	Year	County
1	Jno. R. Wilson	Dead	Non Citz	Lydia A Wilson	Dead	Non Citz
2	No1			Julia Wilson	"	Sugar Loaf
3	No1			" "	"	" " "
4	No1			" "	"	" " "
5	No1			" "	"	" " "
6	Robt. Morris		Sugar Loaf	" "	"	" " "
7						
8	For child of No.2 see NB (Mar 3, 1905) #510					
9	As to evidence of marriage of No1 see					
10	testimony of C.C. Mathies.					
11	No1 on 1896 roll as Sam R Wilson					
12	No2 " 1896 " " Joseph "					
13	No.1 formerly husband of Julia Wilson (formerly Benton)					
14	1896 Sugar Loaf, No.12849, and who died in 1898.					
15	For child of No2 see NB (Apr 26-06) Card #633					
16	No.1 is now the Husband of Alice Ward on				Date of Application	
17	Choc. Card #2287: See evidence taken 12/17-'02			this day	for Enrollment.	

No1 enrolled Aug 3/99
All others enrolled June 7/99

Choctaw By Blood Enrollment Cards 1898-1914

RESIDENCE: Sugar Loaf   COUNTY. **Choctaw Nation**   Choctaw Roll   CARD NO.
POST OFFICE: Wister, I.T.   *(Not Including Freedmen)*   FIELD NO.   2378

Dawes' Roll No.	NAME		Relationship to Person	AGE	SEX	BLOOD	TRIBAL ENROLLMENT		
							Year	County	No.
I.W. 1490	₁ Reding, Ella	31	First Named	28	F	I.W.			
15916	₂ Kiefer, Ardella	16	Dau	12	"	1/4	1896	Sugar Loaf	5258
	₃								
	₄ Nos 1 and 2 restored to roll by Departmental authority of January 19, 1909 (File 5-51)								
	₅ DISMISSED Action rescinded and under opinion of Assistant Attorney								
	₆ SEP 20 1904 General for Dept of March 24, 1905, Nos 1 and 2 are enrolled.								
	₇ GRANTED See decision of June 6, 1905								
	₈ JUN -6 1905								
	₉								
	₁₀ Enrollment of Nos 1 and 2 cancelled by order of Department March 4, 1904								
	₁₁								
	₁₂								
	₁₃ No1 originally listed on this card as Ella Lucas								
	₁₄ No2 originally listed on this card as Ardella Hickman								
	₁₅ No1 formerly wife of Atch Hickman 1885 Sugar Loaf No 350, and who died Feb 1, 1887								
	₁₆ For children of No2 see NB (Apr 26-06) 788								
	₁₇								

TRIBAL ENROLLMENT OF PARENTS

	Name of Father	Year	County	Name of Mother	Year	County
₁	Edward Hatfield	Dead	Non Citz	Cynthia Hatfield	1896	Non Citz
₂	Atch Hickman	"	Choctaw	No 1		
₃						
₄	Admitted by U.S. Court, Central Dist, Aug 26/97 Case No 16					
₅					ENROLLMENT	
₆	As to residence, see testimony of No.1				OF NOS. Two HEREON APPROVED BY THE SECRETARY	
₇	No.2 on 1896 census roll, as Henrietta Hickman				OF INTERIOR AUG 23 1905	
₈	#5258, page 128		May 8, 1900			
₉					ENROLLMENT HEREON	
₁₀					OF NOS. One APPROVED BY THE SECRETARY	
₁₁					OF INTERIOR AUG 22 1905	
₁₂	No 1 & 2 admitted by Dawes Commission: Case #1243					
₁₃	Judgement [?] of U.S. Ct admitting Nos1&2 vacated and set aside by Decree of					
₁₄	Choctaw Chickasaw Ct Ct Dec 17 '02					
₁₅	No appear [?]					
₁₆					Date of Application for Enrollment. 6/7/99	
₁₇						

278

RESIDENCE: Sugar Loaf								
POST OFFICE: Poteau, I.T.	COUNTY: **Choctaw Nation**				Choctaw Roll *(Not Including Freedmen)*		CARD NO. FIELD NO. 2379	

Dawes' Roll No.	NAME	Relationship to Person First Named	AGE	SEX	BLOOD	TRIBAL ENROLLMENT		
						Year	County	No.
6897	1 Folsom, Sweny W 35	First Named	32	M	3/4	1896	Sugar Loaf	3960
6898	2 " Julia A 38	Wife	35	F	3/4	1896	" "	3961
6899	3 " Carrie L 9	Dau	6	"	3/4	1896	" "	3962
6900	4 " Agnes B	"	9mo	"	3/4			
6901	5 Gilmon, Leonard 19	S.Son	16	M	7/8	1896	Sugar Loaf	4681
6902	6 Kincade, Lela M 15	S.Dau	12	F	3/4			7472
	7							
	8							
	9							
	10							
	11	ENROLLMENT						
	12	OF NOS. 1,2,3,4,5 and 6 HEREON APPROVED BY THE SECRETARY						
	13	OF INTERIOR JAN 17 1903						
	14							
	15							
	16							
	17							

DIED PRIOR TO SEPTEMBER 25, 1902

TRIBAL ENROLLMENT OF PARENTS

	Name of Father	Year	County	Name of Mother	Year	County
1	Ellis W Folsom	Dead	Sugar Loaf	Selina Folsom	Dead	Sugar Loaf
2	Tom Sexton	1896	" "	Judie Sexton	"	"
3	No 1			No 2		
4	No 1			No 2		
5	Gilmon	Dead	Sugar Loaf	No 2		
6	Will Kincade	"	" "	No 2		
7						
8			No1 on 1896 roll as Sweny Folsom			
9			No5 " 1896 " " Lomice Gilmon			
10			No6 " 1896 " " Leler M Kingcade			
11			For child of No.6 see NB (March 3, 1905) Card #580			
12			No4 Affidavit of birth to be supplied. Recd June 8/99			
13			No4 died June – 1901; Proof of death filed Dec 20 1902			
14			No.4 died June - 1901: Enrollment cancelled by Department July 8, 1904			
15					Date of Application for Enrollment.	
16					6/7/99	
17						

279

Choctaw By Blood Enrollment Cards 1898-1914

RESIDENCE:	Sugar Loaf	COUNTY.				CARD NO.
POST OFFICE:	Wister, I.T.	**Choctaw Nation**			Choctaw Roll (Not Including Freedmen)	FIELD NO. 2380

Dawes' Roll No.	NAME		Relationship to Person	AGE	SEX	BLOOD	TRIBAL ENROLLMENT		
							Year	County	No.
6903	1 Jackson, Henry	38	First Named	35	M	Full	1897	Sugar Loaf	6519
DEAD.	2 " Sally DEAD.		Wife	45	F	"	1896	" "	10650
6904	3 " Jacob Jr	10	Son	7	M	"	"	1896	6521
6905	4 Simmon, Willie	20	Ward	17	"	"	"	1896	11205
	5								
	6 No. 2 HEREON DISMISSED UNDER ORDER OF THE COMMISSION TO THE FIVE CIVILIZED TRIBES OF MARCH 31, 1905.								
	7								
	8								
	9								
	10								
	11								
	12								
	13								
	14								
	15 ENROLLMENT OF NOS. 1 and 3&4 HEREON APPROVED BY THE SECRETARY OF INTERIOR JAN 17 1903								
	16								
	17								

TRIBAL ENROLLMENT OF PARENTS

	Name of Father	Year	County	Name of Mother	Year	County
1	Jackson	Dead	Sugar Loaf	Te-ma-thla	Dead	Sugar Loaf
2		"	" "		"	" "
3	No 1			Nancy Jackson	"	" "
4	Jim Simmon	Dead	Sugar Loaf	Martha Simmon	"	" "
5						
6						
7	No2 on 1896 roll as Sally Quinn					
8	No2 Died Jan 1st 1900: Evidence of Death filed June 25th 1902					
9	No.1 now Husband of Mila Moon on Choctaw card #2310. Evidence requested July 16" 1902					
10						
11						
12						
13						
14						
15						
16				Date of Application for Enrollment.	6/7/99	
17						

RESIDENCE: Sugar Loaf
POST OFFICE: Wister, I.T

COUNTY, **Choctaw Nation**

Choctaw Roll
(Not Including Freedmen)

CARD NO.
FIELD NO. 2381

Dawes' Roll No.	NAME		Relationship to Person	AGE	SEX	BLOOD	TRIBAL ENROLLMENT		
							Year	County	No.
6906	1 Harris, Aaron	26	First Named	23	M	Full	1896	Sugar Loaf	5264
6907	2 " Ida	8	Niece	5	F	"	1896	" "	5250
	3								
	4								
	5								
	6								
	7								
	8								
	9								
	10								
	11								
	12								
	13								
	14								
	15	ENROLLMENT OF NOS. 1 and 2 HEREON APPROVED BY THE SECRETARY OF INTERIOR JAN 17 1903							
	16								
	17								

TRIBAL ENROLLMENT OF PARENTS

	Name of Father	Year	County	Name of Mother	Year	County
1	Joseph Harris	Dead	Sugar Loaf	Mih-yo-lo-na	Dead	Sugar Loaf
2				Mutsey Harris	"	" " "
3						
4						
5						
6	No2 is an illegitimate child, father unknown					
7	No1 now Husband to Sillen Alexander Choctaw Card #2402 June 17th 1902					
8	For child of No1 see NB (Mar 3-05) Card #156					
9						
10						
11						
12						
13						
14						
15					Date of Application for Enrollment.	
16					6/7/99	
17						

RESIDENCE: Sugar Loaf	COUNTY.								
POST OFFICE: Wister, I.T.									

Choctaw Nation

Choctaw Roll (Not Including Freedmen)

CARD NO.
FIELD NO. 2382

Dawes' Roll No.	NAME		Relationship to Person	AGE	SEX	BLOOD	TRIBAL ENROLLMENT		
							Year	County	No.
6908	1 Potts, Forbis	41	First Named	38	M	7/8	1896	Sugar Loaf	10153
I.W. 717	2 " Ada	31	Wife	26	F	I.W.			
14735	3 " Florence	2	Dau	1½	"	7/16			
14736	4 " Willie Arthur	2	Son	2½ mo	M	7/16			
	5								
	6								
	7								
	8								
	9								
	10	ENROLLMENT OF NOS. 2 HEREON APPROVED BY THE SECRETARY OF INTERIOR MAY -7 1904							
	11								
	12								
	13								
	14								
	15	ENROLLMENT OF NOS. 1 HEREON APPROVED BY THE SECRETARY OF INTERIOR JAN 17 1903			ENROLLMENT OF NOS. 3 and 4 HEREON APPROVED BY THE SECRETARY OF INTERIOR MAY 20 1903				
	16								
	17								

TRIBAL ENROLLMENT OF PARENTS

	Name of Father	Year	County	Name of Mother	Year	County
1	William Potts	Dead	Wade	Sally Willis	1896	Wade
2	Jas Merchant	"	Non Citz	Eliz. Merchant	Dead	Non Citz
3	No 1			No 2		
4	No 1			No.2		
5						
6						
7						
8						
9	No2 See Decision of March 2 '04					
10	No3 Affidavit of birth to be supplied. Recd June 8/99					
11	No.4 Enrolled Oct. 11th 1900					
12	Evidence of marriage of Nos 1&2 in jacket					
13						
14	For children of Nos 1&2 see NB (March 3-1905) Card #141.					
15						
16				Date of Application for Enrollment.	6/7/99	
17	P.O. Howe, I.T. 12/13 '02					

Choctaw By Blood Enrollment Cards 1898-1914

RESIDENCE: Sugar Loaf   COUNTY. **Choctaw Nation**   **Choctaw Roll**   CARD NO.
POST OFFICE: Conser, I.T.   *(Not Including Freedmen)*   FIELD NO. 2383

Dawes' Roll No.	NAME		Relationship to Person Named	AGE	SEX	BLOOD	TRIBAL ENROLLMENT		
							Year	County	No.
6909	₁ Perry, Dixon	51	First Named	48	M	Full	1896	Sugar Loaf	10108
I.W. 718	₂ " Nancy	61	Wife	58	F	I.W.	1896	" "	14925
	3								
	4								
	5								
	6								
	7								
	8								
	9								
	10	ENROLLMENT OF NOS. ~~ 2 ~~ HEREON APPROVED BY THE SECRETARY OF INTERIOR MAY -7 1904							
	11								
	12								
	13								
	14								
	15	ENROLLMENT OF NOS. 1 HEREON APPROVED BY THE SECRETARY OF INTERIOR JAN 17 1903							
	16								
	17								

TRIBAL ENROLLMENT OF PARENTS

	Name of Father	Year	County	Name of Mother	Year	County
1	Daniel Perry	Dead	Sugar Loaf	Elizabeth Perry	Dead	Sugar Loaf
2	Jim Hurst	"	Non Citz		"	Non Citz
3						
4						
5						
6	No2 See Decision of March 2 '04					
7	As to marriage, see testimony of No1 and that of Dixon Battiest					
8						
9						
10						
11						
12						
13						
14						
15					Date of Application for Enrollment.	
16					6/7/99	
17						

283

Choctaw By Blood Enrollment Cards 1898-1914

RESIDENCE: Sugar Loaf	COUNTY. **Choctaw Nation**	**Choctaw Roll** (Not Including Freedmen)	CARD NO.
POST OFFICE: Howe, I.T.			FIELD NO. 2384

Dawes' Roll No.	NAME	Relationship to Person First Named	AGE	SEX	BLOOD	TRIBAL ENROLLMENT		
						Year	County	No.
6910	1 Hitcher, Dicey 25		22	F	Full	1896	Sugar Loaf	8495
6911	2 " William 1	Son	1mo	M	"			
	3							
	4							
	5							
	6							
	7							
	8							
	9							
	10							
	11							
	12							
	13							
	14							
	15							
	16							
	17							

ENROLLMENT
OF NOS. 1 and 2 HEREON
APPROVED BY THE SECRETARY
OF INTERIOR JAN 17 1903

TRIBAL ENROLLMENT OF PARENTS

	Name of Father	Year	County	Name of Mother	Year	County
1	William Moore	1896	Sugar Loaf	Ellen Moore	1896	Sugar Loaf
2	Henry Hitcher		Chickasaw	No 1		
3						
4						
5						
6			On 1896 roll as Lycie Moore			
7						
8			Husband on Chickasaw Card No 1447 – 7-5492			
9			No.2 Born Sept 26 and Enrolled Oct. 28, 1901			
10						
11						
12						
13						
14						
15						
16				Date of Application for Enrollment.	6/7/99	
17						

RESIDENCE: Sugar Loaf		COUNTY. **Choctaw Nation**				**Choctaw Roll** *(Not Including Freedmen)*	CARD No.	
POST OFFICE: Houston, I.T.							FIELD No.	2385

Dawes' Roll No.	NAME		Relationship to Person	AGE	SEX	BLOOD	TRIBAL ENROLLMENT		
							Year	County	No.
6912	1 Perry, Charles T	31	First Named	28	M	1/2	1896	Sugar Loaf	10111
6913	2 " Martha	25	Wife	22	F	1/4	1896	" "	10112
6914	3 " Myrtle	7	Dau	4	"	3/8	1896	" "	10113
6915	4 " Maud	5	"	2	"	3/8			
6916	5 " Charles Raymond	1	Son	3wks	M	3/8			
	6								
	7								
	8								
	9								
	10								
	11								
	12								
	13								
	14								
	15	ENROLLMENT OF NOS. 1,2,3,4,5 HEREON APPROVED BY THE SECRETARY OF INTERIOR JAN 17 1903							
	16								
	17								

TRIBAL ENROLLMENT OF PARENTS

	Name of Father	Year	County	Name of Mother	Year	County
1	Nail Perry	1896	Sugar Loaf	Eliza A Perry	Dead	Sugar Loaf
2	Abel Harris	1896	" "	Susan Harris	1896	Non Citz
3	No 1			No 2		
4	No 1			No 2		
5	No 1			No 2		
6						
7						
8	As to marriage of parents of No2, see Card No 2272					
9						
10	No.4 Affidavit of birth to be supplied. Recd 6/2/99					
11	No1 on 1896 roll as Charlie Perry					
12	No.5 Enrolled May 3, 1901					
13	For child of Nos 1&2 see NB (March 3, 1905) #1060					
14						
15				#1 to 4		
16				Date of Application for Enrollment.	6/7/99	
17						

| RESIDENCE: | Sugar Loaf | COUNTY. | **Choctaw Nation** | **Choctaw Roll** | CARD No. |
| POST OFFICE: | Conser, I.T. | | | *(Not Including Freedmen)* | FIELD No. 2386 |

Dawes' Roll No.	NAME		Relationship to Person First Named	AGE	SEX	BLOOD	TRIBAL ENROLLMENT		
							Year	County	No.
6917	₁ Watson, Mary	25	First Named	22	F	1/2	1896	Sugar Loaf	2216
	₂ DIED PRIOR TO SEPTEMBER 25 1902 John H		Son	1½	M	1/4			
6919	₃ " Beulah M	3	Dau	1mo	F	1/4			
14737	₄ " Magdenlena		Dau	15mo	F	1/4			
	₅								
	₆								
	₇								
	₈								
	₉								
	10								
	11								
	12								
	13								
	14								
	15	ENROLLMENT OF NOS. 1,2,3 HEREON APPROVED BY THE SECRETARY OF INTERIOR JAN 17 1903				ENROLLMENT OF NOS 4 HEREON APPROVED BY THE SECRETARY OF INTERIOR MA& 20 1903			
	16								
	17								

TRIBAL ENROLLMENT OF PARENTS

	Name of Father	Year	County	Name of Mother	Year	County
₁	Isom Camp	Dead	Sugar Loaf	Seanna Camp	1896	Sugar Loaf
₂	Andrew Watson	1896	Non Citz	No 1		
₃	" "	1896	" "	No 1		
₄	" "		" "	No 1		
₅						
₆						
₇			No1 on 1896 roll as Mary Camp			
₈			For child of No.1 see NB (March 4 1905) #1129			
₉			No2 died July 7, 1899: Proof of death filed Dec 20 1902			
10			No4 Born Oct 14" 1901: Enrolled Dec 22ⁿᵈ 1902			
11						
12						
13						
14						
15				#1 to 3		
16				DATE OF APPLICATION FOR ENROLLMENT.	6/7/99	
17						

286

RESIDENCE: Sugar Loaf COUNTY. PO Chickasha I.T. 1902

POST OFFICE: Wister, I.T.

Choctaw Nation   Choctaw Roll   CARD No. 2387

Dawes' Roll No.	NAME	Relationship to Person First Named	AGE	SEX	BLOOD	TRIBAL ENROLLMENT		
						Year	County	No.
✓	1 Wooldridge, Eli		45	M	1/4			
✓	2 " Fannie	Wife	40	F	I.W.			
✓	3 " Hattie	Dau	20	"	1/8			
✓	4 " Vivian A	"	1	"	1/8			
	5							
	6 1,2,3 DENIED CITIZENSHIP BY THE CHOCTAW AND CHICKASAW CITIZENSHIP COURT							
	7							
	8							
	9 Nº4 DISMISSED							
	10 MAY 23 1904							
	11							
	12							
	13							
	14							
	15							
	16							
	17							

TRIBAL ENROLLMENT OF PARENTS

	Name of Father	Year	County	Name of Mother	Year	County
1	John Wooldridge	Dead	Non Citz	Anna Wooldridge	1896	Choctaw
2	George Loveless	1896	" "	Eliz. A Walker	Dead	Non Citz
3	No 1			No 2		
4	No 1			No 2		
5						
6	Nos 1,2 and 3 denied by Com in 96 Case #1379					
7	Nos 1-2-3 were admitted by U.S. Court Central Dist. Aug 30/97, Case No 161					
8	As to residence see testimony of No1					
9	No4 Affidavit of birth to be supplied. Recd June 16/99					
10						
11						
12						
13						
14	REFUSED FEB 16 1907					
15						
16	DISMISSED FEB 16 1907			Date of Application for Enrollment.	6/7/99	
17						

Choctaw By Blood Enrollment Cards 1898-1914

RESIDENCE: Sugar Loaf COUNTY. **Choctaw Nation** **Choctaw Roll** CARD NO.
POST OFFICE: Howe I.T. *(Not Including Freedmen)* FIELD NO. **2388**

Dawes' Roll No.	NAME		Relationship to Person	AGE	SEX	BLOOD	TRIBAL ENROLLMENT		
							Year	County	No.
6920	1 Johnson Martha	25	First Named	22	F	1/4	1896	Sugar Loaf	6503
6921	2 " Deller	7	Dau	4	F	1/8	1896	" "	6504
6922	3 " William E	5	Son	2	M	1/8			
6923	4 " Lynard	2	Son	19mo	M	1/8			
	5								
	6								
	7								
	8								
	9								
	10								
	11								
	12								
	13								
	14								
	15	ENROLLMENT OF NOS. 1,2,3,4, HEREON APPROVED BY THE SECRETARY OF INTERIOR JAN 17 1903							
	16								
	17								

TRIBAL ENROLLMENT OF PARENTS

	Name of Father	Year	County	Name of Mother	Year	County
1	Sam Hickman	1896	Non Citz	Margaret Hickman	Dead	Sugar Loaf
2	Sam Johnson	1896	Non Citz	No 1		
3	" "		" "	No 1		
4	" "		" "	No 1		
5						
6						
7						
8			Nº4 Born Feby 23, 1901, enrolled Sept 23, 1902			
9						
10			For child of No1 see NB (Apr 26-06) Card #501			
11			" " " " (Mar 3-05) " #804			
12						
13						
14						
15					#1 to 3 inc	
16				Date of Application for Enrollment.	6/7/99	
17	P.O. Reichert IT 4/7/05					

288

Choctaw By Blood Enrollment Cards 1898-1914

RESIDENCE: Sugar Loaf COUNTY. **Choctaw Nation** **Choctaw Roll** *(Not Including Freedmen)* CARD NO.
POST OFFICE: Wister I.T. FIELD NO. 2389

Dawes' Roll No.	NAME		Relationship to Person	AGE	SEX	BLOOD	TRIBAL ENROLLMENT		
							Year	County	No.
6924	1 Jefferson Frazier	26	First Named	23	M	Full	1896	Sugar Loaf	6514
6925	2 " Nancy	26	Wife	23	F	"	1896	" "	6515
6926	3 " Thomas	6	Son	3	M	"	1896	" "	6516
	4								
	5								
	6								
	7								
	8								
	9								
	10								
	11								
	12								
	13								
	14								
	15	ENROLLMENT OF NOS. 1,2,3, HEREON							
	16	APPROVED BY THE SECRETARY							
	17	OF INTERIOR JAN 17 1903							

TRIBAL ENROLLMENT OF PARENTS

	Name of Father	Year	County	Name of Mother	Year	County
1	Wattus Jefferson	Dead	Sugar Loaf	Hitty Jefferson	1896	Sugar Loaf
2	Robinson Perry	1896	" "	Amy Perry	Dead	Skullyville
3	No 1			No 2		
4						
5						
6			No1 On 1896 roll [sic] Frazier Jefferson			
7						
8						
9						
10						
11	Nos 1 and 2 have separated: No.` is now husband of Lena Harris Choc C. #2316					
12	No2 is now wife of Thomas Quinn on Choc Card #2322: Evidence of marriage					
13	to be supplied – 12/18 02					
14						
15					Date of Application for Enrollment.	
16					6/7/99	
17						

289

Choctaw By Blood Enrollment Cards 1898-1914

RESIDENCE: Sugar Loaf COUNTY. **Choctaw Nation** **Choctaw Roll** CARD NO.
POST OFFICE: Wister I.T. *(Not Including Freedmen)* FIELD NO. 2390

Dawes' Roll No.	NAME	Relationship to Person First Named	AGE	SEX	BLOOD	TRIBAL ENROLLMENT		
						Year	County	No.
6927	1 Jefferson Hittie DIED PRIOR TO SEPTEMBER 25 1902		63	F	Full	1896	Sugar Loaf	6517
14738	2 Patterson Isabelle 19	Dau	16	F	"	1896	" "	6518
14739	3 Patterson James Oscar 1	Gr Son	2mo	M	1/2			
	4							
	5							
	6							
	7							
	8							
	9							
	10							
	11							
	12							
	13							
	14							
	15	ENROLLMENT OF NOS. 1 HEREON APPROVED BY THE SECRETARY OF INTERIOR JAN 17 1903				ENROLLMENT OF NOS. 2 and 3 HEREON APPROVED BY THE SECRETARY OF INTERIOR MAY 20 1903		
	16							
	17							

TRIBAL ENROLLMENT OF PARENTS

	Name of Father	Year	County	Name of Mother	Year	County
1	Nak-i-che	Dead			Dead	
2	Wattus Jefferson	"	Sugar Loaf	No 1		
3	Elick Patterson		non-citizen	N°2		
4						
5						
6	No.1 Died April 8th 1900" Proof of death filed Dec'r 23 1902					
7	N°2 is now wife of Elick Patterson non citizen. Evidence of marriage filed Oct. 27 1902					
8	N°3 Born Aug. 18, 1902. Enrolled Oct. 27, 1902					
9	See letter as to No2					
10						
11	For child of No.2 see NB (March 3, 1905) #1418					
12						
13						
14						
15						
16				Date of Application for Enrollment.	6/7/99	
17	P.O. Page, I.T. 12/12 '02					

Choctaw By Blood Enrollment Cards 1898-1914

RESIDENCE: Sugar Loaf	COUNTY. **Choctaw Nation**					**Choctaw Roll** *(Not Including Freedmen)*	CARD NO.	2391
POST OFFICE: Wister I.T.							FIELD NO.	

Dawes' Roll No.	NAME	Relationship to Person First Named	AGE	SEX	BLOOD	TRIBAL ENROLLMENT Year	County	No.
6928	1 Folsom Israel 26		23	M	Full	1896	Sugar Loaf	3972
	2							
	3							
	4							
	5							
	6							
	7							
	8							
	9							
	10							
	11							
	12							
	13							
	14							
	15							
	16							
	17							

ENROLLMENT
OF NOS. 1 HEREON
APPROVED BY THE SECRETARY
OF INTERIOR JAN 17 1903

TRIBAL ENROLLMENT OF PARENTS

	Name of Father	Year	County	Name of Mother	Year	County
1	Isaac Folsom	Dead	Sans Bois		Dead	Sans Bois
2						
3						
4						
5	Names of father & mother to be forwarded					
6						
7						
8						
9						
10						
11						
12						
13						
14						
15				Date of Application for Enrollment.		
16	No 1 is now husband of Rhoda Burties on Choc Card #2768				6/7/99	
17	Marriage certificate to be supplied					

291

RESIDENCE:	Sugar Loaf	COUNTY.	**Choctaw Nation**	**Choctaw Roll**	CARD No.	
POST OFFICE:	Summerfield, I.T.			*(Not Including Freedmen)*	FIELD No.	**2392**

Dawes' Roll No.	NAME		Relationship to Person	AGE	SEX	BLOOD	TRIBAL ENROLLMENT		
							Year	County	No.
6929	₁ Pike, James	24	First Named	21	M	1/2	1896	Sugar Loaf	10156
6930	₂ " Emiline	24	Wife	21	F	1/2	1896	Wade	3346
6931	₃ " Alfred	3	Son	10mo	M	1/2			
14740	₄ " Marion	1	Son	14mo	M	1/2			
	₅								
	₆								
	₇								
	₈								
	₉								
	10								
	11								
	12								
	13								
	14								
	15	ENROLLMENT OF NOS. 1,2,3 HEREON APPROVED BY THE SECRETARY OF INTERIOR Jan 17 1903				ENROLLMENT OF NOS. 4 HEREON APPROVED BY THE SECRETARY OF INTERIOR May 20 1903			
	16								
	17								

TRIBAL ENROLLMENT OF PARENTS

	Name of Father	Year	County	Name of Mother	Year	County
₁	Albert Pike	Dead	Skullyville	Eliza Pike	Dead	Sugar Loaf
₂	John Durant	"	Wade		"	Wade
₃	No.1			No.2		
₄	No 2			No 2		
₅						
₆						
₇			No2 on 1896 roll as Emeline Durant			
₈			No.3 Enrolled September 26th 1900			
₉			Nº4 Born Oct 12, 1901. Enrolled Dec. 24, 1902. For child of No.2 see NB (March 3, 1905) #977			
10						
11						
12						
13						
14					#1&2	
15					Date of Application for Enrollment	
16					6/7/99	
17	P.O. Talihina I.T. 4/4/05					

Choctaw By Blood Enrollment Cards 1898-1914

RESIDENCE: Sugar Loaf   COUNTY. **Choctaw Nation**   **Choctaw Roll**   CARD No.
POST OFFICE: Conser I.T.   *(Not Including Freedmen)*   FIELD No. 2393

Dawes' Roll No.	NAME	Relationship to Person First Named	AGE	SEX	BLOOD	TRIBAL ENROLLMENT		
						Year	County	No.
6932	1 Carshall Zack T 30	First Named	27	M	Full	1896	Sugar Loaf	2226
	2							
	3							
	4							
	5							
	6							
	7							
	8							
	9							
	10							
	11							
	12							
	13							
	14							
	15	ENROLLMENT OF NOS. 1 HEREON APPROVED BY THE SECRETARY						
	16	OF INTERIOR JAN 17 1903						
	17							

TRIBAL ENROLLMENT OF PARENTS

	Name of Father	Year	County	Name of Mother	Year	County
1	Mi-cha-tub-bee	Dead	Sugar Loaf	Betsy Mi-cha-tub-bee	Dead	Sugar Loaf
2						
3						
4						
5						
6						
7	Nº1 is husband of No2 on Choc Card #2360 12/14 '02					
8						
9						
10						
11						
12						
13						
14						
15						
16				Date of Application for Enrollment.	6/7/99	
17						

Choctaw By Blood Enrollment Cards 1898-1914

Dawes' Roll No.	NAME		Relationship to Person First Named	AGE	SEX	BLOOD	TRIBAL ENROLLMENT		
							Year	County	No.
6933	1 Simpson Sally Ann	66	First Named	63	F	Full	1896	Sugar Loaf	11190
14741	2 Sam Ann	16	Ward	13	F	"	1896	" "	11192
14742	3 " Emma	14	Ward	11	F	"	1896	" "	11193
	4								
	5								
	6								
	7								
	8								
	9								
	10								
	11								
	12								
	13								
	14								
	15								
	16								
	17								

ENROLLMENT OF NOS. 1 HEREON APPROVED BY THE SECRETARY OF INTERIOR JAN 17 1903

ENROLLMENT OF NOS. 2 and 3 HEREON APPROVED BY THE SECRETARY OF INTERIOR MAY 20 1903

TRIBAL ENROLLMENT OF PARENTS

	Name of Father	Year	County	Name of Mother	Year	County
1	Na-lah-ta-be	Dead	Skullyville		Dead	Skullyville
2	Jackson Sam	"	"	Eliza Jackson	"	"
3	" "	"	"	" "	"	"
4						
5						
6						
7						
8						
9						
10						
11						
12						
13						
14						
15						Date of Application for Enrollment.
16						6/7/99
17						

294

Choctaw By Blood Enrollment Cards 1898-1914

RESIDENCE: Sugar Loaf	COUNTY.			**Choctaw Nation**		**Choctaw Roll** *(Not Including Freedmen)*	CARD NO.	
POST OFFICE: Poteau, I.T							FIELD NO.	2395

Dawes' Roll No.	NAME	Relationship to Person	AGE	SEX	BLOOD	TRIBAL ENROLLMENT		
						Year	County	No.
6934	1 Walker, Edward E ⁶	First Named	3	M	1/2	1896	Sugar Loaf	12885
	2							
	3							
	4							
	5							
	6							
	7							
	8							
	9							
	10	ENROLLMENT						
	11	OF NOS. 1 HEREON						
	12	APPROVED BY THE SECRETARY OF INTERIOR JAN 17 1903						
	13							
	14							
	15							
	16							
	17							

TRIBAL ENROLLMENT OF PARENTS

	Name of Father	Year	County	Name of Mother	Year	County
1	Ed. E. Walker	Dead	Sugar Loaf	Leamon Welch	1896	Non Citz
2						
3						
4						
5	No1 on 1896 roll as Ed. E. Walker					
6	Mother on Card No D215					
7						
8	No.1 is on Creek census card #2474					
9	3/23/23 See Old Creek Card No. 2474					
10						
11						
12	See Choctaw cards #4768.					
13	No 215 and 4770					
14						
15					Date of Application for Enrollment.	
16					6/7/99	
17						

295

Choctaw By Blood Enrollment Cards 1898-1914

RESIDENCE: Sugar Loaf COUNTY.
POST OFFICE: Howe I.T.

Choctaw Roll *(Not Including Freedmen)*

CARD NO.
FIELD NO.

Dawes' Roll No.	NAME	Relationship to Person First Named	AGE	SEX	BLOOD	TRIBAL ENROLLMENT Year	County	No.
6935	1 McCurtain Joel 26	First Named	23	M	Full	1896	Sugar Loaf	9140
6936	2 Collin Wesley Ann 23	Wife	20	F	Full	1896	" "	9141
6937	3 Collin Webster 1	Son of No2	2mo	M	"			
	4							
	5							
	6							
	7							
	8							
	9							
	10							
	11							
	12							
	13							
	14							
	15							
	16							
	17							

ENROLLMENT
OF NOS. 1,2,3 HEREON
APPROVED BY THE SECRETARY
OF INTERIOR JAN 17 1903

TRIBAL ENROLLMENT OF PARENTS

	Name of Father	Year	County	Name of Mother	Year	Coun
1	Frank McCurtain	Dead	Sugar Loaf	Sophia McCurtain	Dead	Sugar Loa
2	Jim Washington	"	Skullyville	Missouri McNoel	1896	" "
3	Buckner Collin	1896	Gaines	No2		
4						
5						
6						
7						
8	No2 was divorced from Joe McCurtain Jany 13, 1901 and was married to Buckner Collin					
9	Choc Card 2406 Aug 29, 1901. Evidence of marriage filed March 6, 1902					
10	No3 Born Jany 5, 1902 enrolled March 6, 1902					
11						
12						
13						
14						#1&2
15						Date of Application for Enrollment.
16						
17						6/7/99

Choctaw By Blood Enrollment Cards 1898-1914

RESIDENCE: Sugar Loaf   COUNTY. **Choctaw Nation**   **Choctaw Roll** *(Not Including Freedmen)*   CARD No.

POST OFFICE: Howe, I.T   FIELD No. 2397

Dawes' Roll No.	NAME	Relationship to Person First Named	AGE	SEX	BLOOD	TRIBAL ENROLLMENT Year	County	No.
6938	1 Franklin, Lizzie 25		22	F	Full	1896	Sugar Loaf	3954
6939	2 Folsom, Ida 6	Dau	3	"	"	1896	" "	3955
6940	3 ~~Per nella~~ DIED PRIOR TO SEPTEMBER 25 1902	"	2	"	"			
	4							
	5							
	6							
	7							
	8							
	9							
	10							
	11							
	12							
	13							
	14							
	15	ENROLLMENT OF NOS. 1,2,3, HEREON APPROVED BY THE SECRETARY OF INTERIOR JAN 17 1903						
	16							
	17							

TRIBAL ENROLLMENT OF PARENTS

	Name of Father	Year	County	Name of Mother	Year	County
1	Jas Franklin	Dead	Sugar Loaf	Co-ma	Dead	Sugar Loaf
2	Alex Folsom	1896	" "	No 1		
3	" "	1896	" "	No 1		
4						
5						
6						
7			No 1 on 1896 roll as Lizzie Folsom also on			
8			1896 roll Page 96, No 3977, as Lizzie Folsom,			
9			Sugar Loaf Co			
10			No 3 Died in 1901. Proof of death filed Dec 23rd 1902			
11						
12						
13						
14						
15						
16				Date of Application for Enrollment.	6/7/99	
17						

297

Choctaw By Blood Enrollment Cards 1898-1914

RESIDENCE:	Sugar Loaf			COUNTY.						
POST OFFICE:	Howe, I.T.						**Choctaw Nation**	**Choctaw Roll** *(Not Including Freedmen)*	CARD No. FIELD No.	2398

Dawes' Roll No. 6941	NAME	Relationship to Person	AGE	SEX	BLOOD	TRIBAL ENROLLMENT		
						Year	County	No.
941	1 McNoel, Eastman 39	First Named	36	M	Full	1896	Sugar Loaf	9108
6942	2 " Missouri 47	Wife	44	F	"	1896	" "	9109
	3							
	4							
	5							
	6							
	7							
	8							
	9							
	10							
	11							
	12							
	13							
	14							
	15	ENROLLMENT OF NOS. 1 and 2 HEREON APPROVED BY THE SECRETARY OF INTERIOR JAN 17 1903						
	16							
	17							

TRIBAL ENROLLMENT OF PARENTS

	Name of Father	Year	County	Name of Mother	Year	County
1	Histey McNoel	Dead	Sugar Loaf	Betsy Jackson	1896	Sugar Loaf
2	A-tok-la-ma	"	Skullyville		Dead	Skullyville
3						
4						
5						
6						
7						
8						
9						
10						
11						
12						
13						
14						
15				Date of Application for Enrollment		
16				6/7/99		
17						

298

RESIDENCE: Skullyville   COUNTY. **Choctaw Nation**   **Choctaw Roll**   CARD NO.
POST OFFICE: Poteau I.T.   *(Not Including Freedmen)*   FIELD NO.   2399

Dawes' Roll No.	NAME		Relationship to Person First Named	AGE	SEX	BLOOD	TRIBAL ENROLLMENT		
							Year	County	No.
6943	1 Willis Josiah	56	First Named	53	M	Full	1896	Skullyville	12794
6944	2 " Winnie	51	Wife	48	F	"	1896	"	12795
6945	3 " Nancy (DIED PRIOR TO SEPTEMBER 25 1902)	16	Dau	13	F	"	1896	"	12798
6946	4 " Martha	13	Dau	10	F	"	1896	"	12799
	5								
	6								
	7								
	8								
	9								
	10								
	11								
	12								
	13								
	14								
	15	ENROLLMENT OF NOS. 1,2,3 and 4 HEREON							
	16	APPROVED BY THE SECRETARY							
	17	OF INTERIOR JAN 17 1903							

TRIBAL ENROLLMENT OF PARENTS

	Name of Father	Year	County	Name of Mother	Year	County
1		Dead	Skullyville	Ya-wa	Dead	Skullyville
2	O-a-lim-ta-be	"	Sugar Loaf	She-ne-bal	"	Sugar Loaf
3	No 1			Sally Willis	"	Skullyville
4	No 1			" "	"	"
5						
6						
7						
8						
9				proof of death filed Dec 20 1902		
10	No 3 died September - 1901:			" " "		" " "
11						
12						
13						
14						
15					Date of Application for Enrollment.	
16					6/7/99	
17						

Choctaw By Blood Enrollment Cards 1898-1914

RESIDENCE:	Skullyville	COUNTY.	Choctaw Nation		Choctaw Roll	CARD NO.	
POST OFFICE:	Poteau I.T.				(Not Including Freedmen)	FIELD NO.	2400

Dawes' Roll No.	NAME		Relationship to Person	AGE	SEX	BLOOD	TRIBAL ENROLLMENT		
							Year	County	No.
6947	1 Willis David	29	First Named	26	M	Full	1896	Skullyville	12796
6948	2 " Nellie	20	Wife	17	F	"	1896	"ddd	8510
6949	3 " Lou	3	Dau	6mo	"	"			
6950	4 " Bennie	1	Son	6mo	M	"			
	5								
	6								
	7								
	8								
	9								
	10								
	11					-			
	12								
	13								
	14								
	15	ENROLLMENT							
	16	OF NOS. 1,2,3 and 4 HEREON APPROVED BY THE SECRETARY							
	17	OF INTERIOR JAN 17 1903							

TRIBAL ENROLLMENT OF PARENTS

	Name of Father	Year	County	Name of Mother	Year	County
1	Josiah Willis	1896	Skullyville	Sally Willis	Dead	Skullyville
2	Willie Morrow	Dead	Sugar Loaf		"	Sugar Loaf
3	No 1			No 2		
4	Nº 1			Nº 2		
5						
6						
7	No2 On 1896 roll as Nellie Morrow					
8	Nº 4 Born Jany 27, 1902: enrolled Aug 15, 1902					
9						
10	For child of Nos 1&2 see NB (Mar 3rd 1905) Card #124					
11						
12						
13						
14						
15				No3 enrolled Dec 16/99		
16				Date of Application for Enrollment.	6/7/99	
17					→1&2	

322

328

www.ingramcontent.com/pod-product-compliance
Lightning Source LLC
Chambersburg PA
CBHW030236030426
42336CB00009B/121